Knot Tying for Beginners

An Illustrated Guide
to Tying 65+ Most Useful
Types of Knots

Matthew McCoy

TABLE OF CONTENT

End Loops _____ 8

Water Bowline _____ 8

Surgeon's Loop Knot _____ 10

Rapala Knot _____ 12

Poacher's Knot _____ 16

Perfection Loop Knot _____ 18

Non-Slip Mono Knot _____ 20

Honda Knot _____ 23

Double Dragon Loop _____ 26

Double Davy Knot _____ 28

Davy Knot _____ 30

Bimini Twist Knot _____ 33

Basic Knots _____ 38

Overhand Knot _____ 38

Figure 8 Knot _____ 40

Half Hitch Knot _____ 42

Half Knot _____ 45

Noose Knot _____ 47

Sheet Bend _____ 50

Slip Knot _____ 52

Square Knot _____ 55

Boating Knots _____ 58

Alpine Butterfly Bend _____ 58

Alpine Butterfly Loop	61
Anchor Hitch	64
Ashley Stopper Knot	67
Bowline Knot	70
Bowline On A Bight	72
Buntline Hitch	75
Carrick Bend	77
Chain Splice	79
Cleat Hitch (Dock Line)	84
Cleat Hitch (Halyard)	87
Clove Hitch - End Rope	90
Constrictor Knot (Twisting Method)	92
Double Overhand Stopper	94
eStar Stopper Knot	96
Eye Splice	99
Halyard Hitch	106
Heaving Line Knot	109
Icicle Hitch (Loop Method)	113
Lighterman's Hitch	116
Midshipman's Hitch	119
Pile Hitch	122
Rolling Hitch	124
Round Turn & Two Half Hitches	127
Running Bowline	130
Stevedore Stopper	133
Perfection Loop Knot	135
Zeppelin Bend	138
Slim Beauty Knot	141
Uni Knot	145
Trilene Knot	148
Surgeon's Join Knot	151
Snell Knot	154

San Diego Jam Knot	157
Palomar Knot	160
Orvis Knot	163
Nail Knot	166
Improved Clinch Knot	170
FG Knot	173
Egg Loop Knot	179
Dropper Loop Knot	183
Blood Knot	187
Australian Braid Knot	191
Arbor Knot	195
Albright Knot	198
Stopper Knots	201
Stopper Loop	201
Double Matthew Walker Knot	205
Crown Knot	207
Conclusion	209
References	210

© Copyright 2021 Matthew McCoy - All rights reserved.

The content contained within this book may not be reproduced, duplicated or transmitted without direct written permission from the author or the publisher.

Under no circumstances will any blame or legal responsibility be held against the publisher, or author, for any damages, reparation, or monetary loss due to the information contained within this book. Either directly or indirectly. You are responsible for your own choices, actions, and results.

Legal Notice:

This book is copyright protected. This book is only for personal use. You cannot amend, distribute, sell, use, quote or paraphrase any part, or the content within this book, without the consent of the author or publisher.

Disclaimer Notice:

Please note the information contained within this document is for educational and entertainment purposes only. All effort has been executed to present accurate, up to date, and reliable, complete information. No warranties of any kind are declared or implied. Readers acknowledge that the author is not engaging in the rendering of legal, financial, medical or professional advice. The content within this book has been derived from various sources.

Please consult a licensed professional before attempting any techniques outlined in this book.

By reading this document, the reader agrees that under no circumstances is the author responsible for any losses, direct or indirect, which are incurred as a result of the use of the information contained within this document, including, but not limited to, — errors, omissions, or inaccuracies.

Any activity that involves ropes is potentially hazardous. Lives may be at risk – possibly your own. Considerable attention and effort have been made to ensure that these descriptions are accurate. However, many critical factors cannot be controlled, including: the choice of materials; the age, size, and condition of ropes; and the accuracy with which these descriptions have been followed. No responsibility is accepted for incidents arising from the use of this material.

Want these Bonus Books for free?

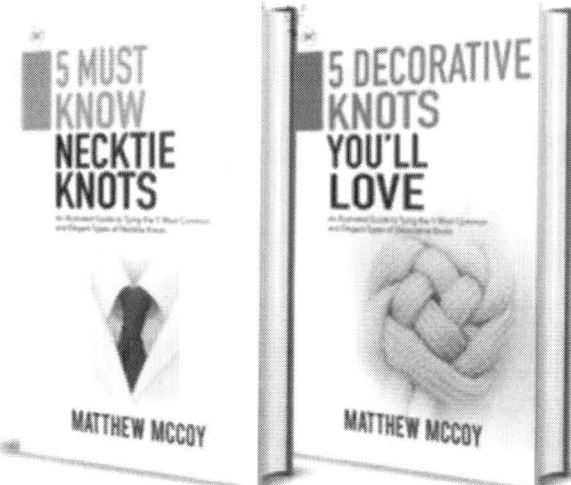

Get FREE, unlimited access to them and all of my new books by joining the Fan Base

Introduction

Congrats on buying Knot Tying for Beginners!

Inside, you'll track down every one of the most widely recognized kinds of bunches assembled in various classifications to make it simple for you to get when to utilize every one of them.

For a quicker and more practical methodology, you will track down every one of the bunches' names recorded in the framework, so you can choose the ideal set to use in your circumstance and effectively discover the page where to figure out how to make it.

Each bunch is outwardly clarified all through delineations of each progression to take. With this aide in your grasp, you won't ever have issues with hitches any longer!

It's way better to know a bunch and not need it than to require one and not know it!

Moving right along, we should begin!

End Loops
Water Bowline

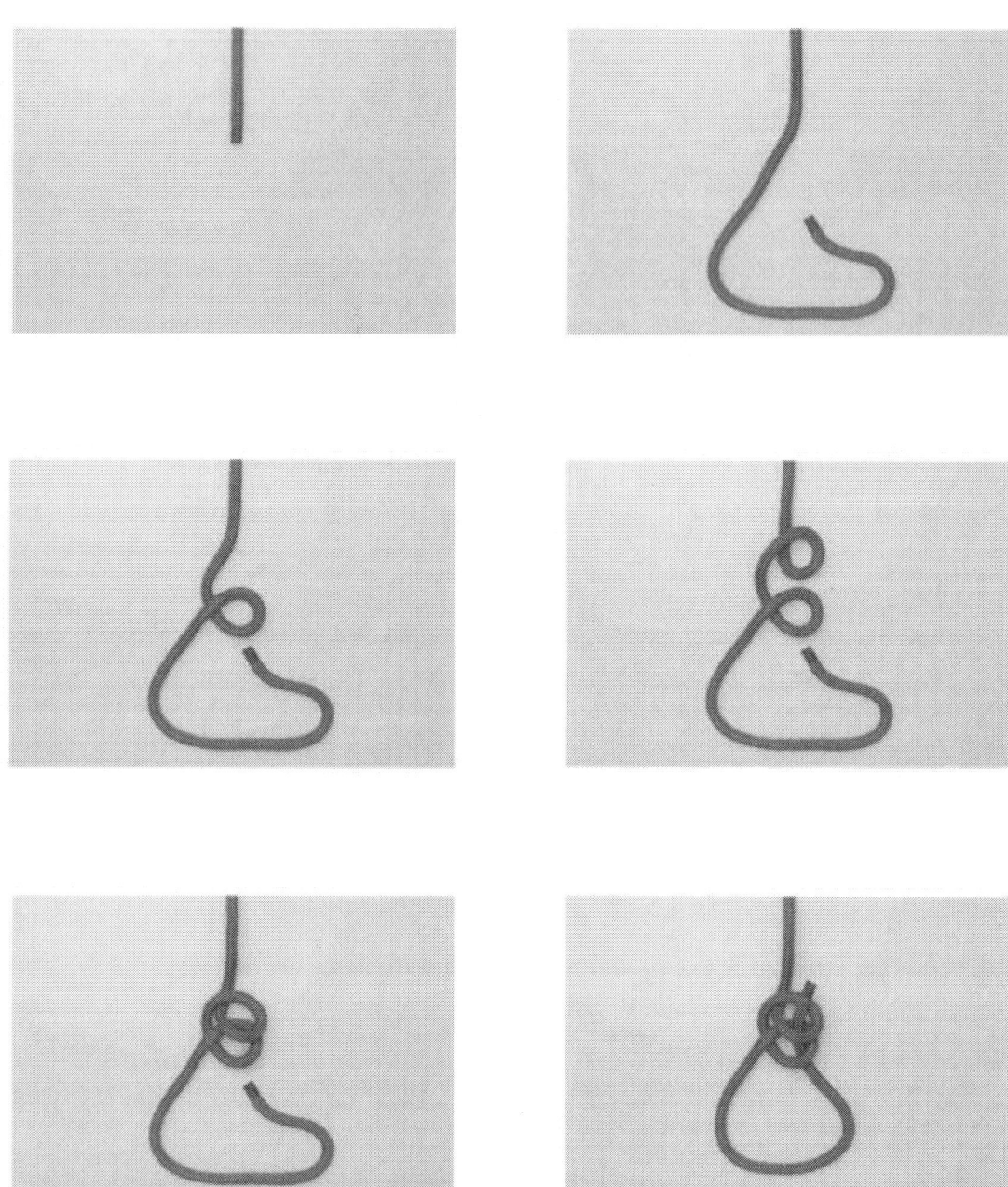

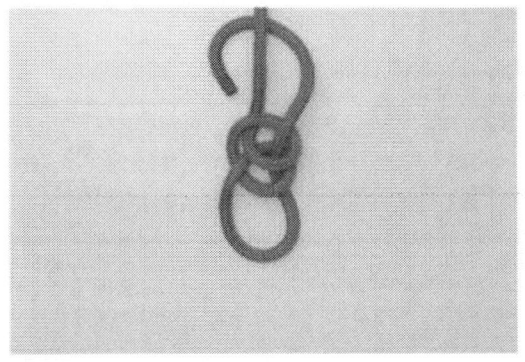 

Utilize sufficient rope to shape the bunch. In the standing end, make one circle, and afterward another. Cross over the two circles as a Clove Hitch. Miss the last part through the Clove Hitch, around the standing end, and down through the Clove Hitch. Fix the Clove Hitch to complete the bunch.

Uses: It makes a safe circle toward the end of a piece of rope.

Benefits: It is a steady bunch that is genuinely simple to tie and review. The additional half hitch, framing a Clove Hitch, gives a safer hold on the last part.

Surgeon's Loop Knot

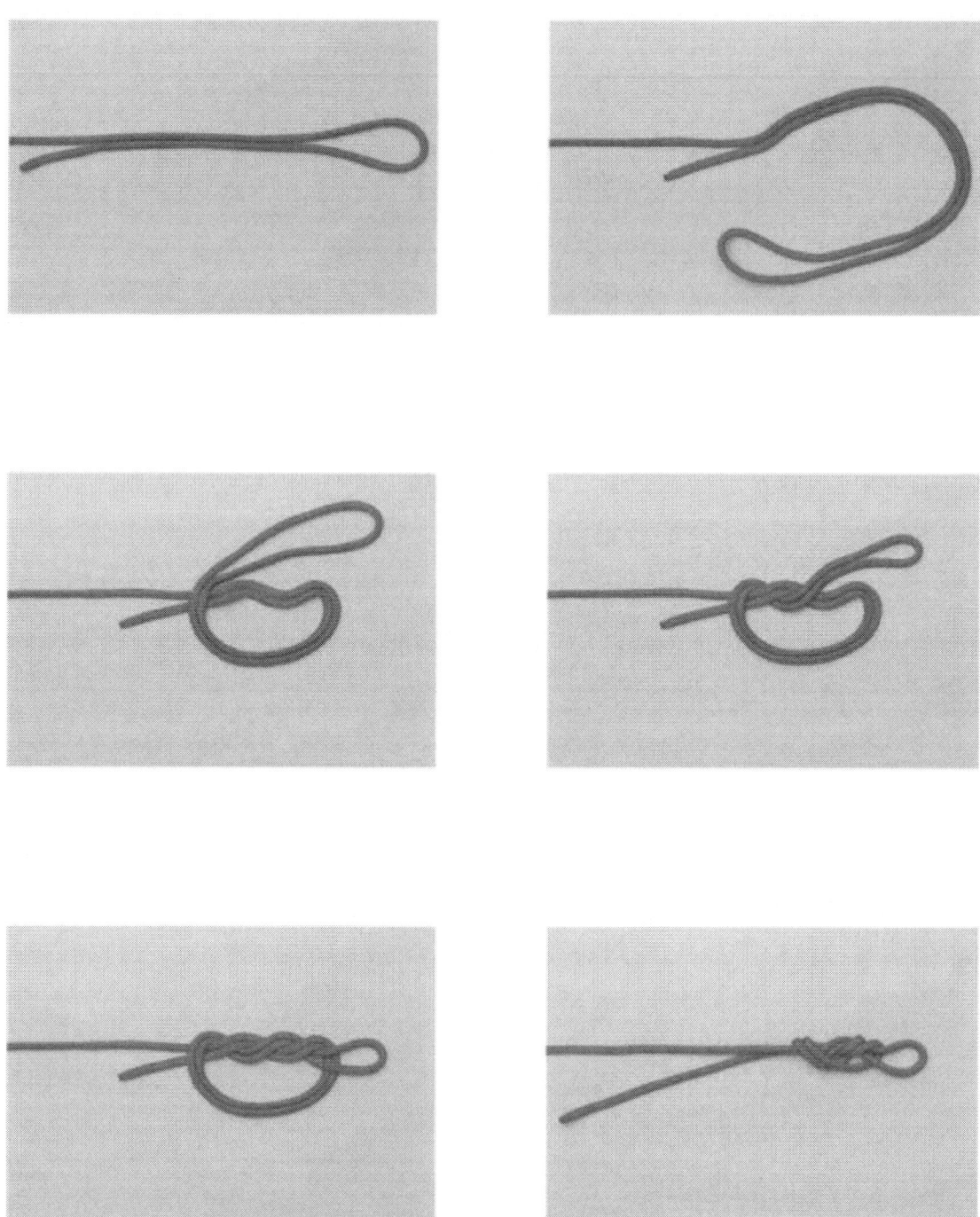

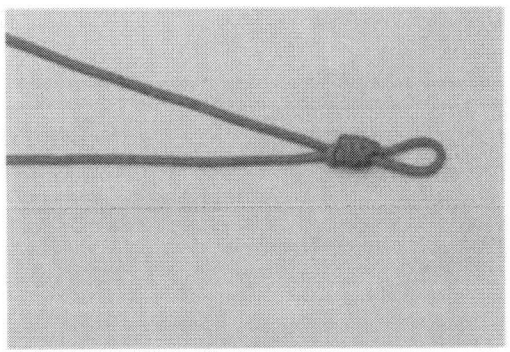 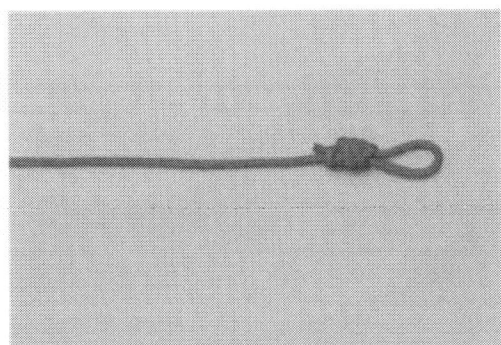

Structure a bight toward as far as it goes and tie an overhand bunch. Pass the bight during a time. Change the bight to make the ideal circle size. Grease up and pull the bunch tight. Trim the end.

Uses: The Surgeon's Loop is a Double Overhand Knot, and it very well may be tied rapidly and effectively toward the end of a line. It isn't unexpected to make a "Circle to Loop" association similarly that can guide two flexible groups into one another. It can likewise make a proper circle that permits the counterfeit draw or fly to move normally.

Benefits: The upside of the Surgeon's Loop is that it is dependable, simple to learn, and a few sources guarantee that it holds a great extent of the appraised line strength.

Rapala Knot

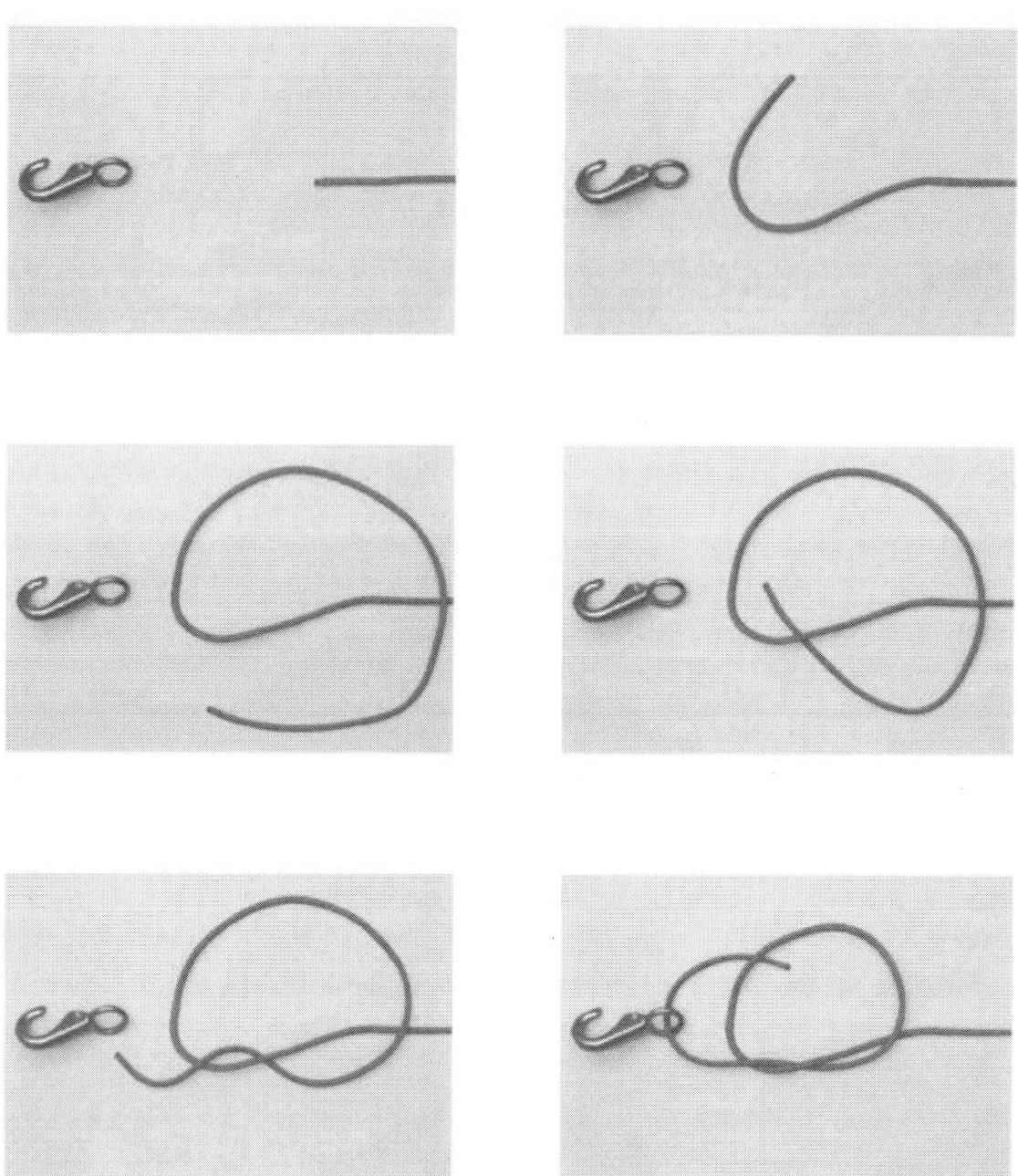

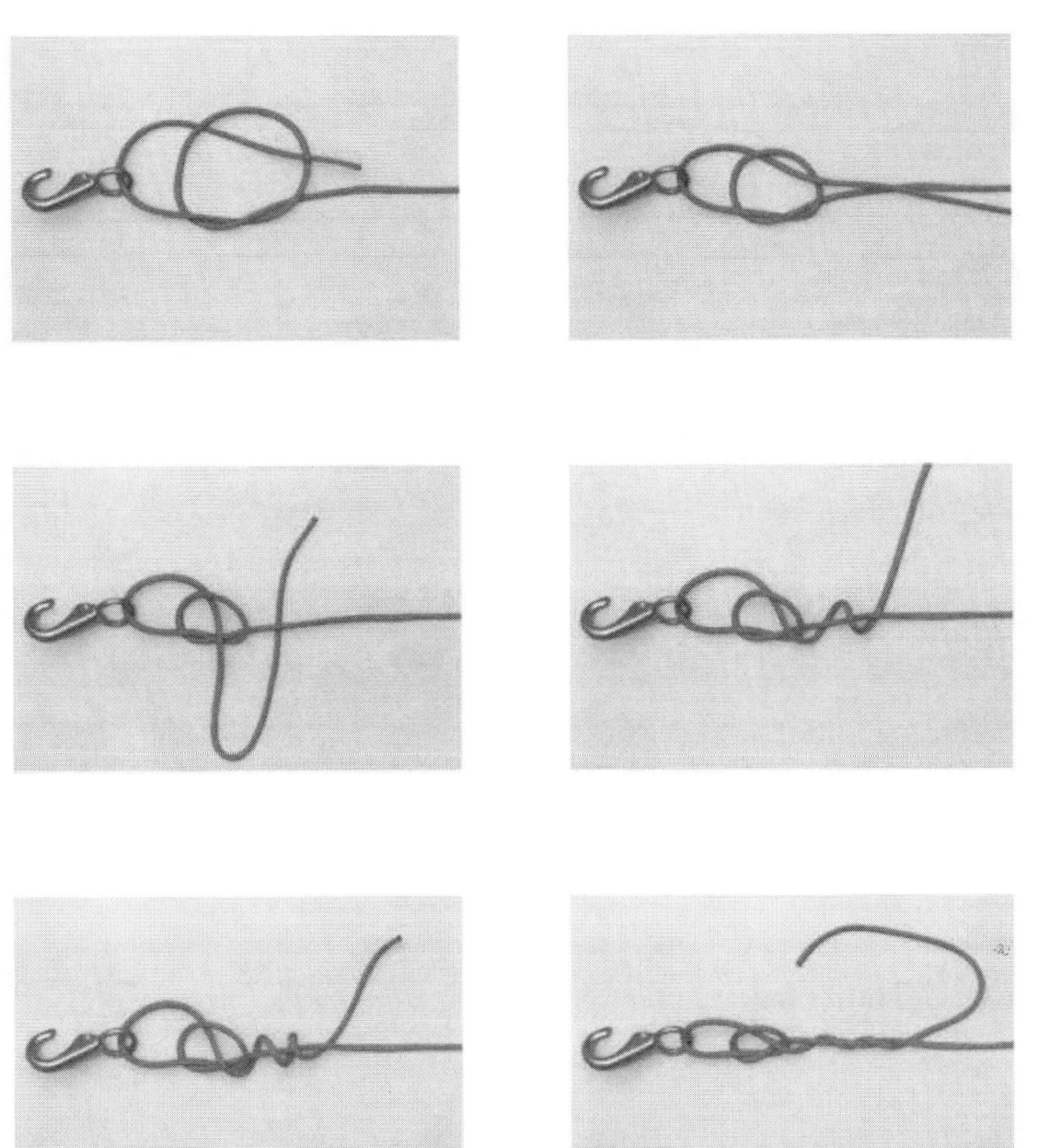

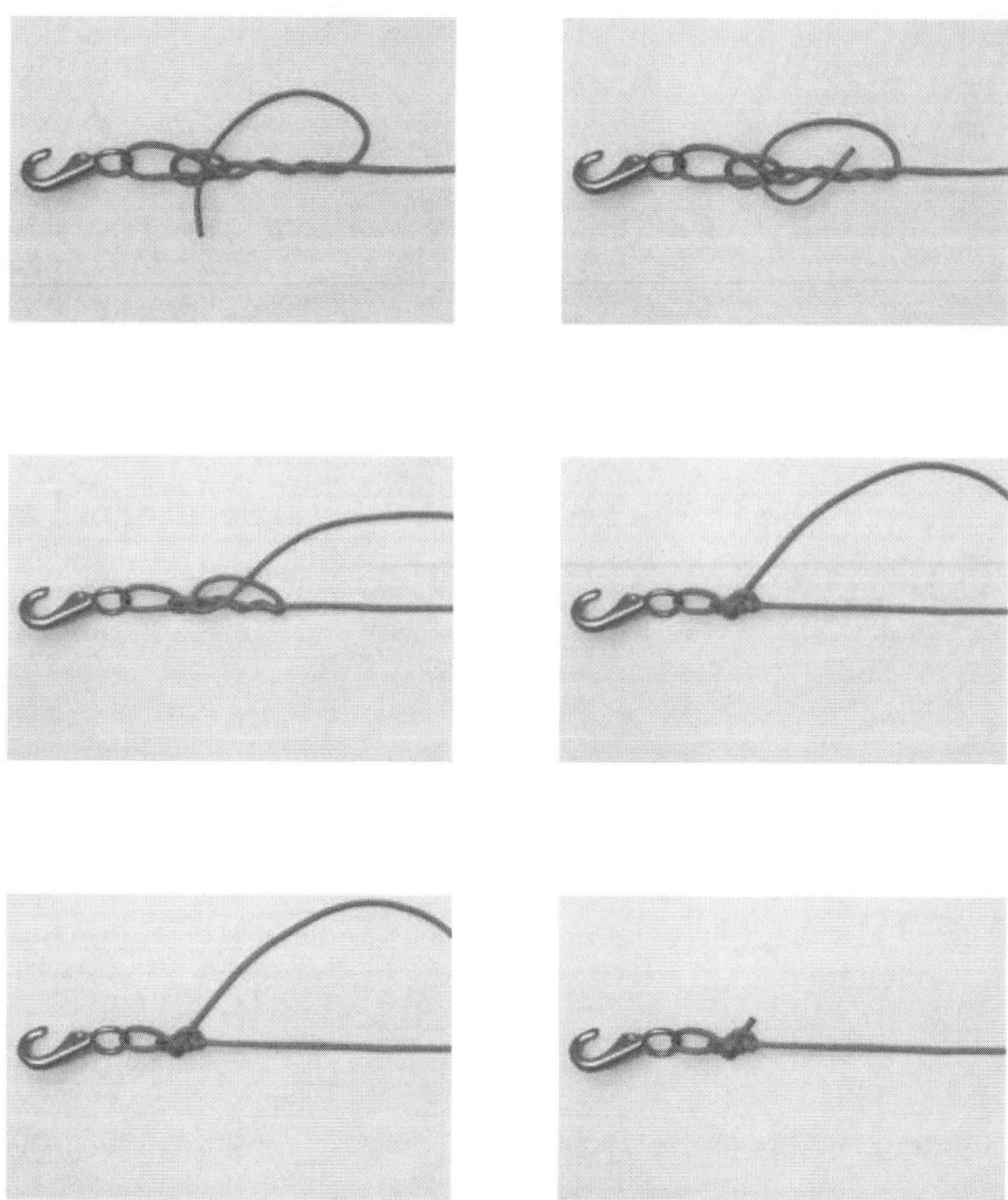

Structure an overhand bunch in the line. Pass the label end through the eye and back through the overhand bunch. Fold the end multiple times over the standing end. Pass the end back through the overhand bunch and afterward through the circle recently framed. Grease up and fix the bunch. Trim the end.

Uses: The Rapala Knot is a non-slip circle hitch generally tied straightforwardly to the draw. The Rapala siblings suggested using their Rapala draws to give a circle that permitted the baits to move uninhibitedly and normally.

On the off chance that a turn or pioneer is fundamental, it is ideal for picking the lightest tackle conceivable to permit the bait to move with a characteristic movement.

History: I am obligated to Lefty Kreh for his set of experiences of this bunch: "The Original Rapala Knot showed one pivot the principle line with the label end then one pass through the Overhand." Kreh tried it and found that it was not especially solid, but he further developed it by adding extra pivots to the primary line. This was the reason for his Non-Slip Mono Loop. A long time later, the Rapala siblings adjusted their depiction to add these additional turns just as the last fold under the label end. Kreh then, at that point, tried this variant and tracked down that the previous fold made it harder to tie and added no solidarity to the Non-Slip Mono.

Benefits: The benefit asserted for the Rapala Knot is that it permits the draw to move normally. It is additionally professed to hold a large portion of the line strength – and this may be normal as the construction of the bunch passes the power to the circle utilizing an enclosed by the middle.

Inconveniences: The label end faces from the snare and along these lines has a more noteworthy inclination to get grass, and so on, during recovery than the Non-Slip Mono (Lefty Kreh email, 2012).

Poacher's Knot

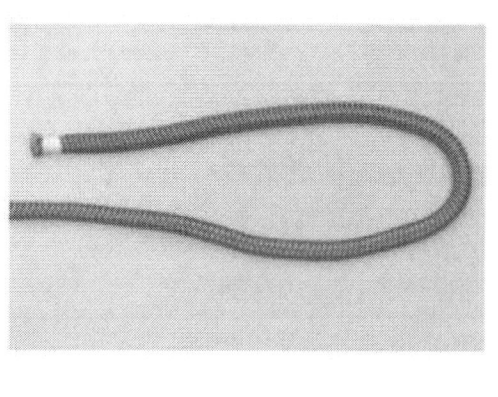
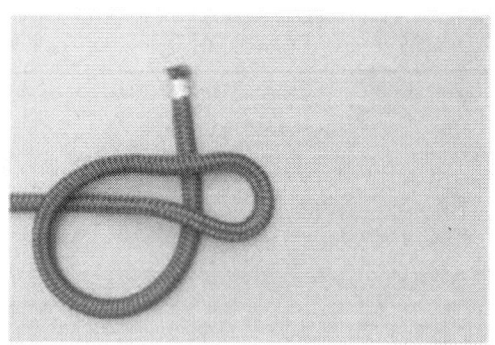

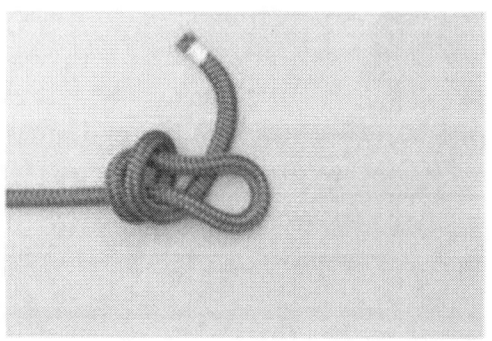

Structure a bight toward the end of the rope. Freely fold the end over the bight twice. Fold the end through these turns to finish the bunch. Pull tight.

Names: The Poacher's Knot is otherwise called a Strangle Snare and a Double Overhand Noose – because the bunch tied around the standing end is referred to as a Strangle Knot and as a Double Overhand Knot.

Tying it: The procedure utilized in the Poacher's Knot activity makes a Double Overhand Knot around the standing end. When learning, a typical slip-up is neglecting to finish the subsequent turn, making just a solitary Overhand bunch that isn't secure.

Perfection Loop Knot

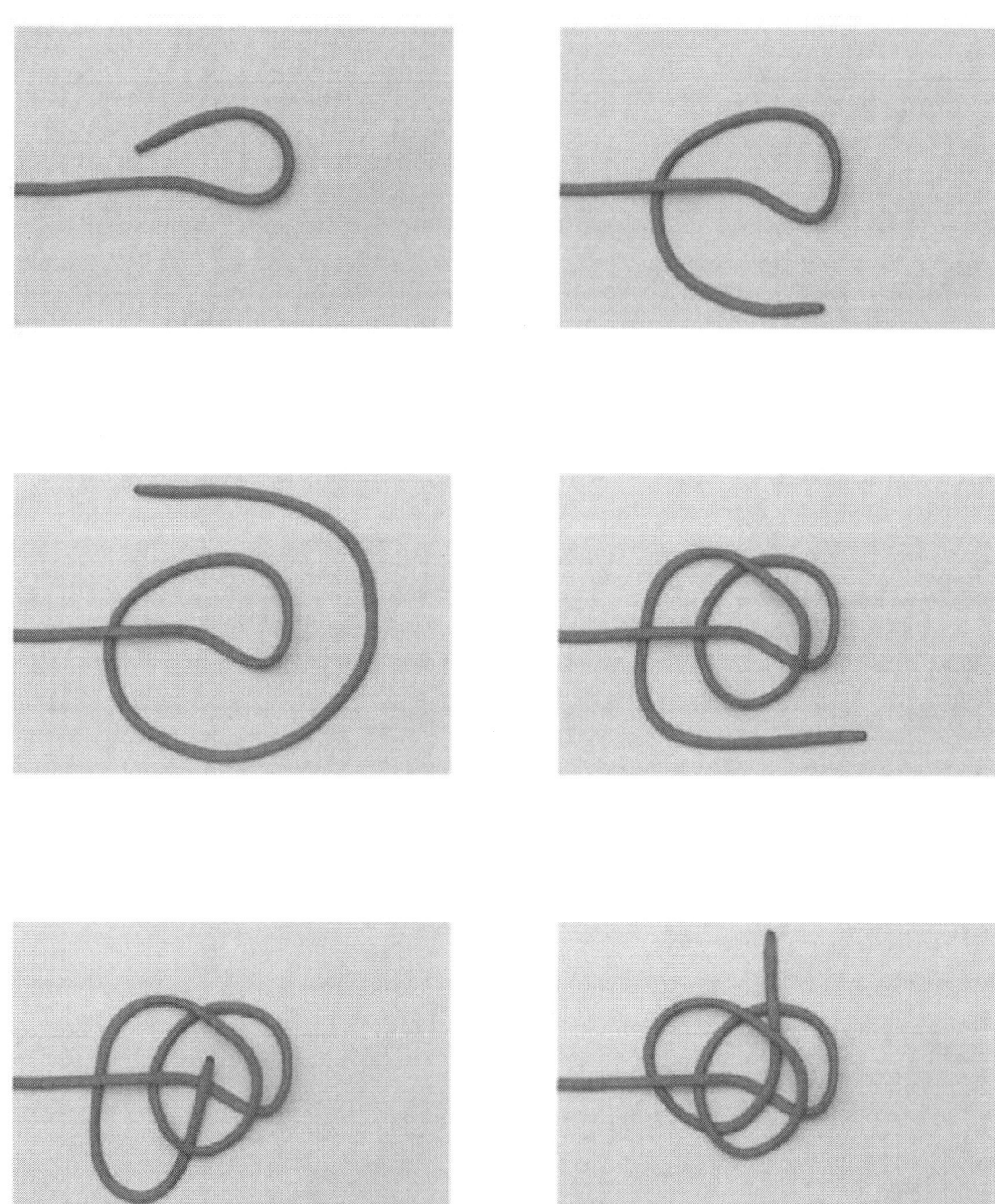

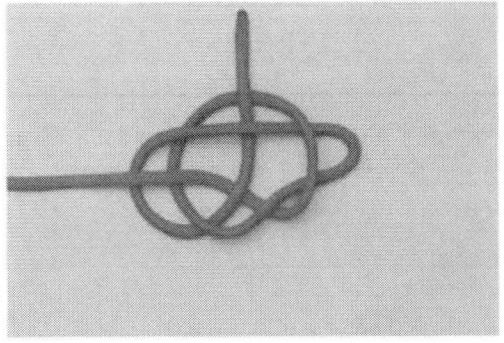

Structure a circle as far as it goes. Structure a subsequent process and lay it on top with the label end under the standing end. Pass the label end between the two circles. Get the top circle through the base circle. Grease up and fix by pulling on the fixed end and the new process. Trim the end.

Uses: The most straightforward approach is to make a little circle toward the end of a pioneer or scarf that will lie totally by the standing end. It is ordinarily used to join a Perfection Loop toward the end of a fly line to a Perfection circle in a Leader utilizing a "Circle to Loop" association.

Benefits: The Perfection Loop Knot makes a steady circle that lines up flawlessly with the standing end. Utilizing a "Circle to Loop" association, The Perfection Loop Knot considers fast and helpful pioneer changes.

Non-Slip Mono Knot

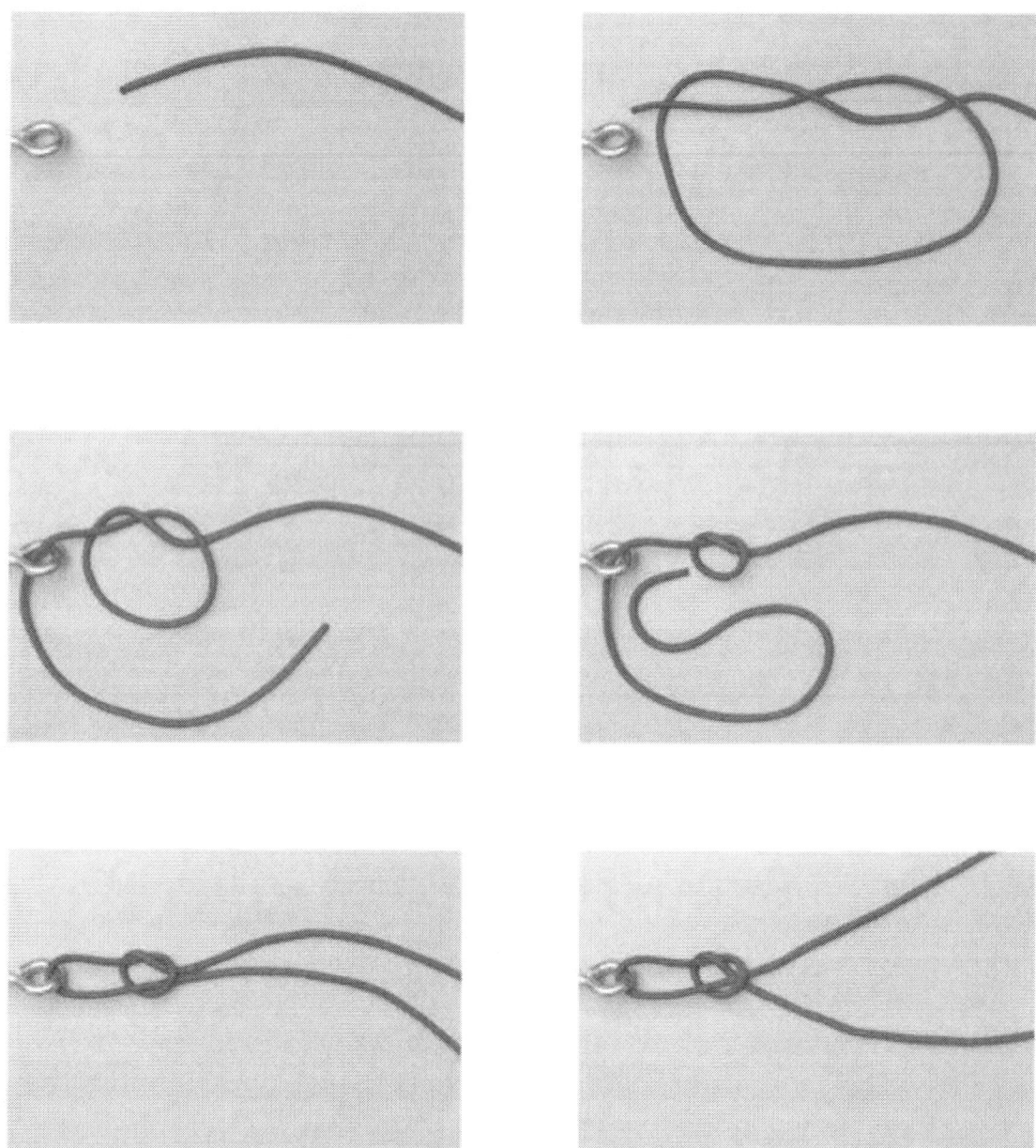

20

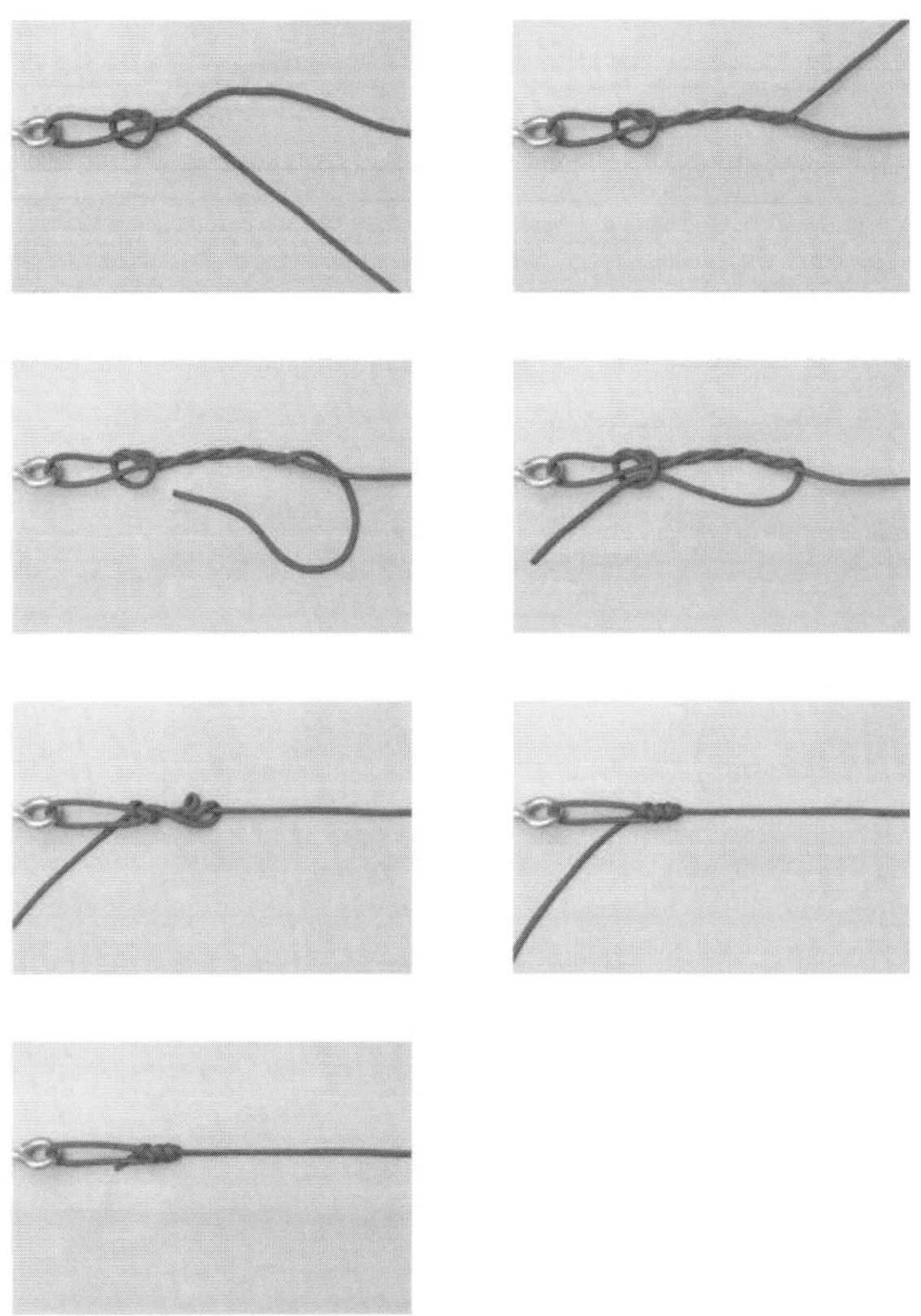

Tie a free overhand bunch and pass the label end through the eye, then, at that point, back through the overhand bunch. Fold the label end over the standing end multiple times and back through the overhand bunch. Grease up, fix and trim the end.

Beginning: The Non-Slip Mono Knot is a higher strength form of the first Homer Rhodes Loop Knot where the label end was just hitched once around the standing line. Lefty Kreh created the Non-Slip Mono during his series of tests to make a solid circle tie and then joined it into the book Practical Fishing Knots which he co-created with Mark Sosin. As needs are, it is frequently known as Lefty Kreh's Loop Knot.

Reason: The Non-Slip Mono makes an excellent fixed circle toward the end of the fishing line. Since the process doesn't hold the bait, it makes an adaptable connection and permits a more regular activity.

Benefits: The Non-Slip Mono Knot is genuinely simple to tie. Lefty Kreh found that the bunch holds the vast majority of the line's appraised strength – to such an extent that the strand broke instead of the bunch in a portion of his tests.

Honda Knot

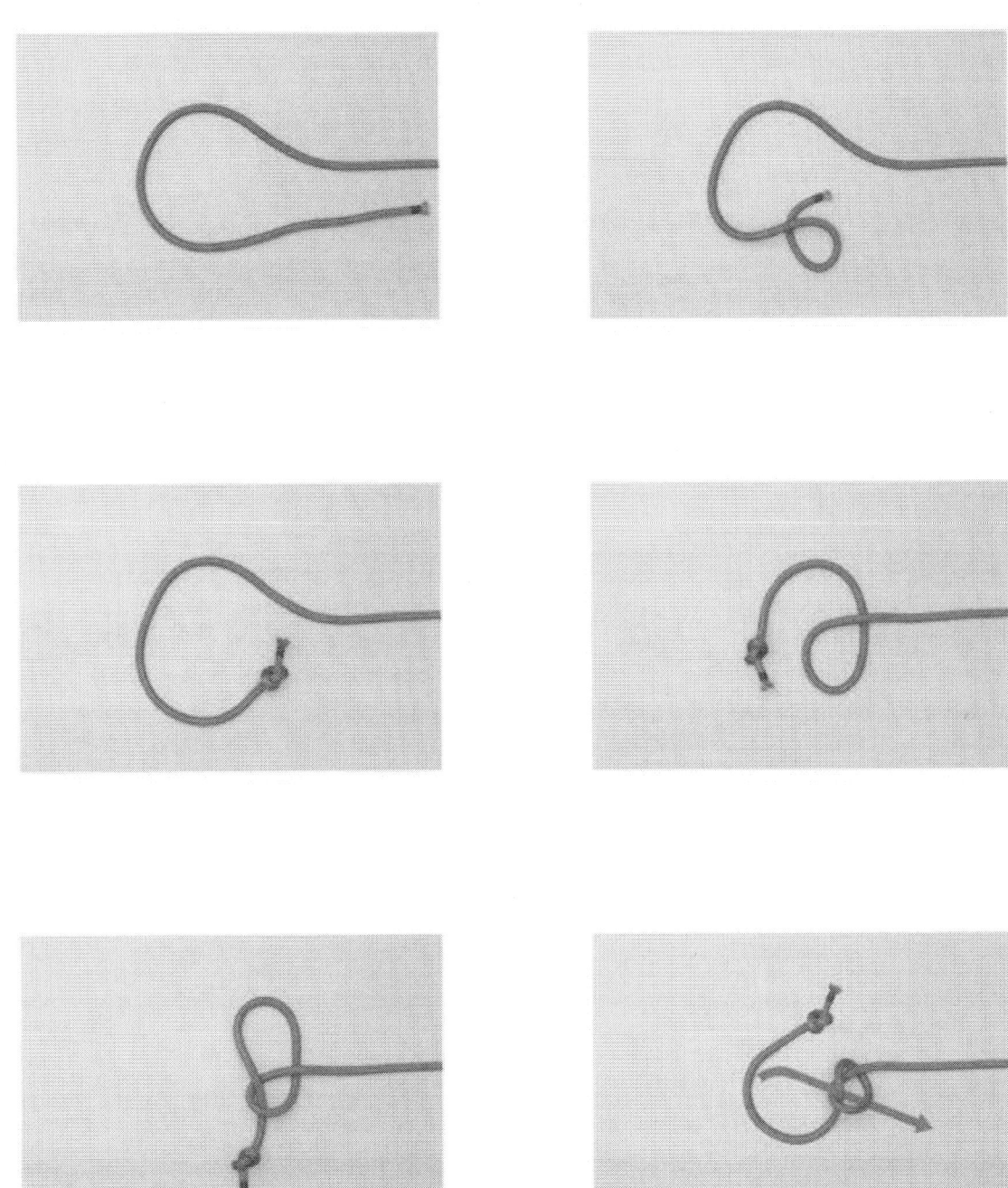

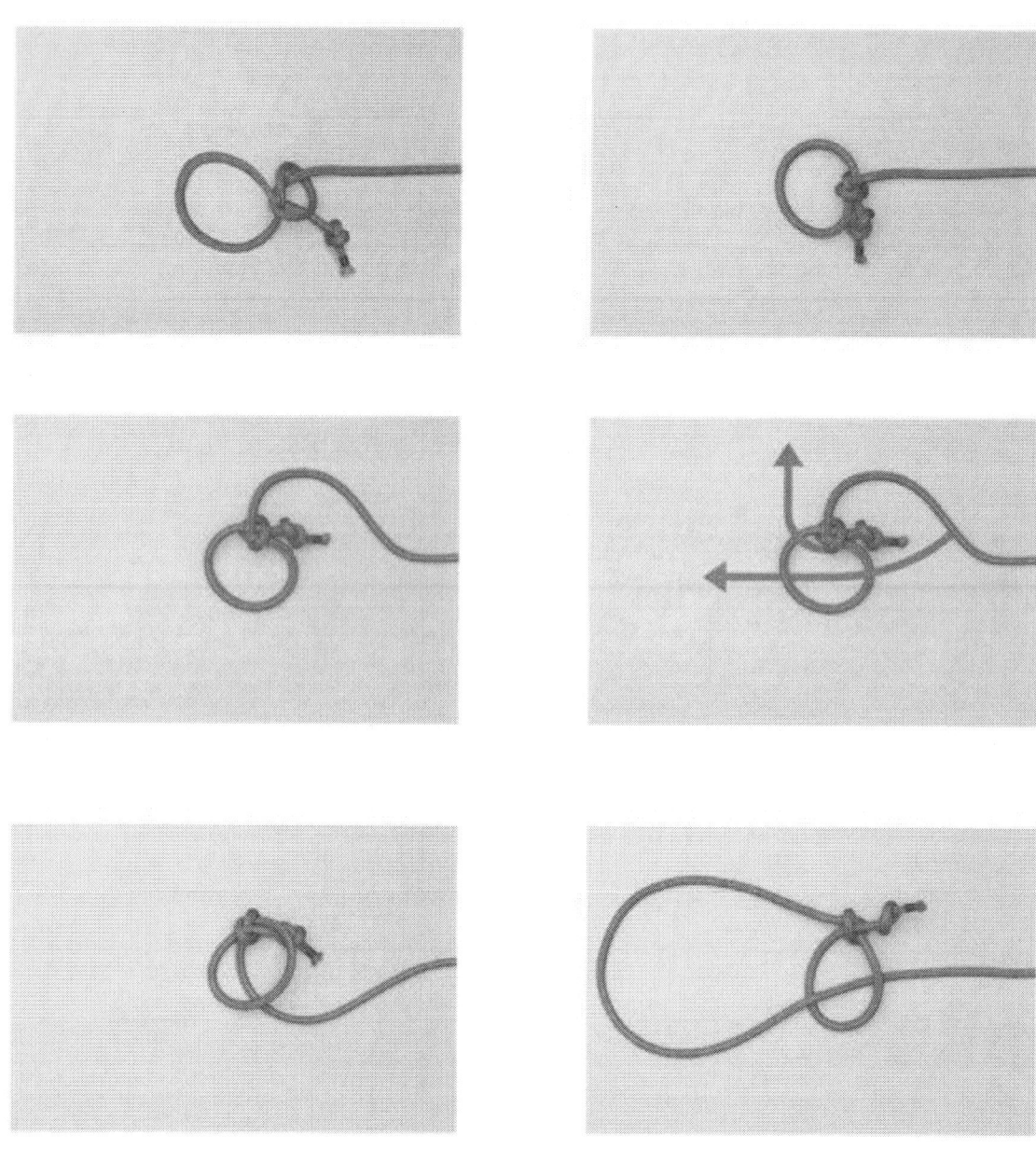

Tie an Overhand Knot eventually, and afterward tie another Overhand Knot. Structure a ring by going to the end overhand and fixing to make the Honda Knot. Then, at that point, get a bight of the rope through the round to shape the Lariat.

Tying it: For the Honda Knot Animation, I utilized the somewhat elastic rope, and it was helpful to reverse the ring and get a bight through to finish the Lariat. A more unbending string is used to keep the crew of the Honda Knot opens and sliding without any problem. Then, at that point, the long end is gotten through the round to make the Lariat.

Double Dragon Loop

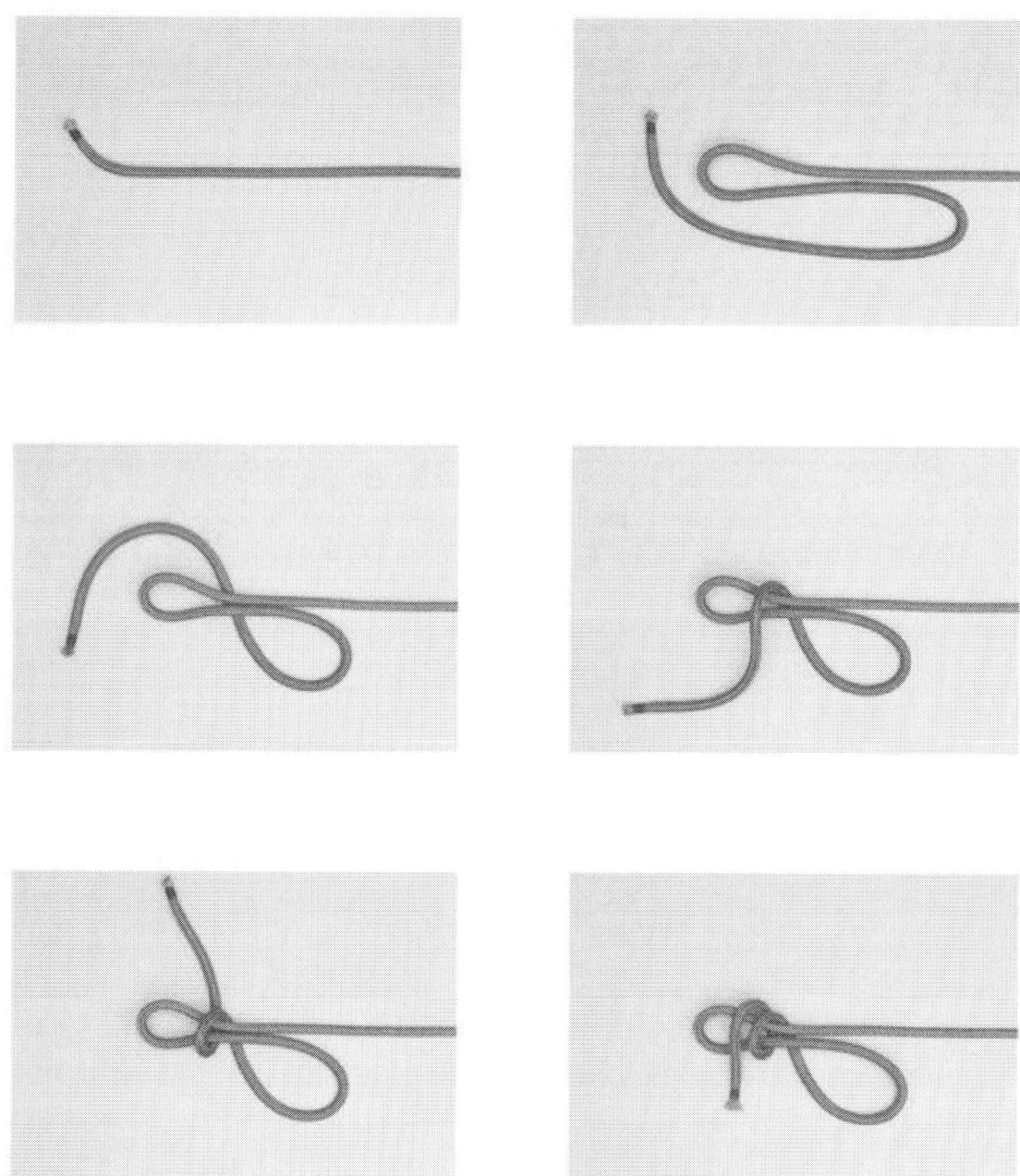

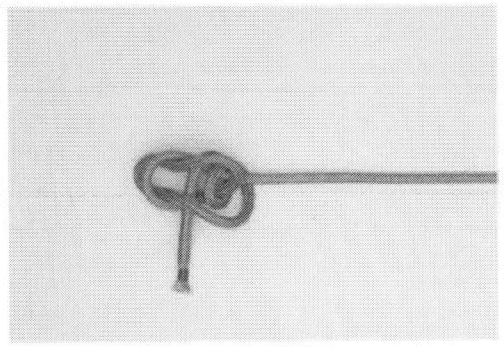

Crease the rope into two bights: a free-end bight and a standing-end bight. Fold the free end over the standing-end bight multiple times. Pass the free-end bight through the standing-end bight and fix.

Uses: The Double Dragon Knot gives a brilliant end of the rope circle that works just like other better-known models. The International Guild of Knot Tyers examines its utilization.

Benefits: It works with high modulus and tricky ropes like Dyneema and is less inclined than the Bowline to shake free. The Double Dragon Knot can be released reasonably without any problem after a weighty burden: flex the circle to permit the rope collar around it to be pushed back. It is likewise satisfying to tie and might recall the method more effectively than some others.

Tying it: There are a few techniques for securing it and can likewise tie it around an item.

Double Davy Knot

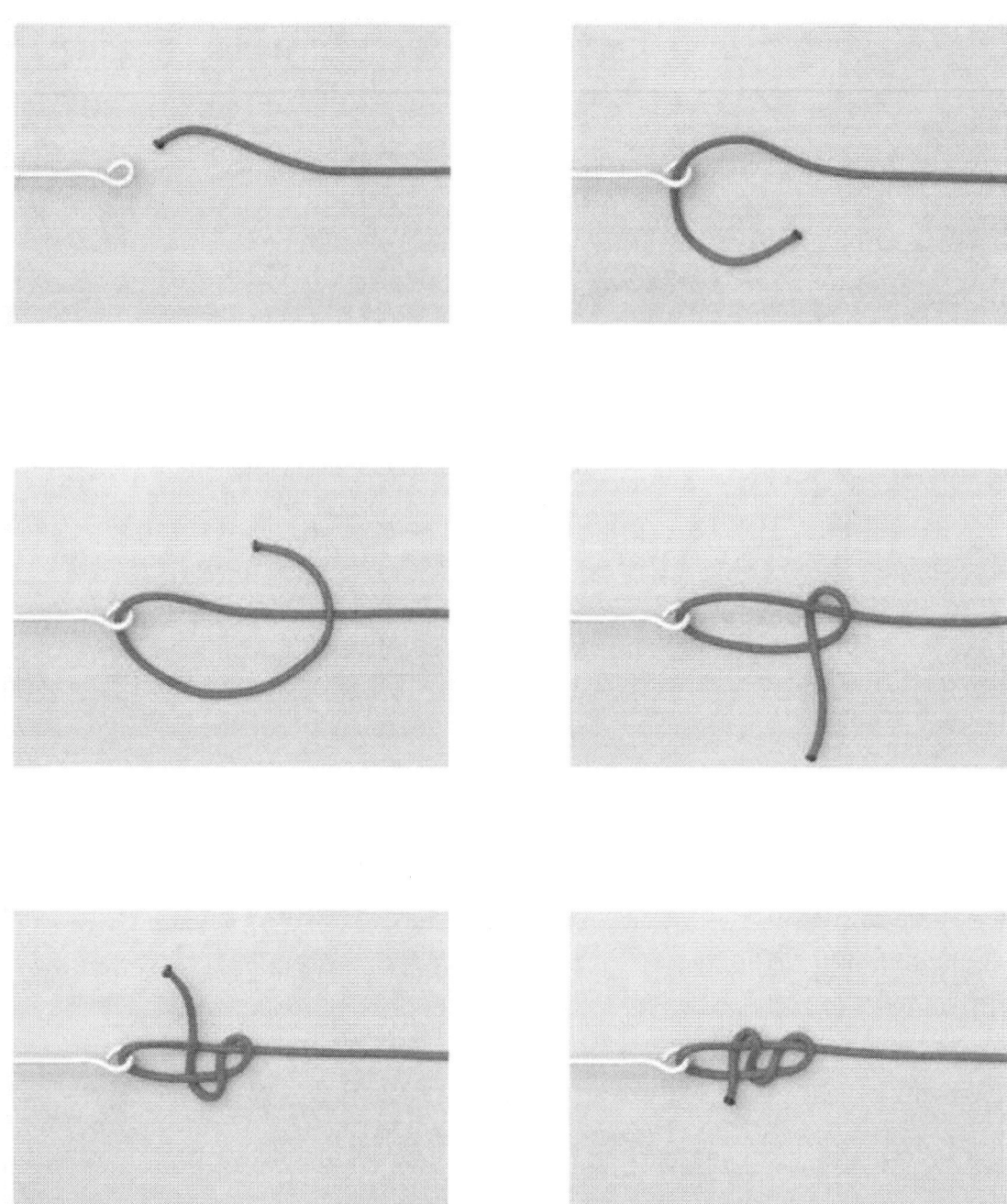

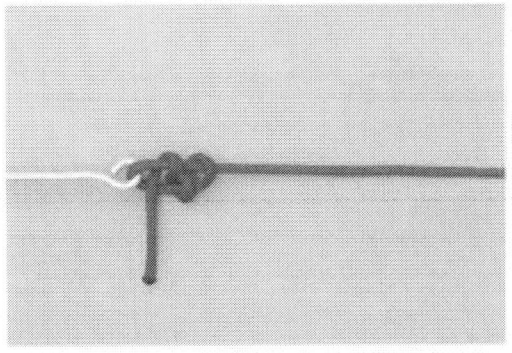
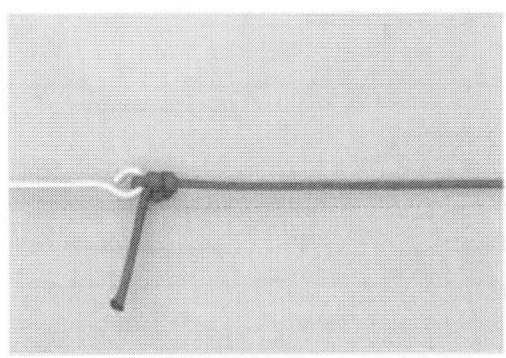
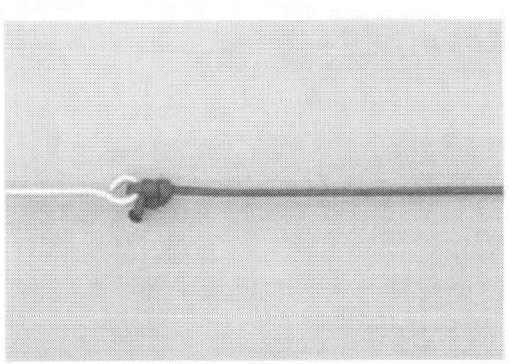

Pass the scarf through the eye, around the running end, and back through the circle to make a half hitch. Proceed around and through the process a subsequent time, then, at that point, around the running end and through the circle a third time. Fix cautiously with the goal that the bunch against the eye encases the label end. Trim the end.

Beginning: The Double Davy Knot is gotten from the first Davy Knot made by Davy Wotton. The goal was a bunch that could, in any case, be tied rapidly, and effectively yet would be safer in certain circumstances.

Fixing it: Like the Davy, the label end should lie against the eye under the bunch. On the off chance that the label end slides from the bunch towards the eye's focal point, the bunch holds considerably less well. Likewise, albeit specific individuals have the label end with their teeth, Davy alerts against this is a direct result of the danger of bacterial defilement.

Relative Diameters of Tippet and Eye Wire: The Davy Knot is bound to slip when the wire distance is more significant, and the Double Davy Knot is liked.

Davy Knot

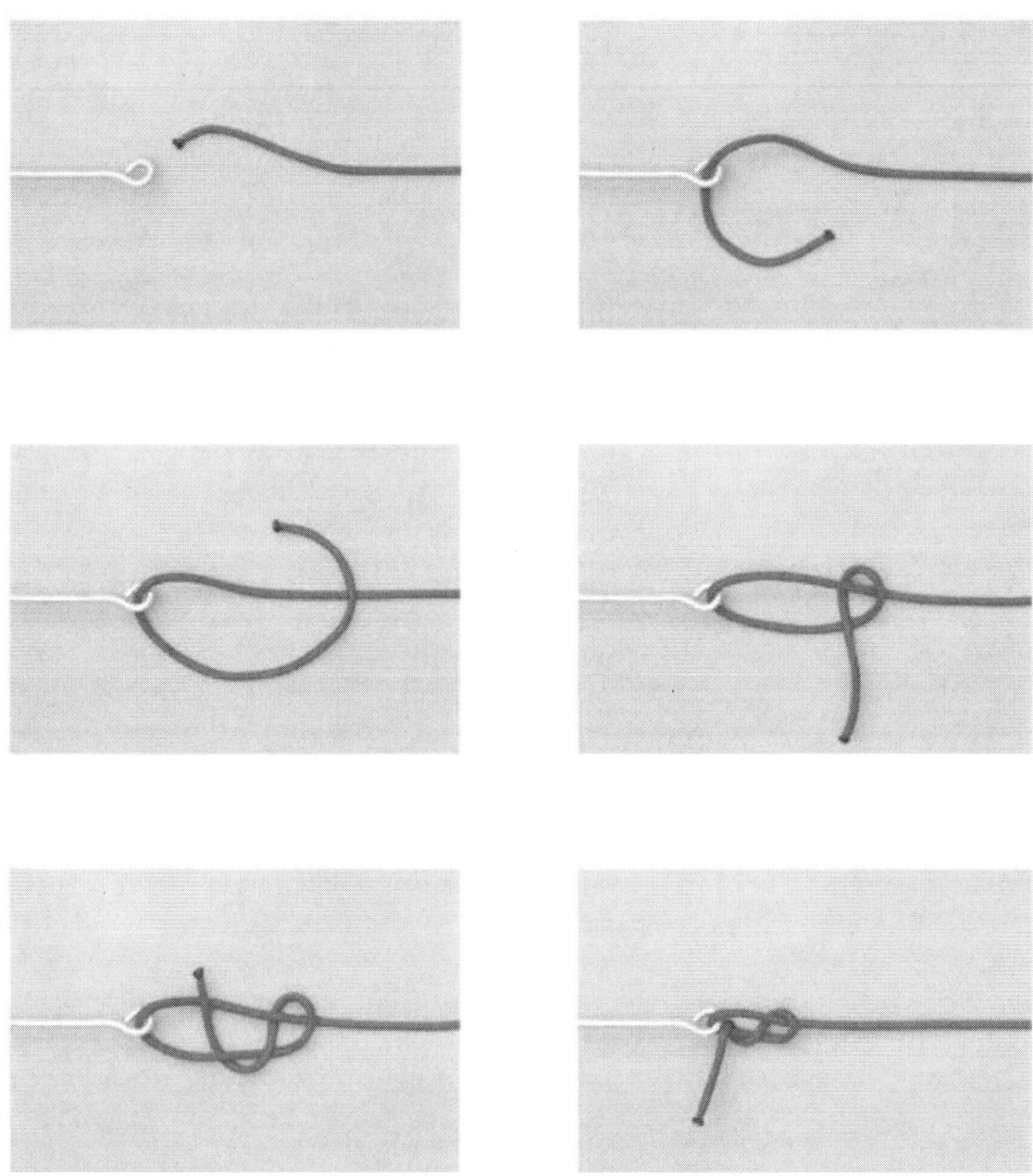

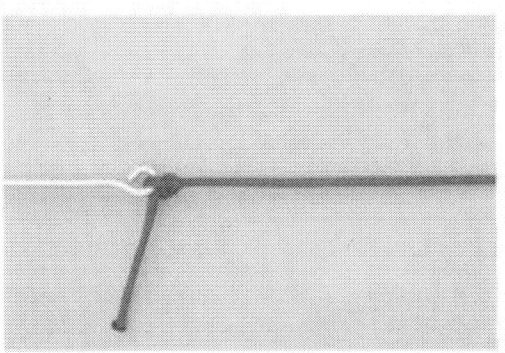 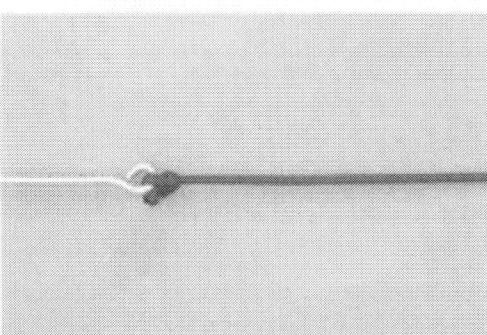

Pass the scarf through the eye, fold it over the running end, and pass it back through the circle to make a half hitch. Proceed around and back through the process a subsequent time. Fix cautiously, so the bunch against the eye encases the label end. Trim the end.

The Davy Knot was made in the 1950s by Davy Wotton when he was contending in the Welsh Fly-Fishing Team. He was testing to discover a bunch he would have the option to tie amazingly rapidly – which bodes well: less time connecting hitches rise to additional time getting fish.

Fixing it: Many authors portray a setting without oil; the bunch is tiny and accessible to the point of slight rubbing to produce heat. With care, the running end can fix the bunch leaving the label end so short that managing might be excessive. Even though it could be simpler to hold the label end with your teeth, Davy himself instructs against doing this because of the danger of bacterial pollution in an excessive number of lakes and streams, especially in case there are beavers or rodents present.

Situating the Tag End: The label end should lie against the eye under the bunch. On the off chance that the label end slides from the bunch towards the eye's focal point, the Davy Knot holds substantially less well.

Relative Diameters of Tippet and Eye Wire: If the scarf is excessively little contrasted with the distance across the wire, the bunch can't grasp the last fold: a heap spreads the circle open and deliveries the label end. In any case, this can frequently be addressed utilizing another fold to make the Double Davy Knot.

Benefits: The Davy Knot is tiny and efficient. With training, it very well may be tied to spending just the littlest measure of scarf length. It can likewise be connected incredibly quickly, even in cold and off-kilter conditions. It has been asserted that the Davy Knot is amazingly impressive by examination with different bunches; that likely could be valid. Cases that it holds 100% of the line strength should be bogus. Cautious tests propose a lot more modest rate, e.g., around 50 – 60%. Davy himself says it is "a most loved bunch for the people who contend in International Fly fishing contests."

Disservices: Some clients have discovered it holds ineffectively when the interlaced line is utilized; however, this issue might also be settled using the Double Davy Knot.

Bimini Twist Knot

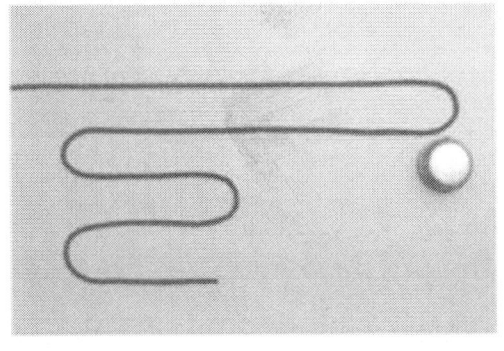 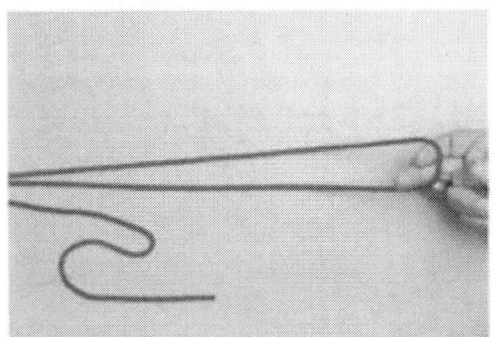

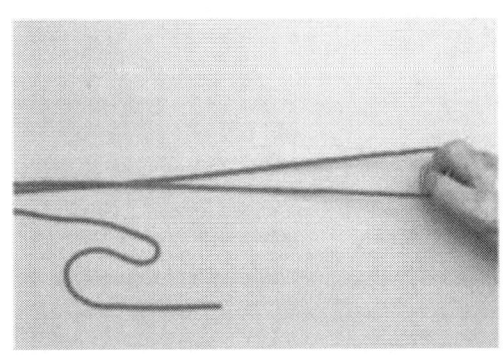 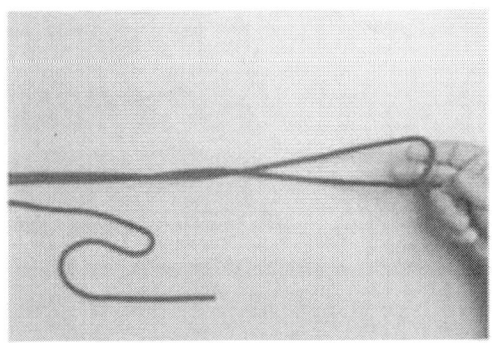

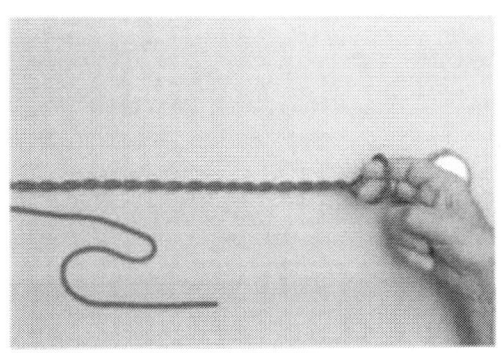 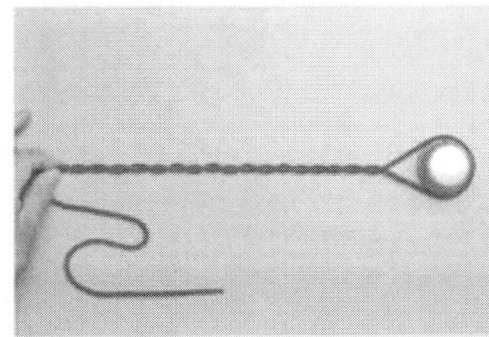

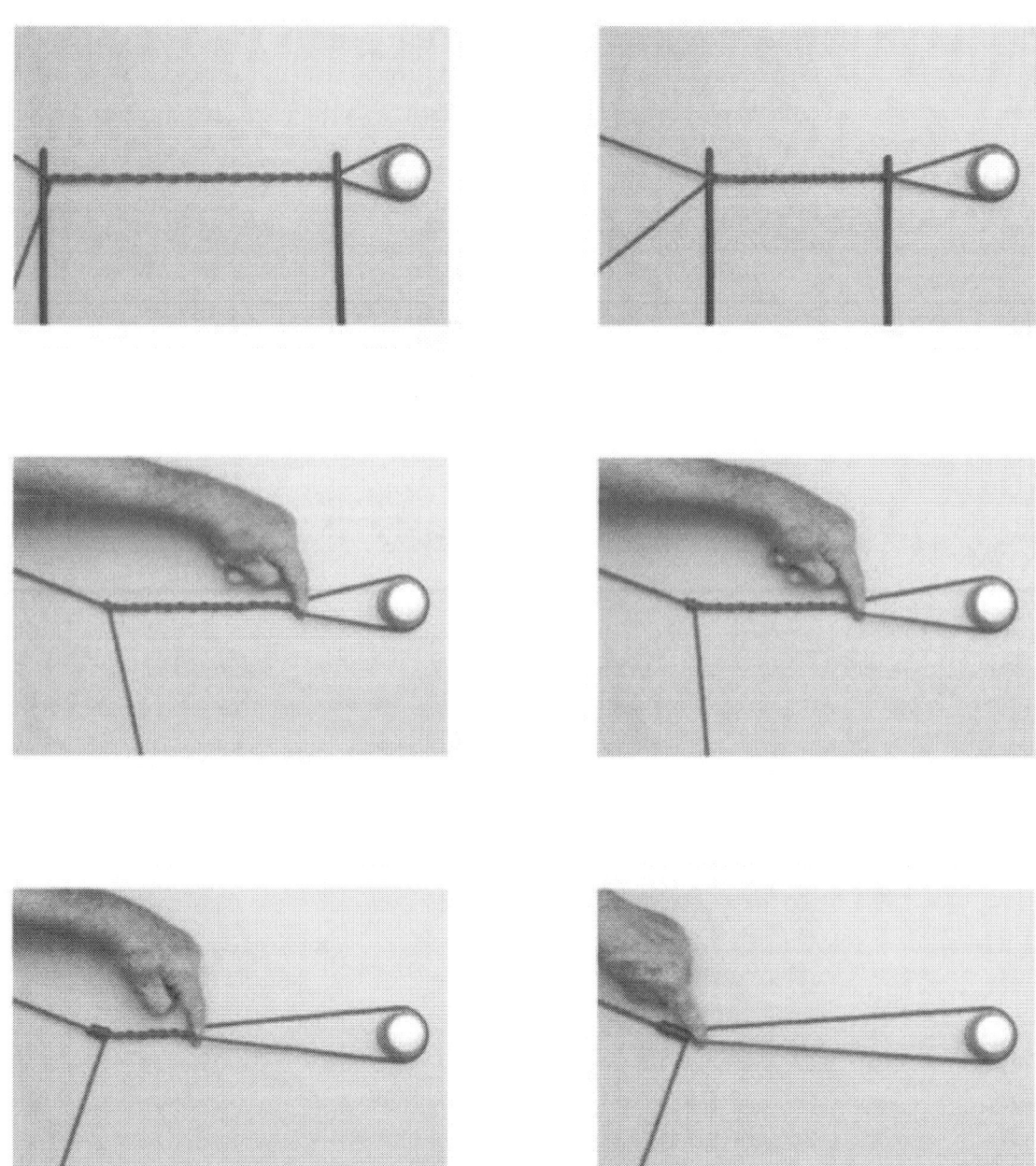

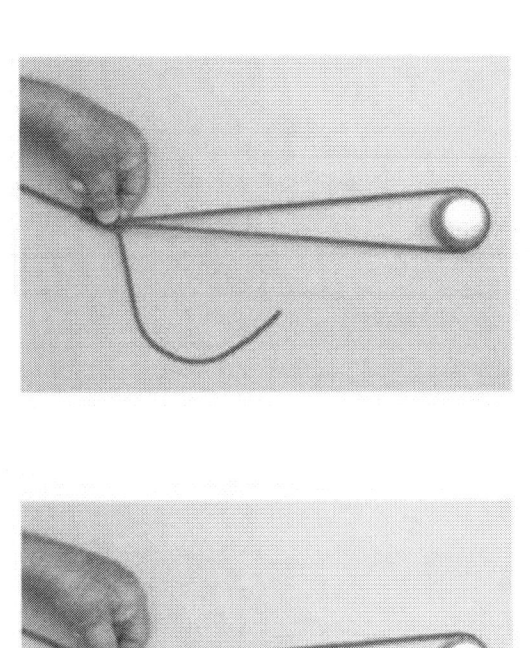
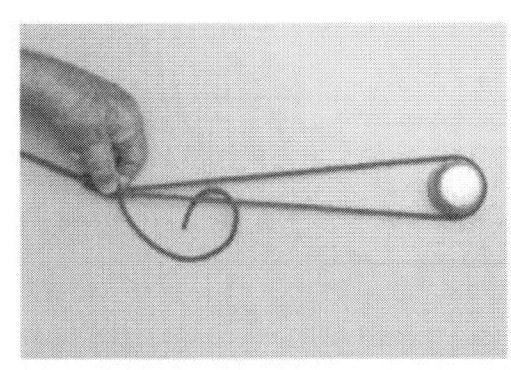
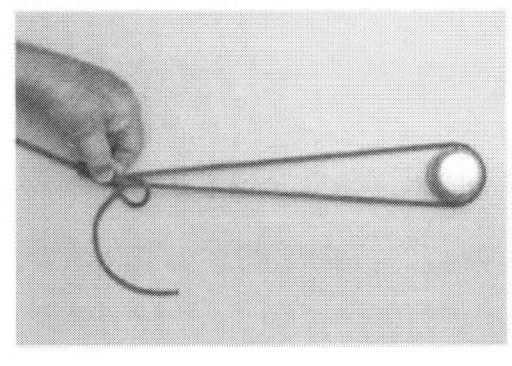
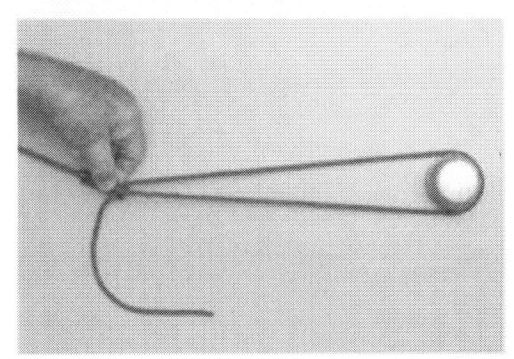
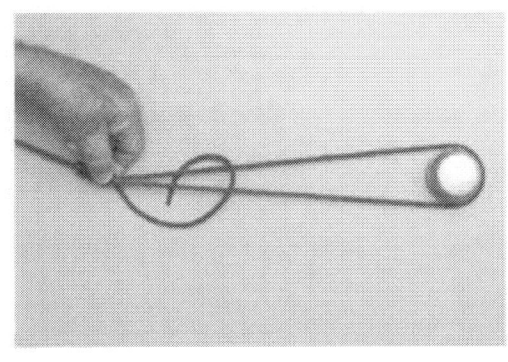
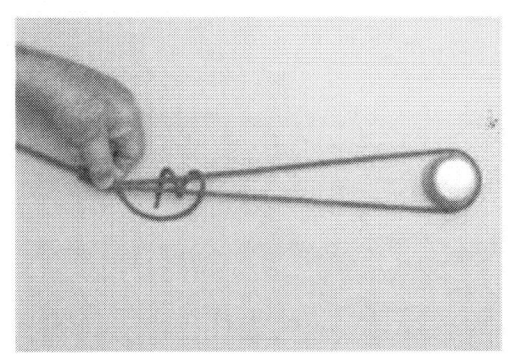

35

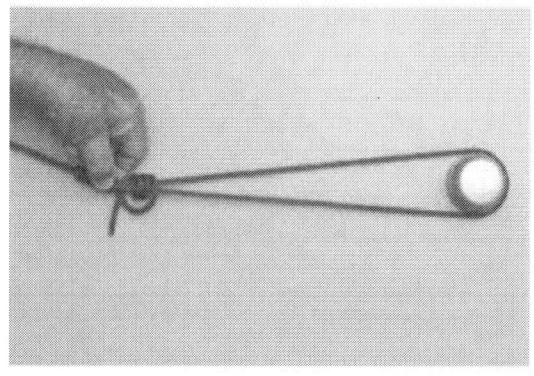 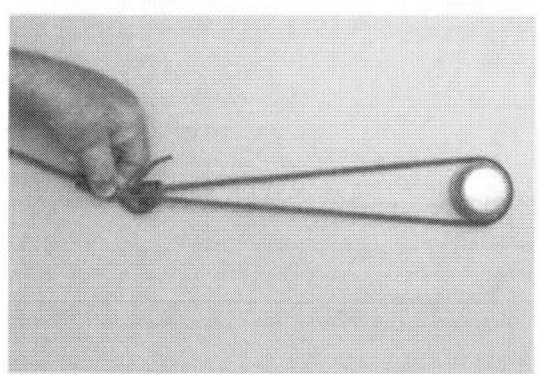

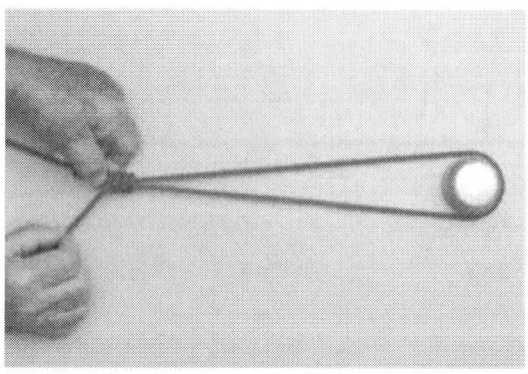 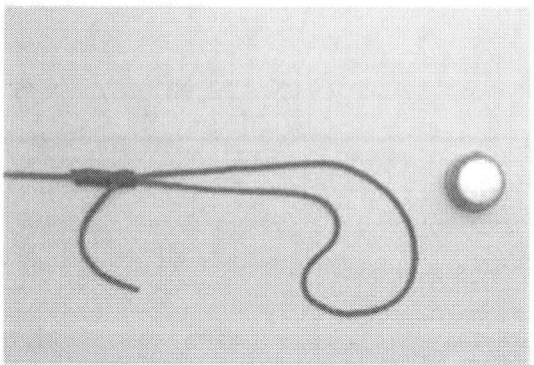

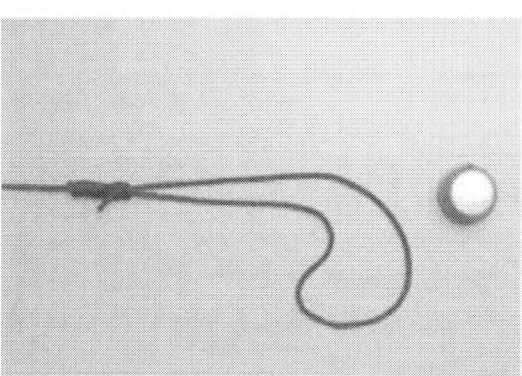

With a long label end, structure a circle and curve it no less than 20 complete turns. With finger and thumb (sticks here), pack the turns to make the label end twist firmly around the turns. Hold the bunch and secure it with a Half Hitch and multi-circle hitch (fold label end between the lines). Fix and trim.

Uses: The Bimini Twist is utilized to make a solid circle as a twofold line pioneer on the end of a fishing line that would then use for a circle-to-circle association.

Tying it: The many strategies depicted to connect the Bimini Twist vouch for its clumsiness. Knees, snares, spare hands, and business tie creators have all been suggested. The activity utilized rope to make the bunch apparent – however, it used just a tiny amount of the necessary number of turns. Albeit one group detailed getting excellent outcomes with around twelve turns, others have shown that this comes up short and suggest about 30 turns for monofilament and more for plait.

Choices: The Bimini Twist activity shows the bunch tied off with a Half Hitch followed by a multi-turn hitch. Numerous anglers do utilize both. Even though they are both shown, the Half Hitch was loosened to permit the liveliness to be done with just the multi-turn hitch. This delivers a smoother completed bunch and is liked by a developing number of anglers.

Benefits: The strength of the Bimini Twist relies on the strain being moved progressively to the bunch over an impressive length. It is better known and more broadly utilized than the Australian Braid – which has comparative properties and might be simpler to learn.

Breaking Strain: The Bimini Twist is professed to protect 100% of the line's breaking strain. Nonetheless, these striking outcomes are recorded under ideal conditions and may likewise be gotten while fishing – cooled, wet, and without too extraordinary a shock load. Cautious research center testing has shown that the bunch fizzles under certain conditions. Abrupt jerks on dry Bimini Twist cause warming because of the grating. This outcome in disappointment at lower breaking strains. Made one severe shock test on a 70 turn Bimini Twist attached with 80 lb monofilament with no pioneer, and it fizzled at around 20 lb.

Basic Knots

Overhand Knot

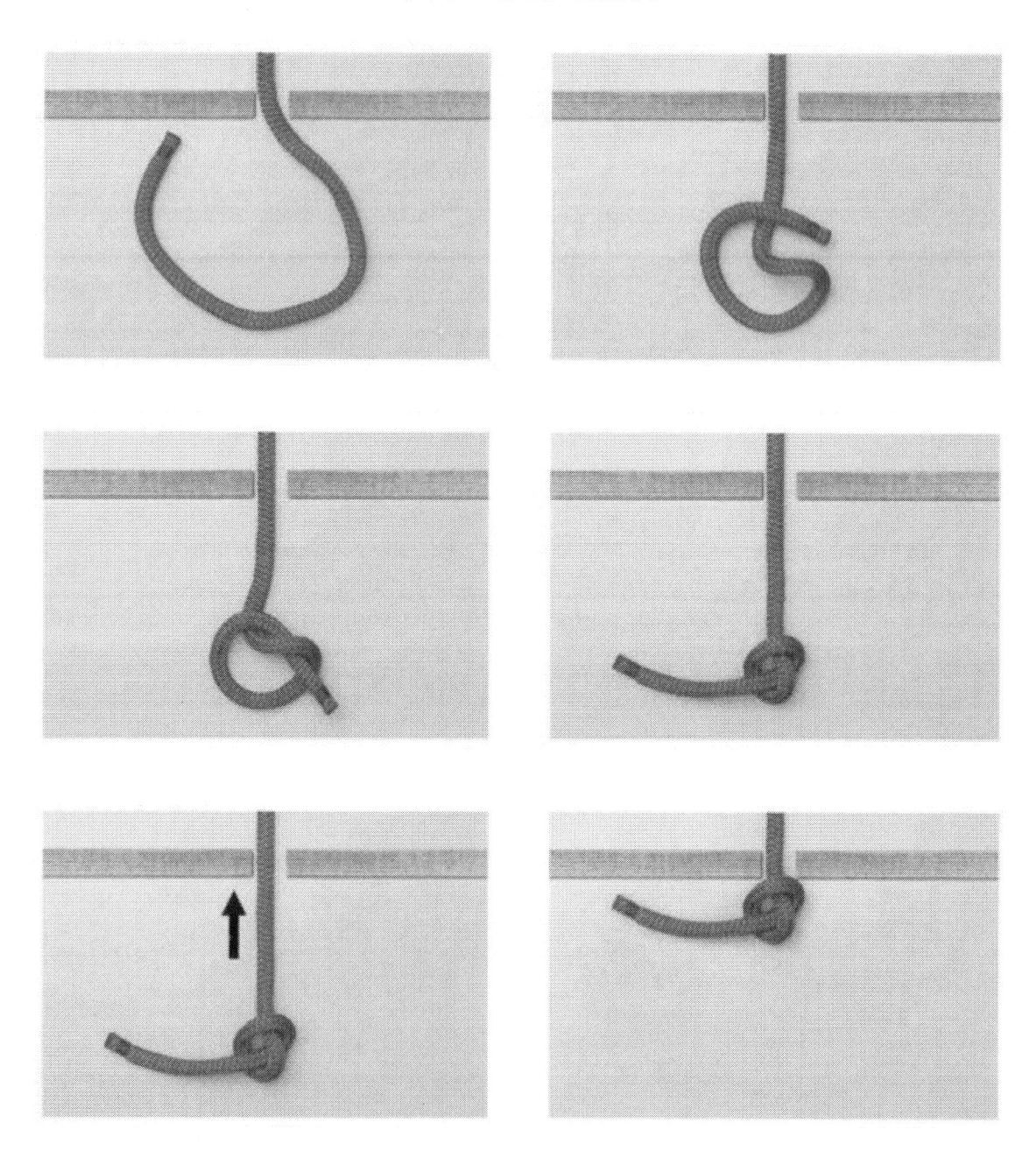

Structure a circle and pass the end through it. Fix it to shape the Overhand Knot. At the point when pulled tight, it can work as a basic plug hitch.

Double Overhand Knot: The main turn is frequently trailed by a second – to make the more oversized plug hitch, the Double Overhand Knot.

Suggestions: As a plug, the Overhand Knot enjoys one benefit: it is one of only a handful of exceptional plug hitches that can be tied firmly facing an article or a bunch. Although the Double Overhand makes a decent plug "Bunch," the Ashley Stopper Knot is liked when a much bigger plug tie is required.

Figure 8 Knot

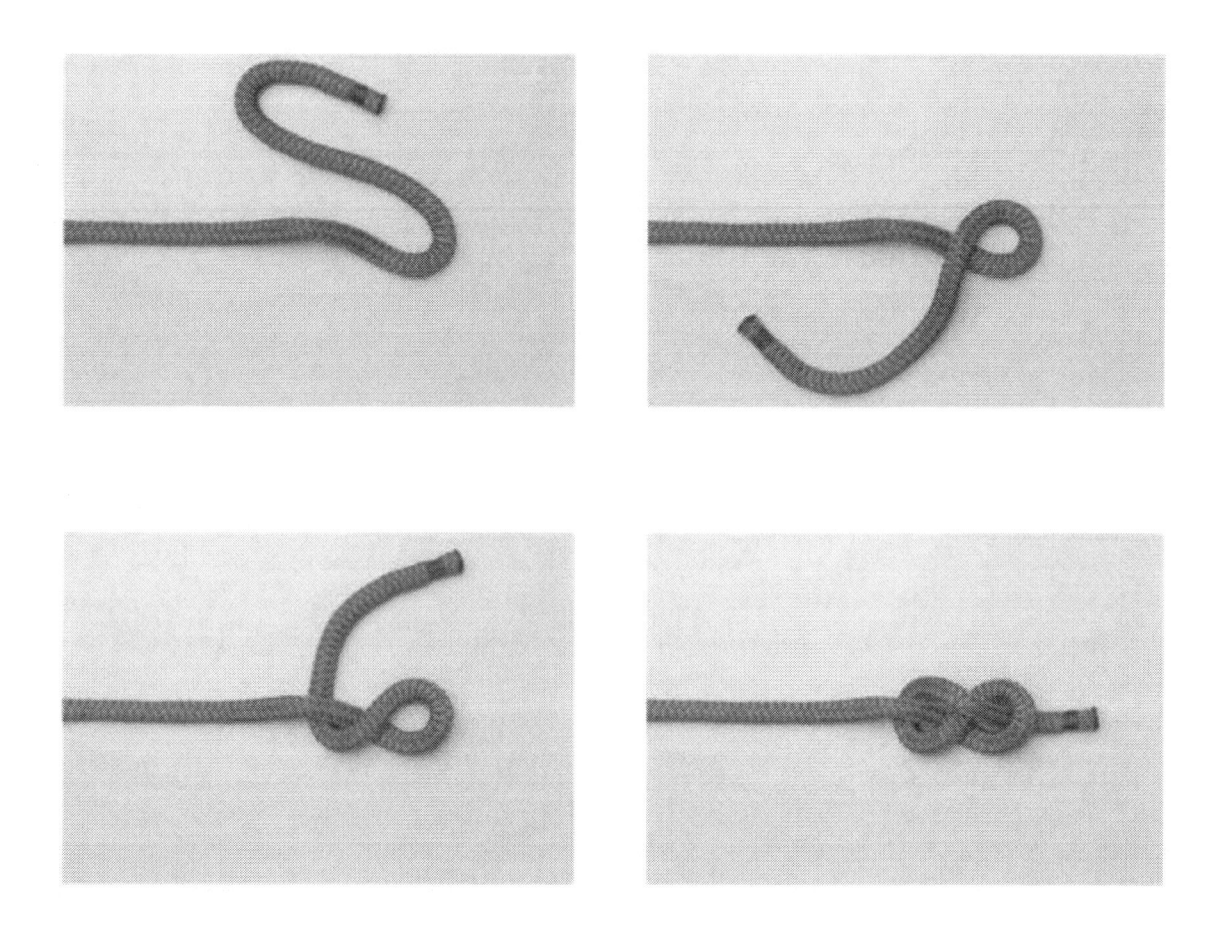

Pass the tail over itself to form a loop. Continue under and around the standing end. Complete the knot by passing the bottom down through the loop.

Take care to avoid coming up through the loop, which merely forms an overhand knot. It would still be a stopper knot but smaller and much harder to undo when pulled tight.

Uses: The Figure 8 Knot provides a quick and convenient stopper knot to prevent a line sliding out of sight, e.g., up inside the mast. Its virtue is that it doesn't bind even after it has been jammed tightly against a block; it can be undone easily. This virtue is also, occasionally, a vice. The Figure 8 Knot can fall undone and then has to be retied.

Comparison: The Figure 8 Knot should be compared to other standard stopper knots. It is much better than the simple Overhand Knot, which is smaller and can bind so tightly that it can be tough to undo. However, the Double Overhand Knot, the Stevedore Stopper Knot, and the Ashley Stopper Knot all make better Stopper knots because they are more significant and more stable. For slippery ropes, the EStar Stopper Knot is the best.

Climbing: For climbing, where safety is paramount, the Double Overhand Knot is the preferred Stopper knot. However, the Figure 8 Knot is vital to climbers because it is the basis for tying the Figure 8 Bend (Rope Join), the Figure 8 Loop Follow Through, and the Double Figure 8 Loop.

Half Hitch Knot

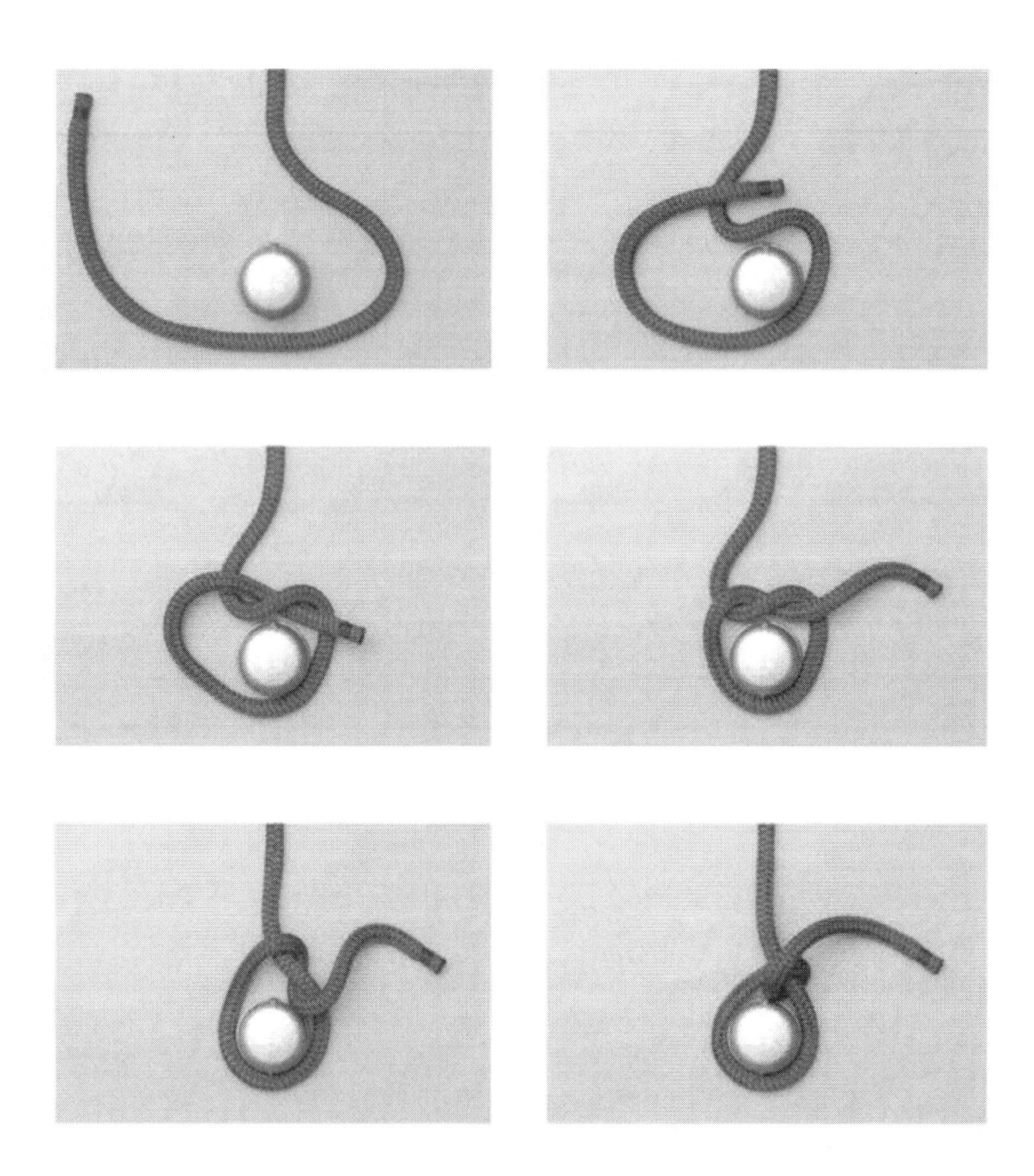

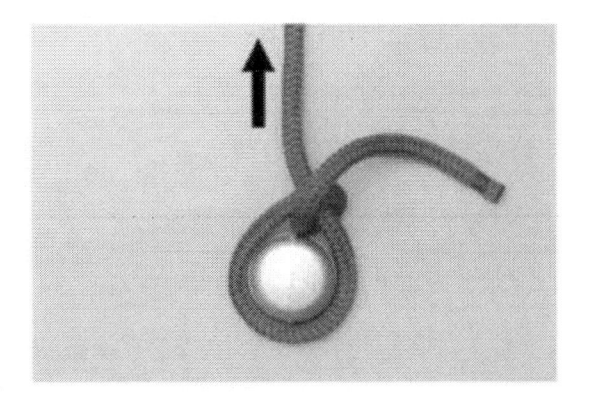

Structure a circle around the object. Pass the end around the standing end and through the process. Fix into a Half Hitch, intended to take a heap (Arrow) on the fixed end. Add a subsequent Half Hitch to make the bunch secure. These means delineate the standard strategy for tying Half Hitches.

Tying it: As displayed in the liveliness, the Half Hitch Knot can be overturned from resembling an overhand bunch into the ordinary look of a Half Hitch. In this liveliness, Half Hitch shows how it is usually tied – wrapping it around the standing end and tucking it under itself.

Two Half Hitches: The central Half Hitch Knot is almost consistently followed by a second – or more. It is standard to pass the rope the same way around to make both Half Hitches. This creates a Clove Hitch around the standing end. When the subsequent Half Hitch is switched, it makes a Cow Hitch round the standing back.

Suggestions: Although two Half Hitches do make a total "Hitch," it is wiser to initially pass the rope around the post or bollard the next opportunity to make the Round Turn and Two Half Hitches. This is safer and gives more straightforward control of the heap while tying the Half Hitches.

Half Knot

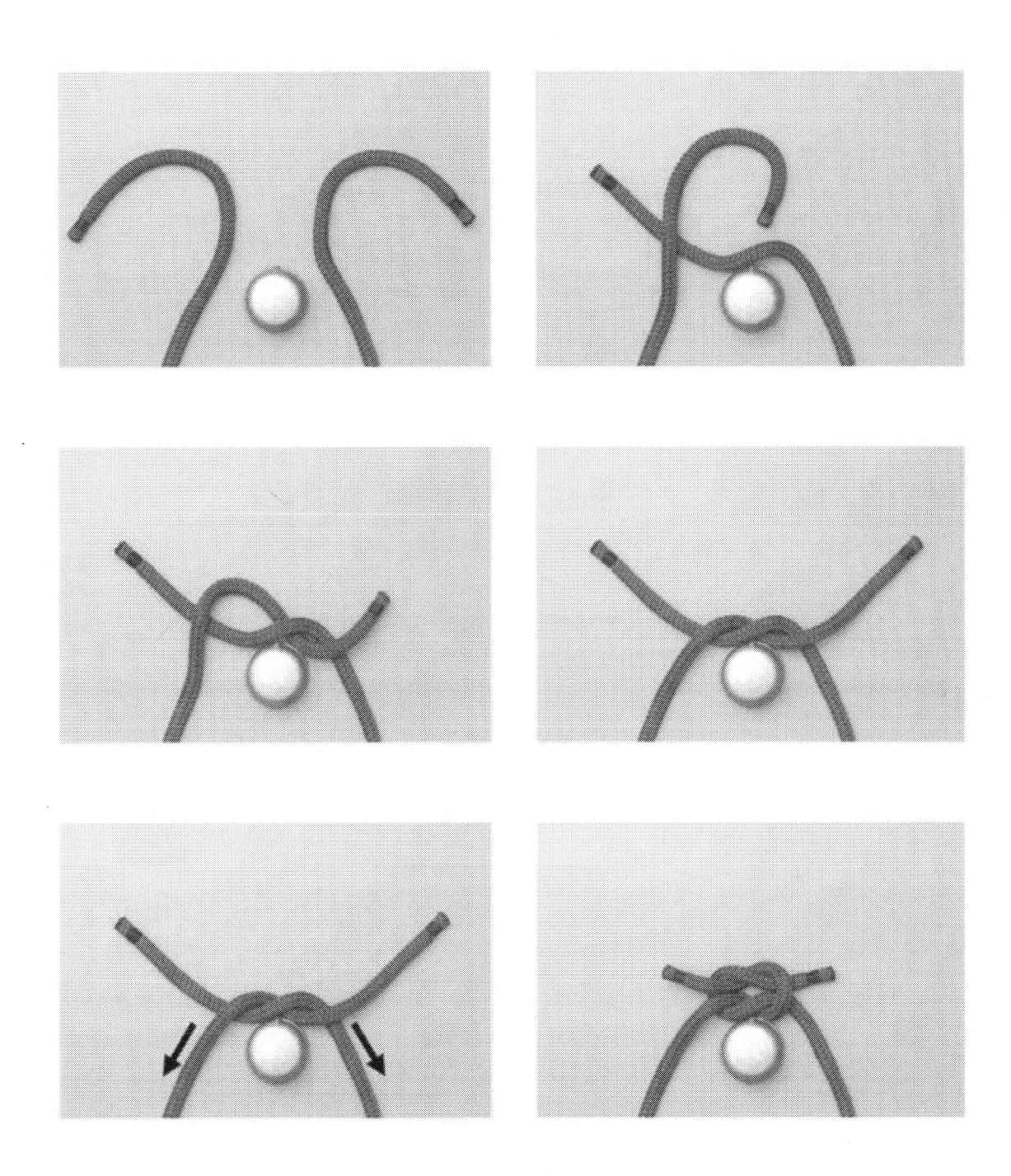

Get the two closures over one another. Ignore one end and afterward under the other to make the Half Knot - which takes the heap (bolts) in the two ropes. Add a subsequent Half Knot to make the whole bunch - the Square (Reef) hitch.

45

Tying it: As displayed in the movement, one end is wrapped around the other to create a balanced bunch. The balance is significant because the Half Knot can, as it were, "tie" when tied like this.

Two Half Knots: The central Half Knot is almost consistently followed by a second – or more. Make sure to observe what direction you tied it, e.g., "Directly over Left." This is significant because to connect the Square accurately (Reef) Knot, the following Half Knot should be "Leftover Right." When the subsequent Half Knot is a rehash of the main, it makes a Granny Knot.

Suggestions: Although two Half Knots make an acceptable "Bunch," its utilization should be limited. The bunch made, the Square (or Reef) tie, is infamous for its ability to upset and slip and should never utilize it for bare burdens.

Macrame: In Macrame, the Half Knot is regularly tied around a focal center of at least two strands. Contingent upon how it is connected, different names know it. When attached with rehashed indistinguishable Half Knots, the outcome is a winding or Banister Bar); when tied with substituting left and right Half Knots, the outcome is known as the Solomon Bar.

Noose Knot

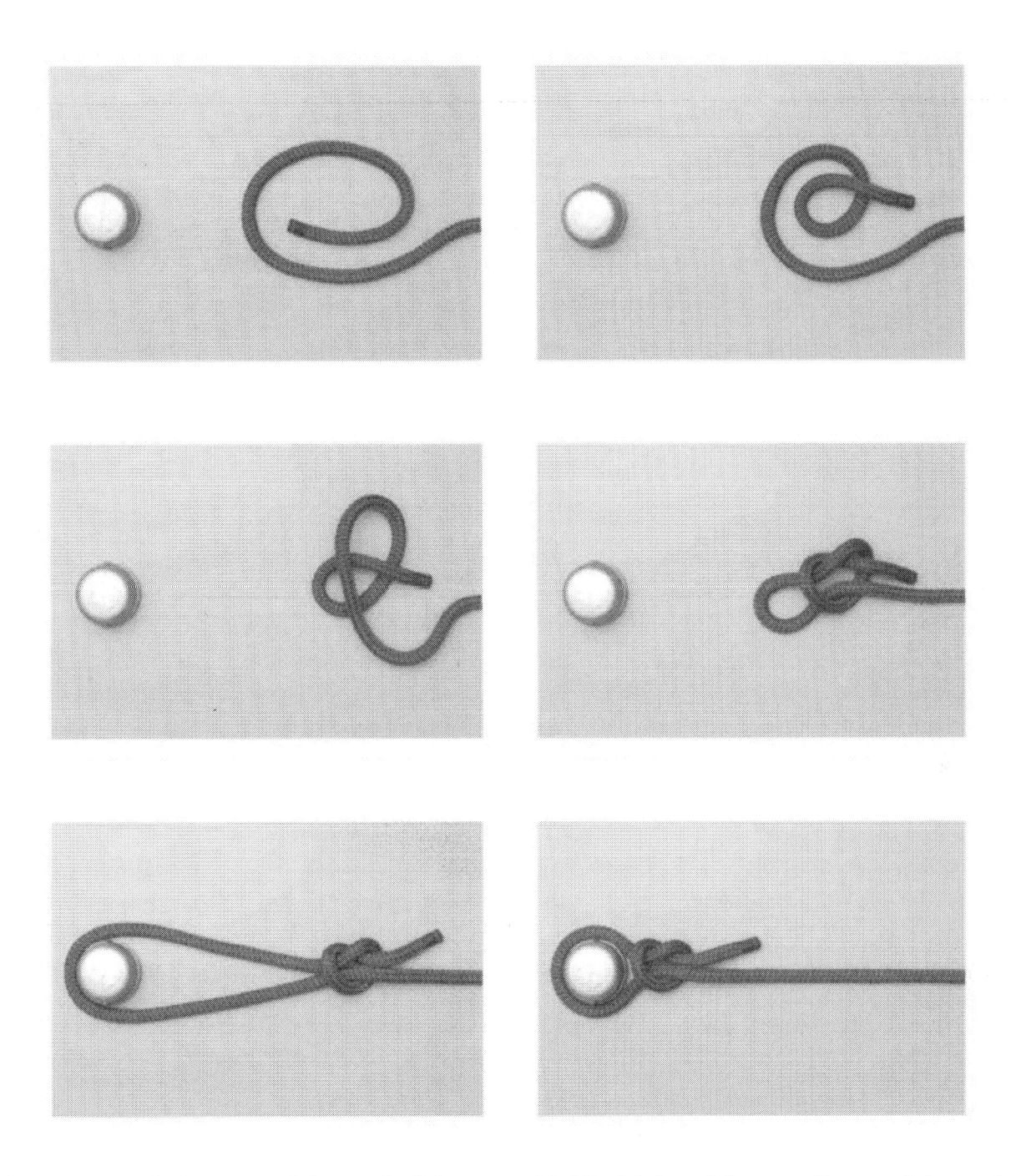

Structure a circle toward the end of the rope. Fold a bight of the standing end through the process. Make the bight bigger and pass it around the item. Pull on the upright end to fix the Noose.

Uses: The basic Noose Knot is indistinguishable in construction to the Slip Knot, except that the bight to be embedded is shaped from the long end – and not the short one. It has been utilized as a catch to get little creatures, and it isn't the Hangman's Knot.

The Noose Knot is a much of the time-tied bunch – being utilized in the Arbor Knot and weaving as the principal circle when projecting on – where it is regularly connected as a Noose and called a Slip Knot. It has numerous different uses, including dealing with the string when tying up a bundle.

The Hangman's Knot is identified with the straightforward Noose; Aside from that, many turns are folded over the circle. Its alleged benefit for hanging was helpful: fair use was planned to bring about a wrecked neck – causing a quick passing. It is purposely not shown here (see underneath).

"Noose" Name Confusion: It is disastrous that "noose" is utilized in various ways: 1. The bunch portrayed on this page; 2. An elucidating term for circle ties that fix under a burden; and, 3. In some cases applied to the Hangman's Knot. The Uni Knot (Duncan Knot) and the Hangman's Knot are frequently wrongly viewed as something similar to aggravate it. We suggest utilizing "Noose" for this bunch and the proper names, e.g., "Running Bowline" or "Uni Knot," and so forth, for other noose-like bunches.

Tying it: The method utilized in the Noose Knot activity tucks a bight of the long end through a circle. A similar outcome can be acquired nearly as effectively bypassing the end round the item and utilizing the short end to tie a Half Hitch around the long end. Connected this way, it is the initial segment of one variant of the Butcher's Knot used to get meat for broiling – where once more, similarly as in weaving, it is frequently incorrectly named a "Slip Knot."

Risk: The Noose tie is not a Hangman's Knot; **however, it can likewise be lethal.** It should never be tight around somebody's neck, and the bunch can tie and confine the bloodstream. A few Questions on Snopes find out if it is illicit to depict the Hangman's Knot, and it isn't.

Enactment: However, 2009 Louisiana Laws TITLE 14 and New York Article 240.31 both deny the showcase of a Noose due to its utilization as a method for terrorizing. The Louisiana Bill indicates the Hangman's Noose, and the New York State Article utilizes the nonexclusive "noose."

Sheet Bend

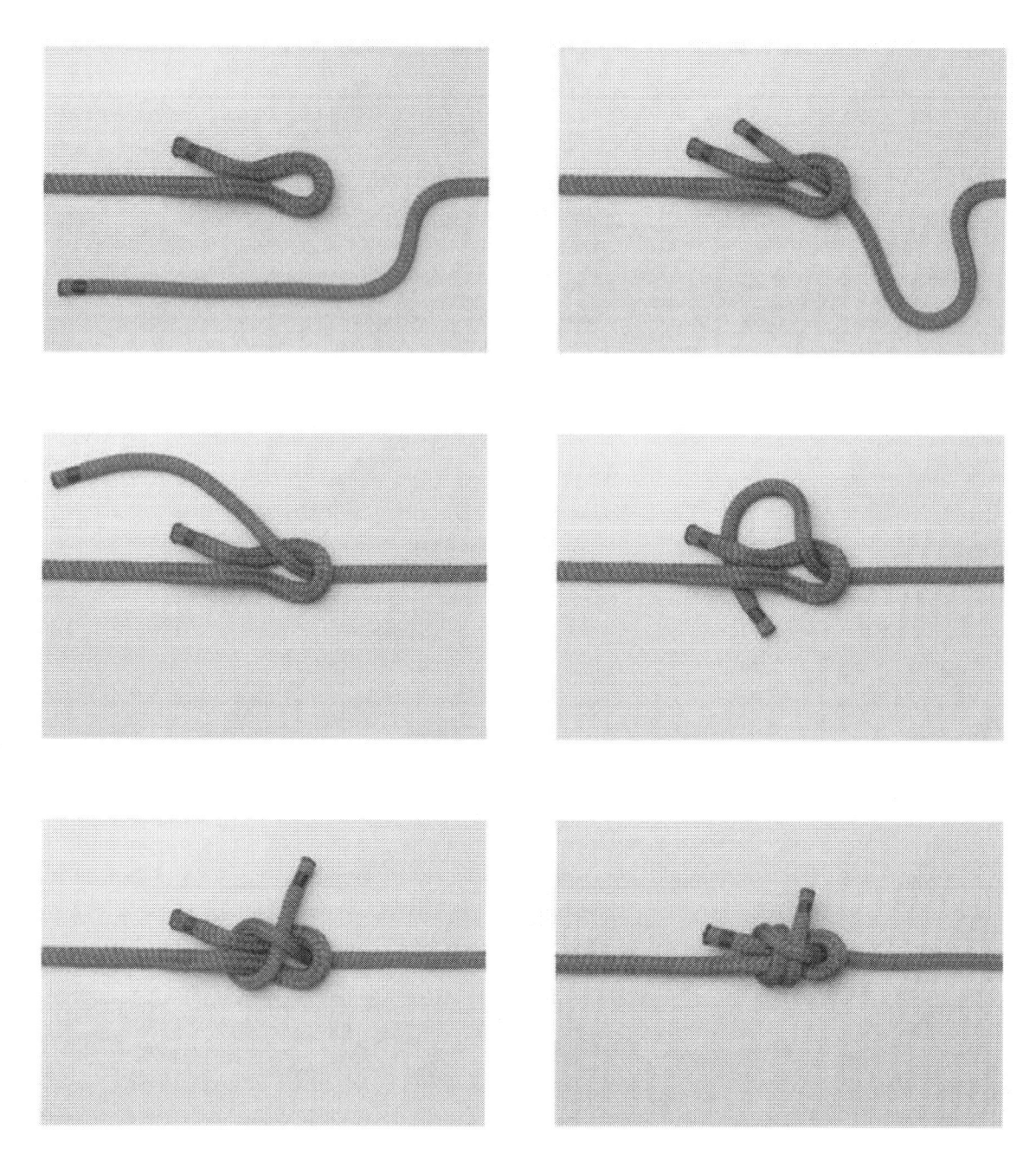

Structure a bight in the thicker rope and hold it in one hand. Pass the more slender string through the bight and behind the tail, and standing ends in a specific order. At last, fold the more modest rope under itself to complete the bunch.

The Double Sheet Bend utilizes a second pivot to the thicker rope. It is suggested when there is an incredible contrast in the widths of the two strings.

Uses: The Sheet Bend or Weaver's Knot is suggested for joining two ropes of varying sizes. The thicker rope should be utilized for the straightforward bight as displayed. Notwithstanding, it functions admirably if the strings are of a similar size.

Caution: For the Animation, the ends were left short, and for essential loads, the ends should be left significantly longer.

Becket Hitch: The Becket Hitch is a very much like bunch. In any case, it is a "Hitch": it doesn't join two ropes; it appends a string to a Becket (a rope handle or an eye). The Blue Rope would be Becket in the activity, and the Red Rope would be attached to it with a Becket Hitch.

Tying it: The Sheet Bend would supplant the Square (Reef) connect; aside from that, it's anything but a limiting bunch – the two closures should be accessible in your grasp with no heap on the ropes. (The Square Knot – with every one of its shortcomings – can be tied tight against a sailor package and remains typically tight while the subsequent Half Hitch is connected). The Weaver's Knot is tied in different ways. One way is displayed here. A slip bunch or Noose is linked toward the end of the fleece, and the new piece is strung through the circle. Pulling on the Noose closes attracts the new work.

Double Sheet Bend: When the ropes are remarkably divergent in size, the tail of the more modest yarn can be taken twice round the bight in the more extensive string to make the twofold sheet twist.

Design: When accurately tied, the two tails of the Sheet Bend lie on a similar side of the bunch. The elective variant – with the tails on inverse sides – is less dependable.

Slip Knot

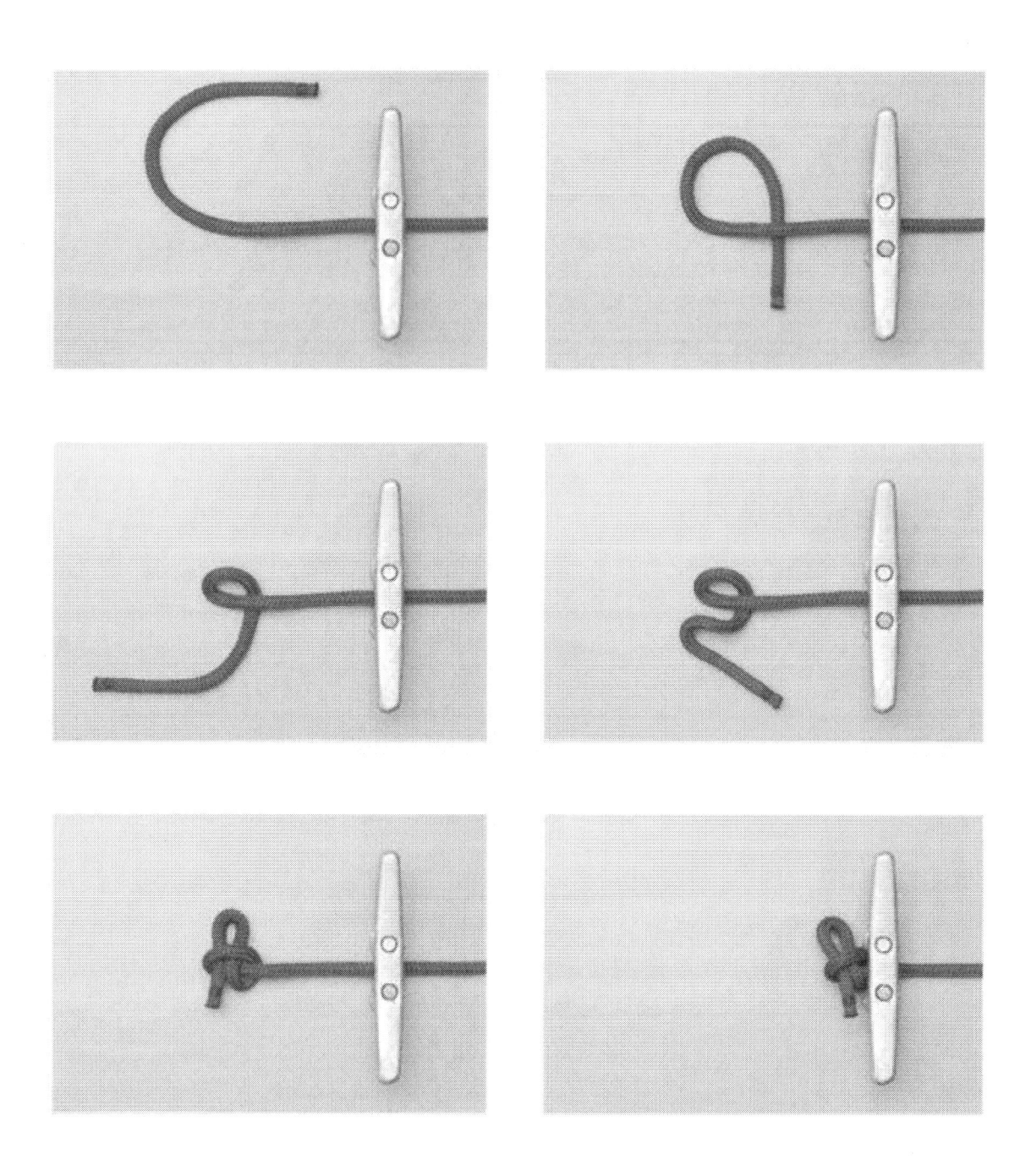

Structure a circle toward the end of the rope. Set up a bight in the short end. Fold the bight through the circle and fix. The bunch can be utilized as an impermanent plug hitch.

Uses: The Slip Knot is indistinguishable in design to the Noose Knot, except that the bight to be embedded is framed from the short end – not the long. The Slip Knot is perhaps the most often tied knot utilized in sewing as the immediate circle when projecting on – where it is known as a slip tie yet now and again connected as a noose. It very well may be utilized as a quick plug hitch – as displayed in the activity.

Disarray: Some scholars apply the expression "Slip Knot" to different bunches – where any circle slides along the standing end. In any case, such bunches also have notable other names, e.g., Bowline on a Bight and different fishing ties that can slide to fix. Further, such groups don't work as Slip Knots. Since they fix under load, they work as nooses. Thus, the conventional abuse of the name Slip Knots is condemned. On this site, Slip Knot is saved for this one bunch.

Slipped Knots: Many bunches can be finished with a bight rather than the end. A group tied this way is depicted as slipped, e.g., a Slipped Rolling Hitch. Slipped Buntline Hitch, Slipped Half Hitch. Hypothetically, they would rapidly loosen the bunch by pulling on the free end to deliver the bight. By and by, this relies upon how much burden has arrived at the bight. For sure, firmly stacked bunches, e.g., a Buntline Hitch, tend to be hard to deliver and exceedingly difficult to pull the last bend of the actual bight out of the fixed turn.

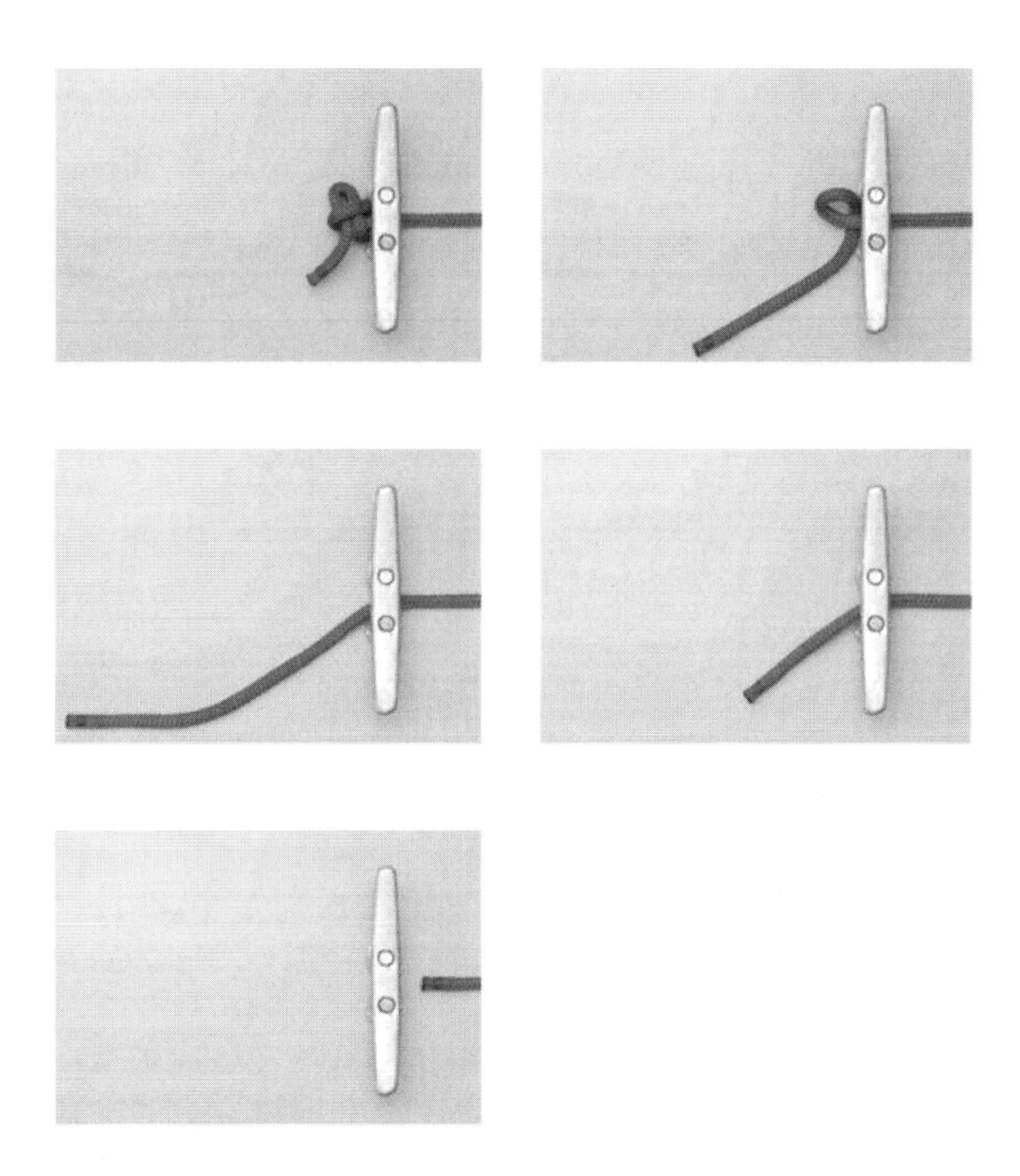

To release the slip tie, just pull on the short end to allow the rope to run free.

Square Knot

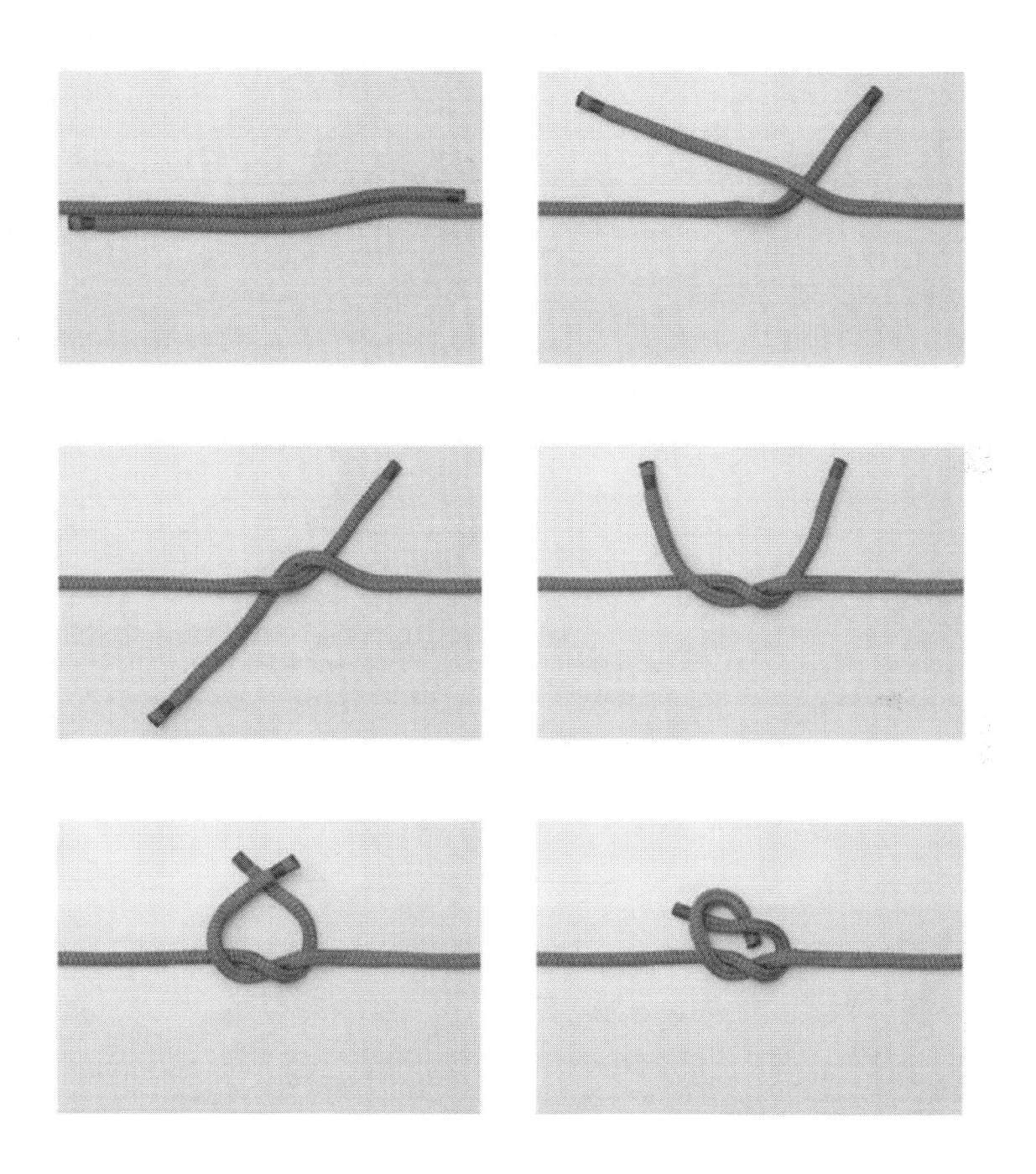

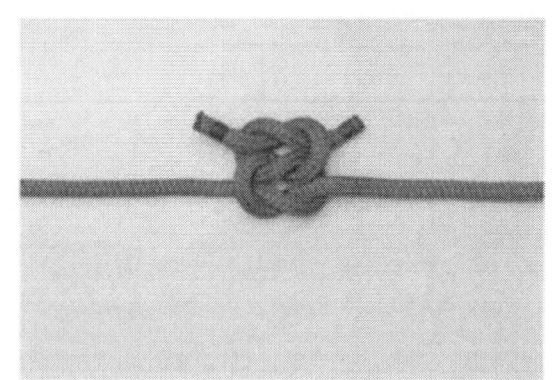

Take two ropes and cross them to shape a half bunch. Cross them a subsequent time and pull the closures tight to frame the Square Knot.

First Knot: The Square (Reef) Knot is generally realized when we tie the bands on our first pair of shoes. Honestly, it is generally a bow that we tie – however, the essential bunch is a Square (Reef) Knot. We likewise learn precisely how unsuitable the bunch is. It slips, it comes unraveled, it jams, and it is all around simple to tie a Granny instead, which acts even less well.

Reason: It is expected to be a limiting bunch and, tied in the suitable material against a bent surface, the primary Half Knot might tie – however, I can't trust it. That is why specialists utilize an additional turn in the main Half Knot to accomplish the limiting required while setting up the subsequent Half Knot.

Caution: Never use it for primary burdens.

Uses: Nevertheless, the Square (Reef) tie has many uses yet not where wellbeing is essential, e.g., you can tie a sail cover over a sail; you can tie the string on a gift, and you can tie the bands on your shoes (on the off chance that they accompany bands). It is additionally one of the many bunches utilized in macramé. All the more significantly, the experience of tying a Square Knot shows the principal cycle of tying a Half Knot or Half Hitch.

Variations: The last Frames of the Animation show a few types: The Granny Knot is offered because it is so generally tied in blunder; Surgeons ordinarily utilize the Double

Throw Knot or Surgical Knot as the initial segment of a Ligature; and the Thief Knot is incorporated for revenue as the last casing, even though it is a pointless bunch. When the Square (Reef) Knot is utilized, it is customary to add extra Half Knots as security – an accolade for how unacceptable a bunch it is. A superior option might be to use two Surgeon's Half Knots, which improve restricting bunches for each stage and a protected, last pack. When the subsequent Half Surgeon's Knots is tied as a bow, it makes a Secure Shoelace Bow.

The Square (Reef) bunch can likewise be tied utilizing bights (circles). For instance, to go through long shoelaces, the bunch can be attached with circles from the beginning. This can't loosen the last "bow" by pulling the ends – however, it makes a protected bunch.

Boating Knots

Alpine Butterfly Bend

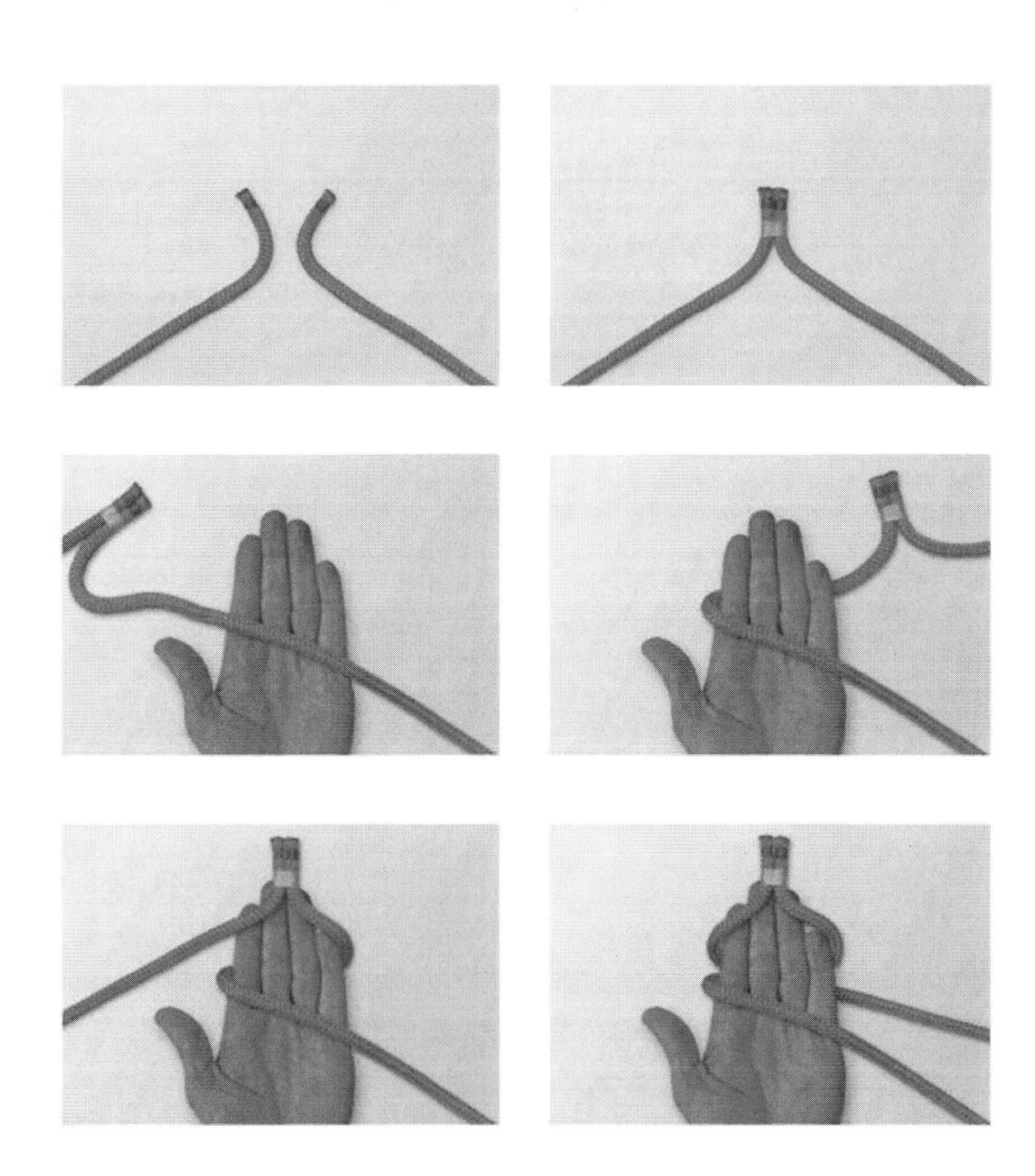

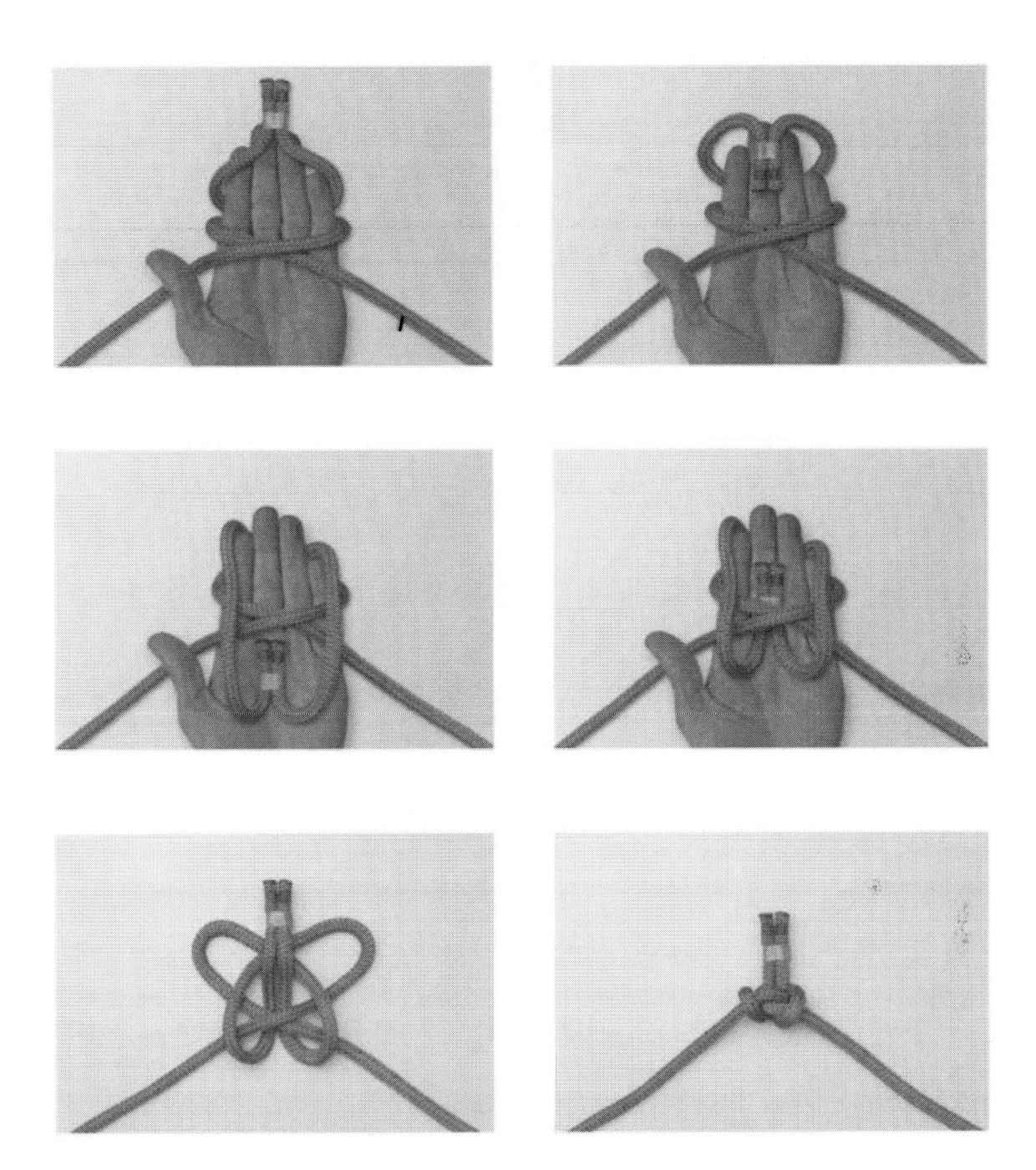

Join the two closures for a brief time. Wind the rope around your hand with the goal that the join is by your fingertips. Go around once more. Overlap the join back and afterward up under different ropes. Push the bunch off your hand and fix to see the presence of the Alpine Butterfly. At last, discharge the transitory join.

Tying it: Several techniques are portrayed for connecting the Alpine Butterfly Bend. We formulated the strategy utilized in the movement, and it enhances other "hand-winding" techniques and finds the intersection and where it is to be tucked. This straightforward strategy sets the Alpine Butterfly Bend separated and makes it one of our favored alternatives.

Variety: Our procedure doesn't need the ends to be joined. After the underlying wrap, fold the end of the main rope between your fingers. Then, fold the end of the second rope alongside the first and complete the wrap at that point. The two ends would then be able to be passed together like tape.

Benefits: The Loop rendition partakes in the standing of dependably tolerating strain between the ends of the circle and either end. In this form, the circle doesn't exist, and the pressure falls between the two ends. The Alpine Butterfly Bend has gained notoriety for strength and dependability. The massive benefit of the Alpine Butterfly Bend is its similitude to the Alpine Butterfly Loop – which means learning just one broadly confided in the tie – and one that is not difficult to fix even after a weighty burden.

Breaking Strain: The Alpine Butterfly Bend, similar to the next comparative bunches, passes the strain around the pair of closures in the center. This twofold thickness ought to limit the wrinkling and help to safeguard strength. To be sure, the bunch is ordinarily portrayed as "one of the most grounded." Nonetheless, some cited breaking strains are as low as 53% to 58% – like breaking strains for some different bunches.

Alpine Butterfly Loop

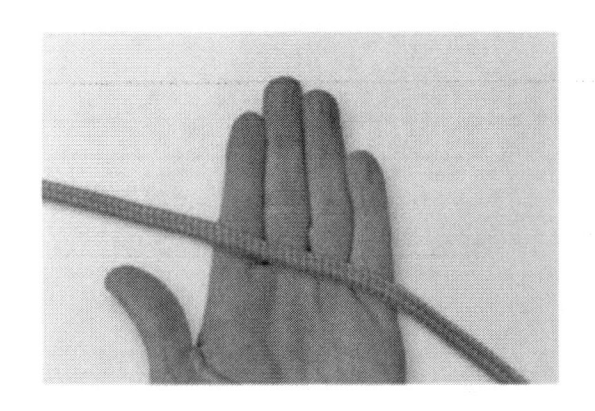

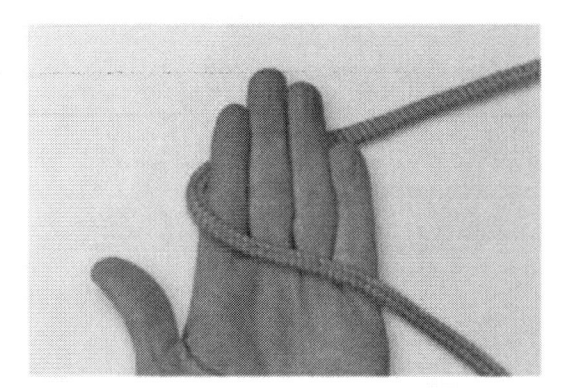

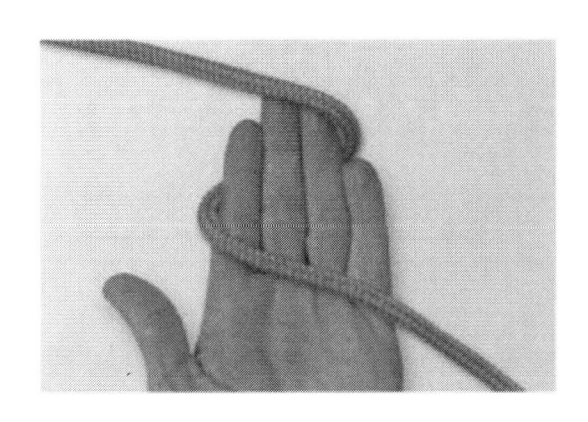

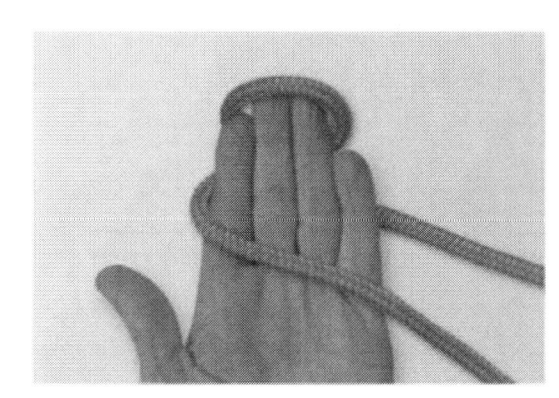

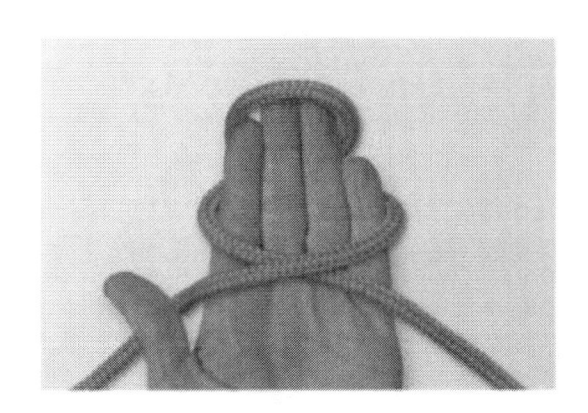

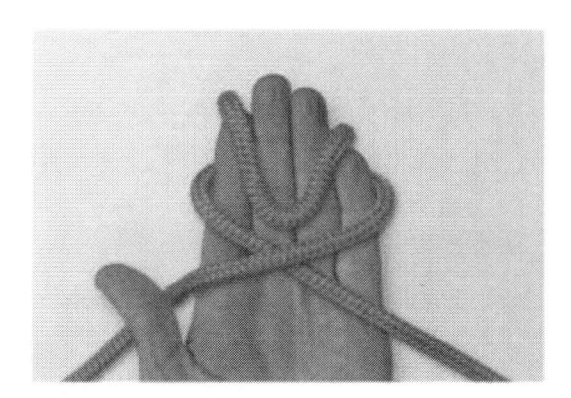

Benefits: The Loop adaptation partakes in the standing of dependably tolerating strain between the ends or between the circle and either end. In this form, the circle doesn't exist, and the pressure falls between the two closures. The Alpine Butterfly Bend has gained notoriety for strength and unwavering quality. The significant benefit of the Alpine Butterfly Bend is its similitude to the Alpine Butterfly Loop – which means learning just one generally confided in the tie – and one that is not difficult to fix even after a substantial burden.

Breaking Strain: The Alpine Butterfly Bend, similar to the next comparable bunches, passes the strain around the pair of ends in the center. This twofold thickness ought to limit the wrinkling and help to safeguard strength. For sure, the bunch is regularly portrayed as "one of the most grounded." Nonetheless, some cited breaking strains are as low as 53% to 58% – like breaking strains for some different bunches.

Uses: The Alpine Butterfly Loop is helpful whenever a protected circle is needed in a rope. A genuine model is a point at which a line of explorers wishes to snare on along the length of a standard string or as a potential choice for the initial segment of a Trucker's Hitch. Likewise, if a length of rope is harmed, it is an excellent method to disconnect the damaged area so the rope might, in any case, be utilized – far more secure than The Sheep Shank.

Tying it: There are a few strategies for tying the Alpine Butterfly Loop. We contrived the strategy that is utilized in the movement. It is an enhancement for other "hand-winding" strategies. It finds the circle: the second intersection of your hand is close to your fingertips and away from the other two turns. This assists you with finding it, get it, and fold it over the two different strands. Setting the bunch usually requires holding the circle in your teeth and pulling the two ends with your hands.

Advantages: The Alpine Butterfly Loop is more steady than either The Bowline on a Bight or The Figure 8 Loop – the two of which might turn over. Even after a substantial burden, the Alpine Butterfly Loop remains sensibly simple to fix, and it is additionally somewhat simpler to tie and more minimal than The Farmer's Loop.

Anchor Hitch

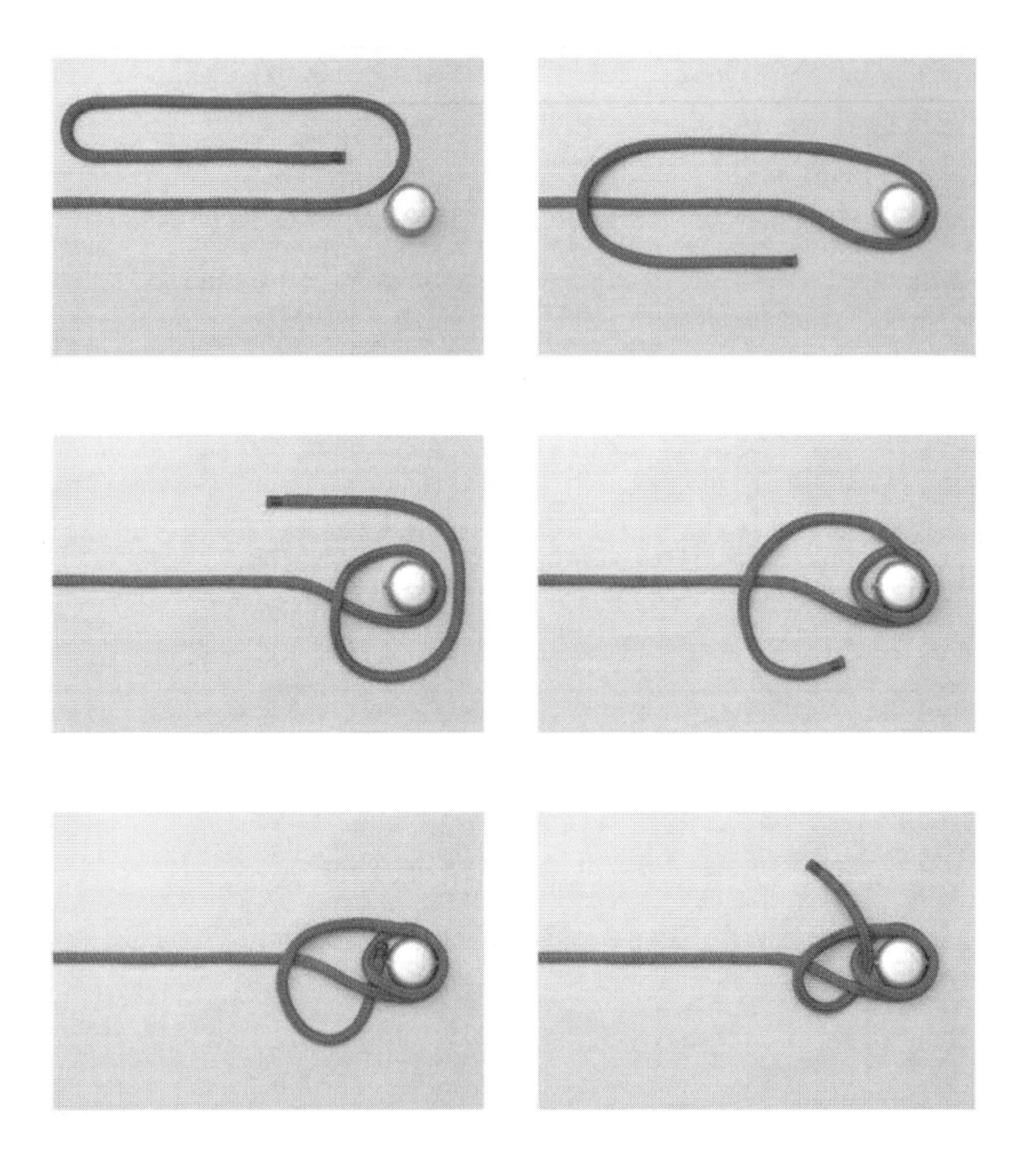

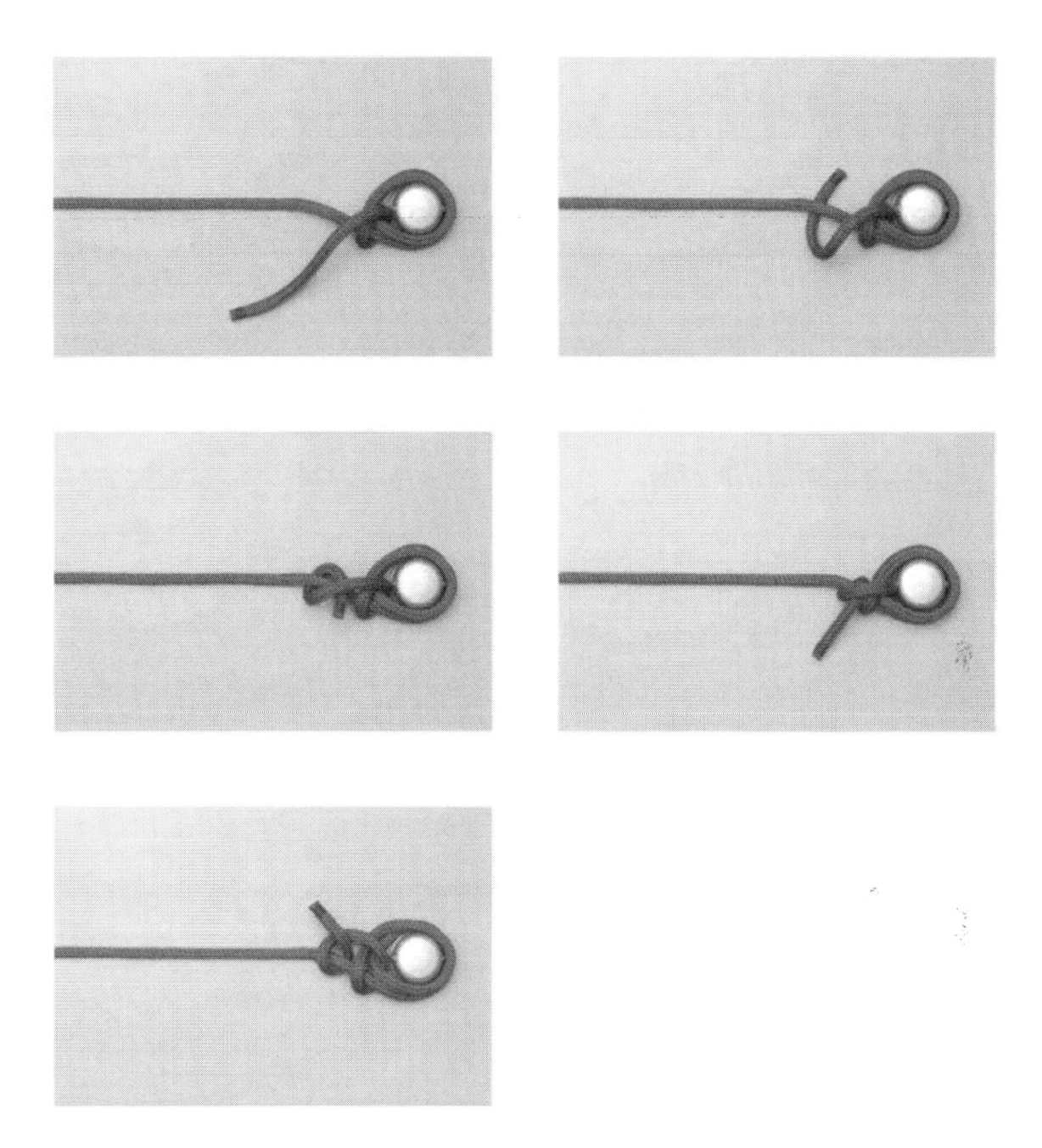

Pass the tail twice around the post keeping the subsequent turn slack. Ignore the tail, the standing end, and go to tie the primary Half Hitch under the first leeway. Proceed around the sheer end to secure the subsequent Half Hitch and complete the bunch.

Uses: The Anchor Hitch or Anchor Bend is otherwise called the Fisherman's Hitch or Fisherman's Bend. It is a fantastic bunch to use for connecting an anchor line to an anchor. To tie a rope to an object, it ought to consistently be known as a hitch.

Notwithstanding, the name Bend gets from when it covered "attached to" and was not confined to joining two ropes.

Correlation: The Anchor Hitch is the same as the Round Turn and Two Half Hitches, so comparable that it is far-fetched if there is a lot of advantage in utilizing one bunch over the other. This is somewhat because many people would add a couple of additional Half Hitches if used either knot to secure an anchor line to an anchor. Many would likewise hold onto the tail of The Anchor Hitch to the standing end for extra security.

Ashley Stopper Knot

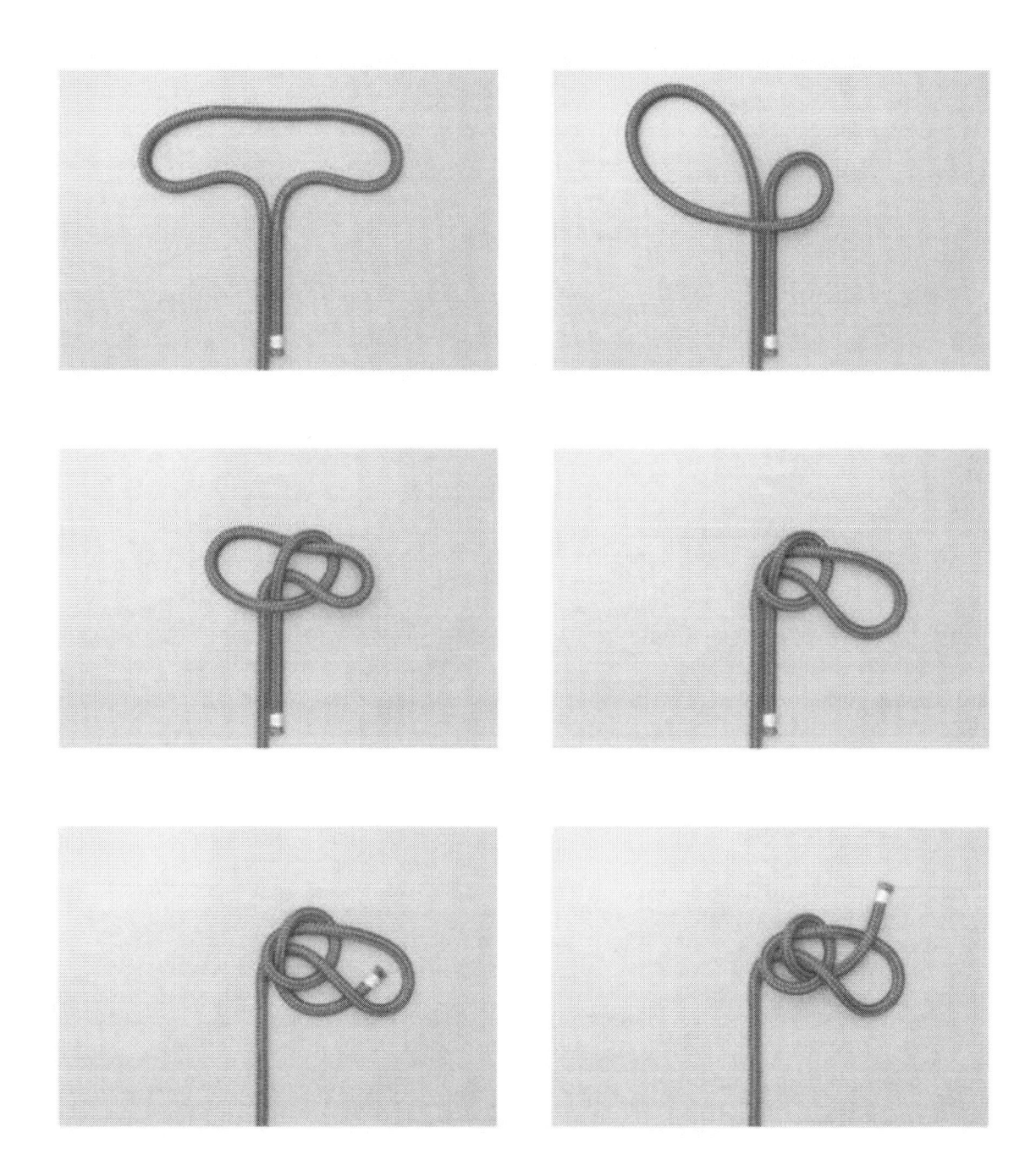

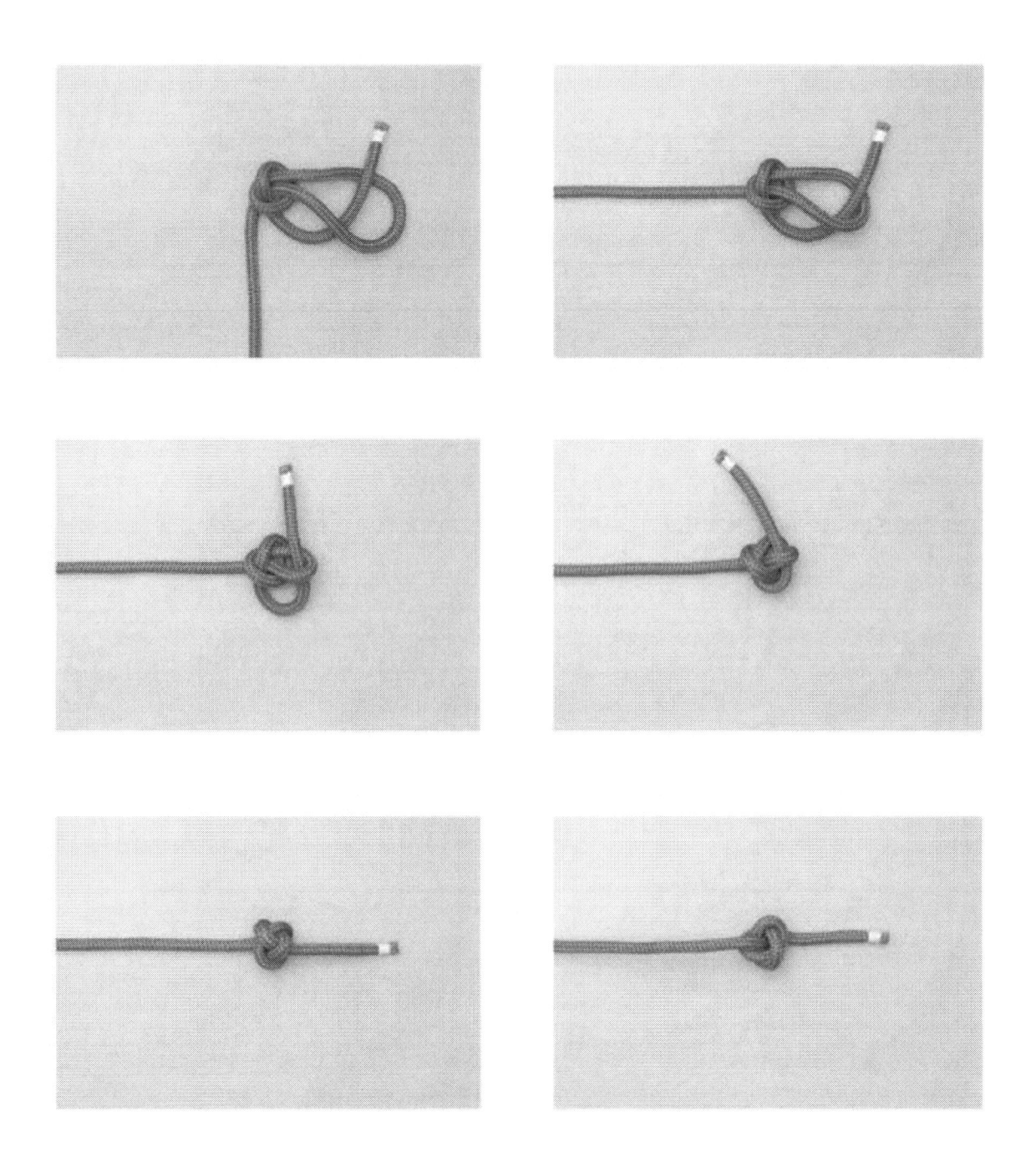

Make a bight and overlay it into two circles. Pass the circle in the standing end through the other loop and afterward fold the tail through it. Fix the Half Knot first. Then, at that point, pull the tail tight lastly, the standing end. The underside of the bunch shows three separate projections.

Uses: It is a tremendous cumbersome plug tie.

Comparative Knots: The Ashley Stopper Knot should be contrasted with different bunches ordinarily utilized as plugs, including the Double Overhand and the Figure 8 Knot, which are exceptionally regular in drifting. In any case, Figure 8 tends to come unraveled unreasonably promptly, and the Stevedore Stopper Knot has the right to be better known. In climbing, the Double Overhand Knot is all the more broadly utilized – in light of current circumstances – it is far doubtful to shake free. It likewise shapes the reason for tying the Double Fisherman's Bend and the Poacher's Knot or Double Overhand Noose. For dangerous ropes, the EStar Stopper is excellent.

Benefits: As a massive, secure, plug the Ashley Stopper Knot has the right to be more broadly known, and it is less inclined to shake free than the figure 8 bunch and is the bulkiest basic plug.

Bowline Knot

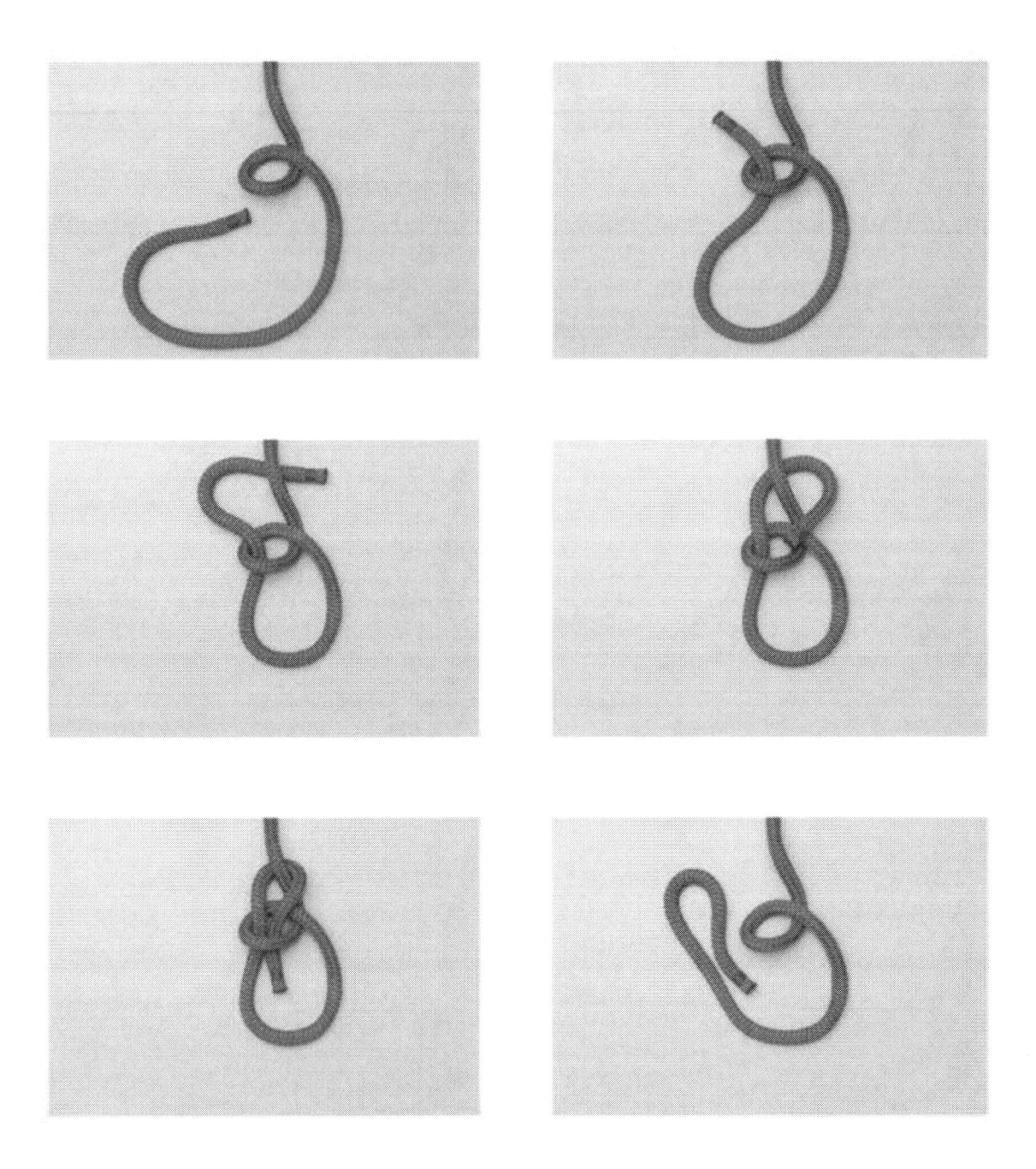

Structure a little circle leaving sufficient rope for the ideal circle size. Pass the end of the rope through the loop like making an overhand bunch. Proceed around the standing end and afterward back through the little circle.

The Bowline is indistinguishable in design to the Sheet Bend - in the two bunches, a bight secures in a circle. Be that as it may, in the Bowline, the tying is completed utilizing the bight, though, in the Sheet Bend, it is common to use the circle.

Uses: The Bowline sensibly closed circle toward the end of a piece of rope. It has many utilizations, e.g., to secure a securing line to a ring or a post. Under load, it doesn't slip or tie. With no heap, it tends to be loosened without any problem. Can you connect two anchors to join two ropes? Its essential inadequacy is that it can't be tied or reduced when a heap is on the standing end. Accordingly, it ought to stay away from when, for instance, a securing line might need to be delivered under load.

Name: The name Bowline gets from "bowline." The Bow Line Knot got the line holding the climate bloodsucker of a square sail forward to forestall it being shocked.

Shakes Undone If Not Loaded: When a Bowline is dumped, it can promptly work its direction unfastened.

One-Handed: The Bowline can be attached with one hand – helpful whenever harmed, fundamental if you are utilizing the other hand to clutch the line or the boat!

Length of Tail End: A discontinuous burden, e.g., on a securing line, may make many bunches slip or release. The Bowline is somewhat open-minded toward such obligations. The by specific texts quote a guideline that expresses that, for wellbeing, the length of remaining detail ought to be multiple times the circuit. A half-inch distance across rope would require a tail more than eighteen inches long, yet this is seldom found by and by.

A mistake is conceivable: Whichever wellbeing hitch is utilized should be reviewed and stress-tried – however, not toward fall!

Bowline On A Bight

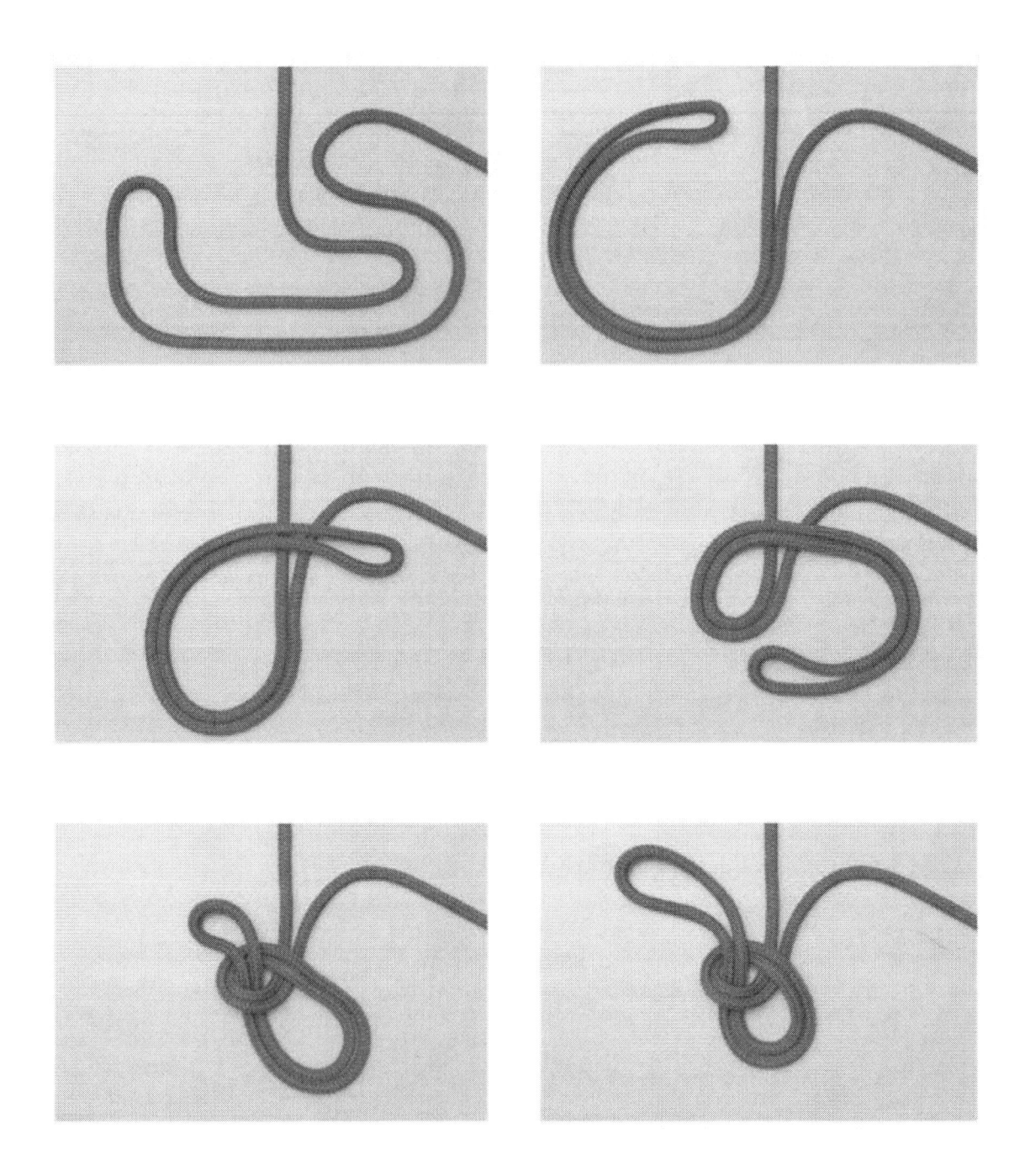

In a piece of rope, structure a bight. Make a circle and pass the end of the bight through it. Open up the bight and bring it around the whole bunch until it surrounds both standing closures. Fix to finish the bunch.

Uses: The Bowline on a Bight makes a solid circle in a piece of rope, and it doesn't slip or tie. It is fulfilling, to begin with, a plain string length and get done with a solid, safe circle in its center.

Tying it: The Bowline on a Bight ought to be not difficult to tie, but since it is at first challenging to envision, it tends to be confounding.

Buntline Hitch

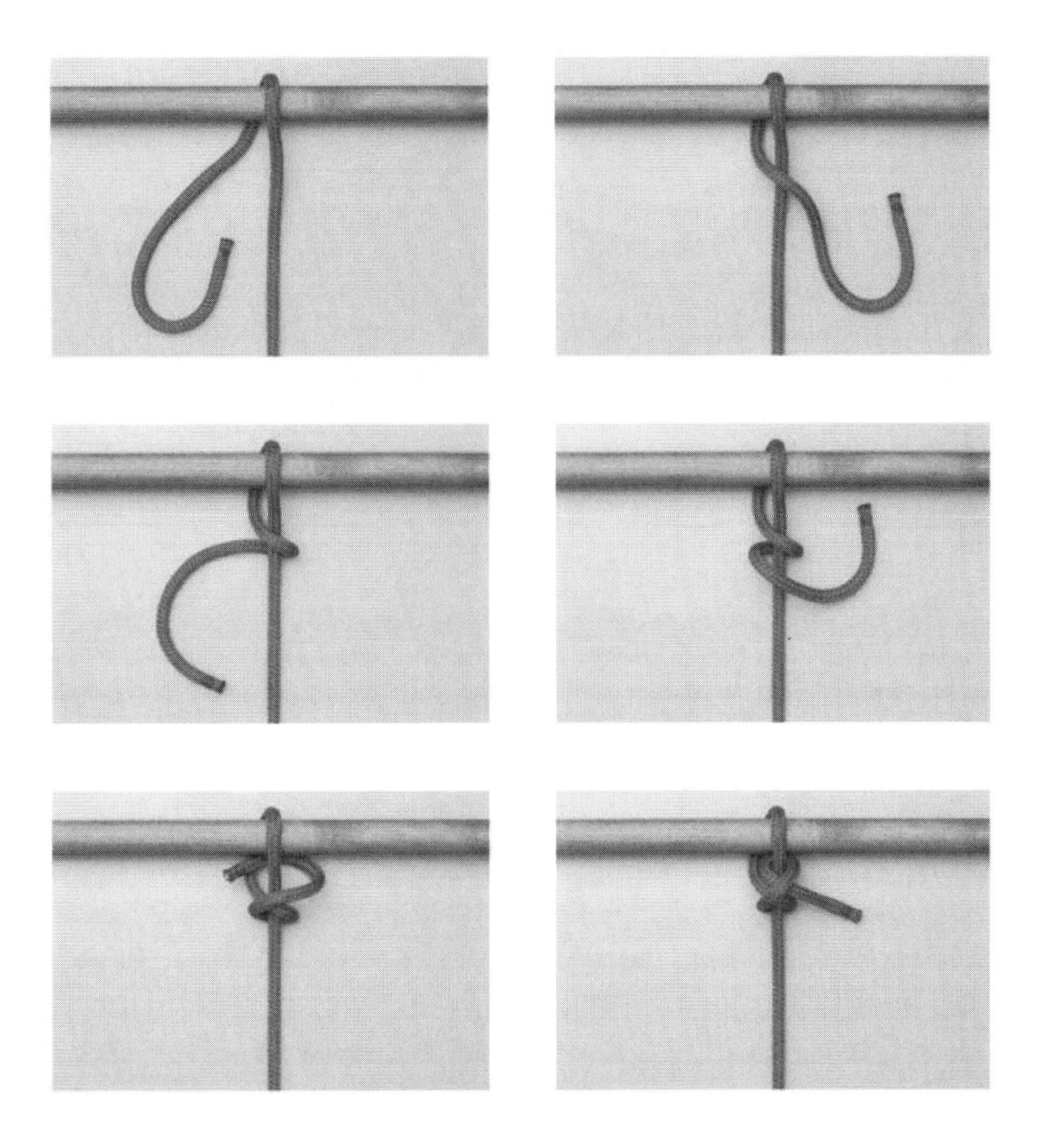

Pass the tail around the post. Make a total turnaround the standing end and afterward through the opening alongside the post. Structure a Half Hitch to finish the bunch.

Uses: The Buntline Hitch was initially utilized to get the buntlines to the foot of the square sails. Constant shaking and jolting by a fluttering sail would, in general, fix this bunch – consequently, it's worth.

Design when complete: the completed Buntline Hitch is a clove hitch around the standing end; however, the clove hitch is transformed when contrasted with the clove hitch in a Round Turn and Two Half Hitches. In any case, while it is being tied, the initial segment of the bunch ought not to be known as a Half Hitch.

Different Uses: Although it isn't self-evident, a similar bunch is generally utilized forties, known as the Four-in-Hand Knot. The thing that matters is only in the material used and the arrangement of the last piece of the bunch, so the two ends arise equally.

Benefits: The Buntline Hitch is safer than two Half Hitches and exceptionally impervious to shaking free.

Inconveniences: The Buntline Hitch tie can't be tied under a heap, and, in the wake of being vigorously stacked, it is more at risk to stick and be off-kilter to deliver than two Half Hitches.

Carrick Bend

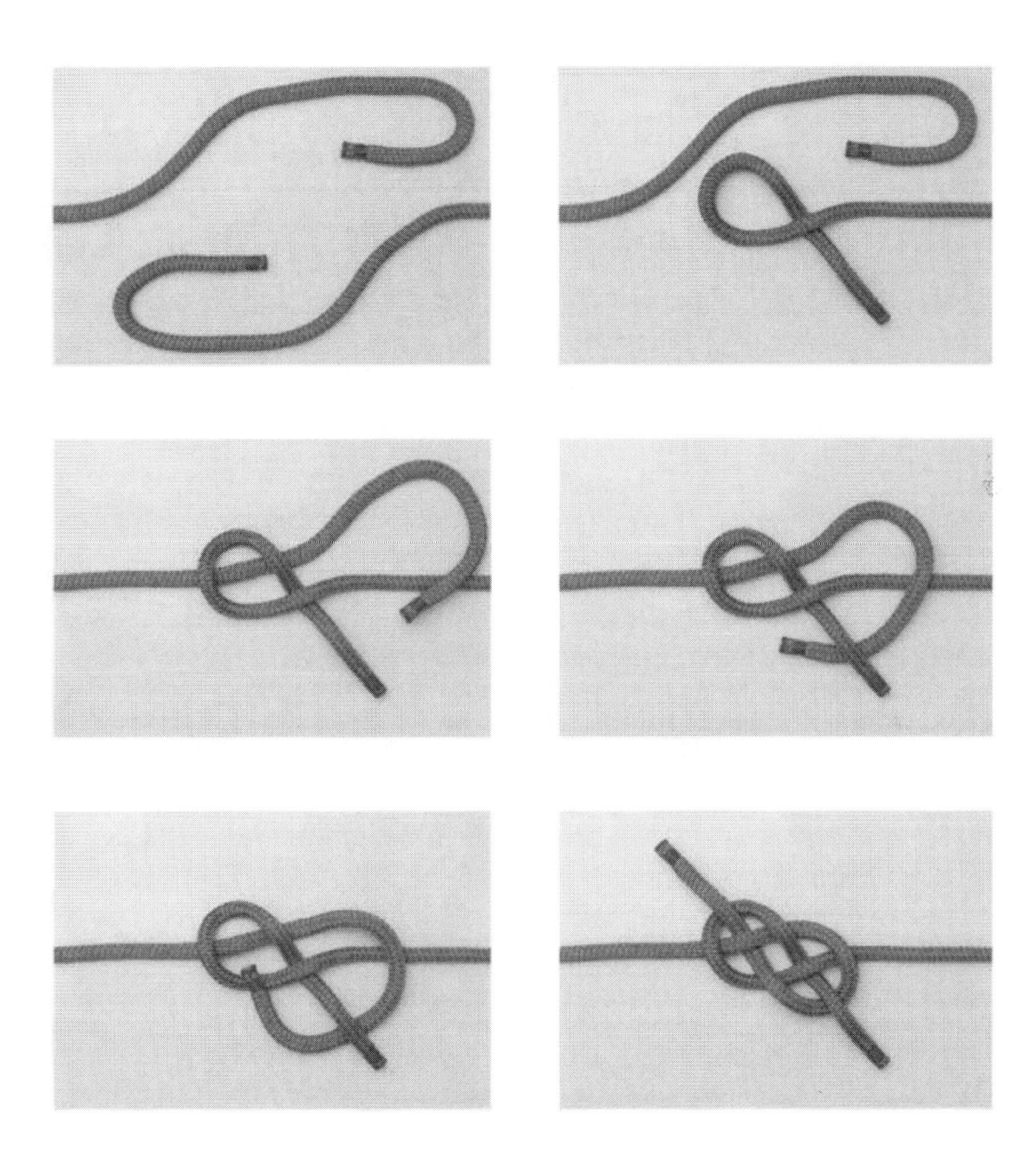

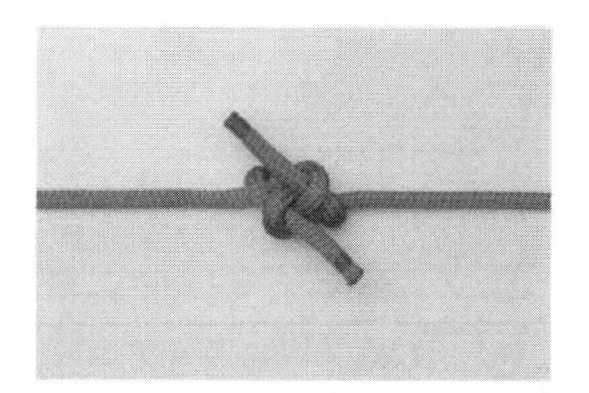

With one rope structure a circle with the tail under the standing end. Pass the other rope under the loop and then over and then under as displayed. String the bottom across the circle passing under itself. Then, at that point, pull both standing closures to fix the bunch.

Uses: The Carrick Bend combines two ropes.

Caution: For the Animation, the ends were left short. For primary burdens, e.g., when Climbing, the ends should be left significantly longer.

Construction: The Carrick Bend twists up under strain, and the alluring, mat-like appearance evaporates. Significantly, the tails lie askew inverse one another; if tied erroneously, an irregular force will continuously work the bunch towards the seats until it is scattered!

Spot: Because the Carrick Bend is solid and enjoys the tremendous benefit of being not difficult to fix, it most likely has the right to be utilized all the more regularly. Nonetheless, it is marginally off-kilter to gather. It is not difficult to commit an error: you can have the two tails on a similar side of the bunch, or one of the intersections might be inaccurate. These different adaptations of this bunch perform undeniably less well.

Chain Splice

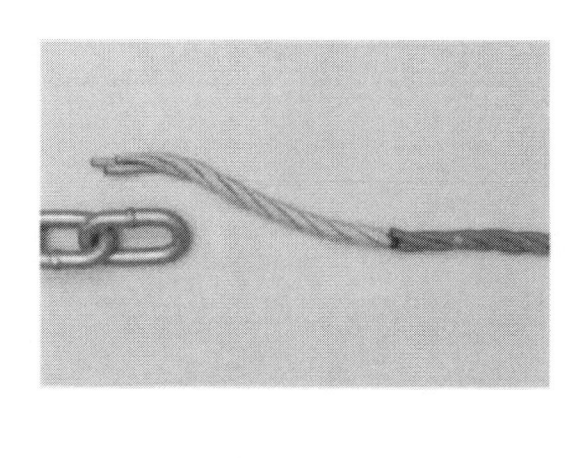

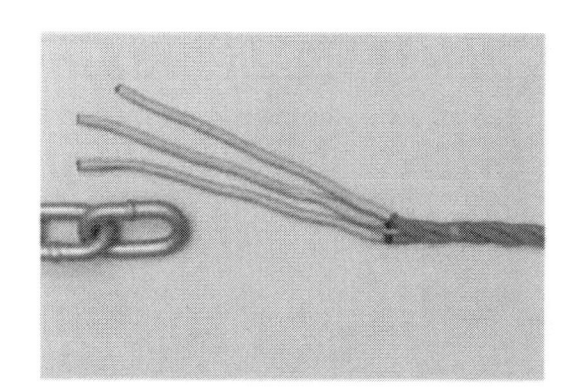

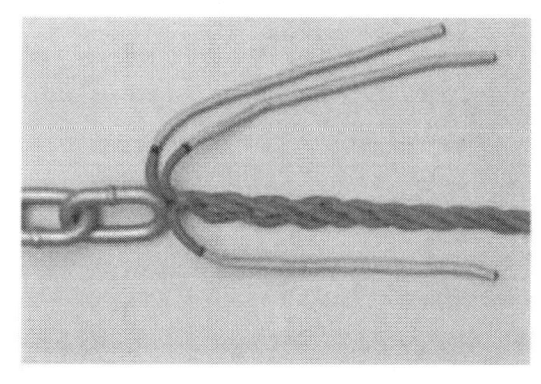

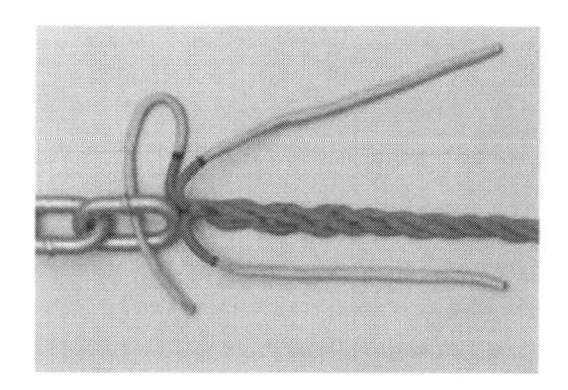

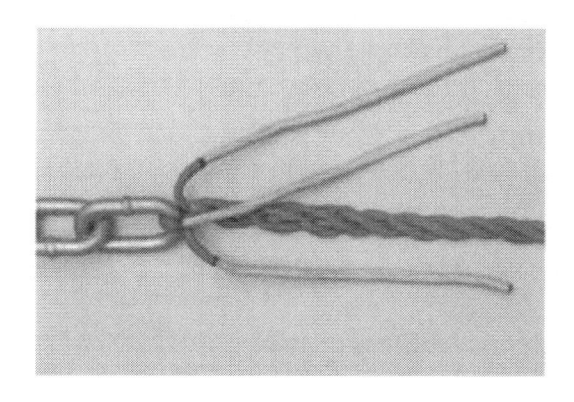

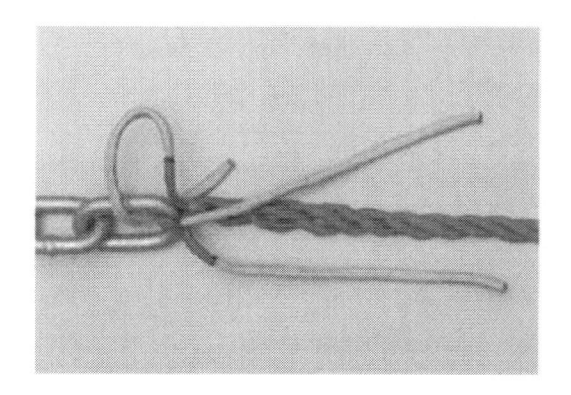

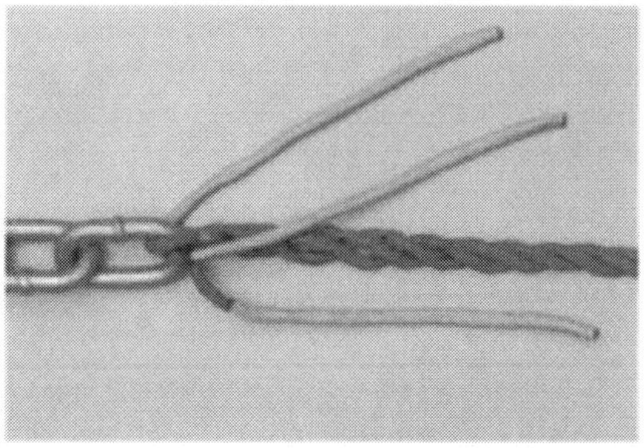

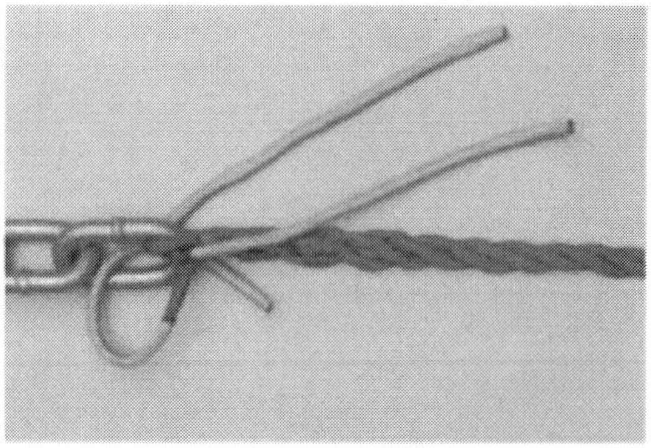

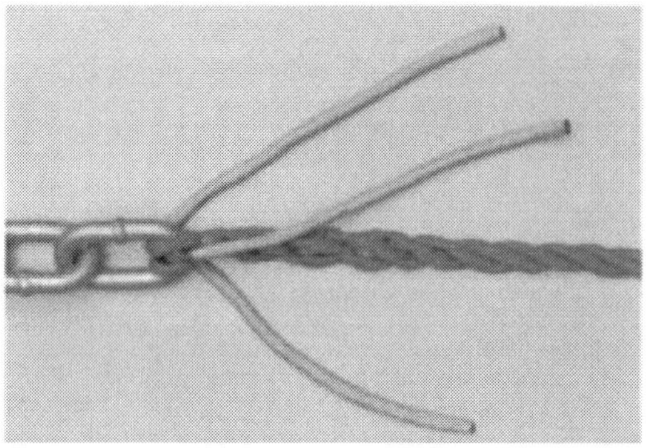

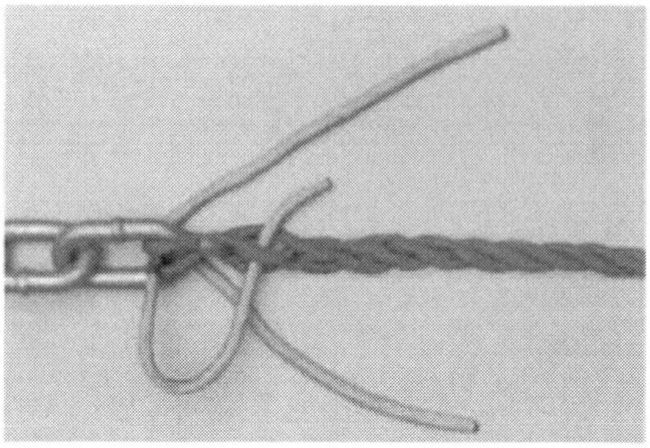

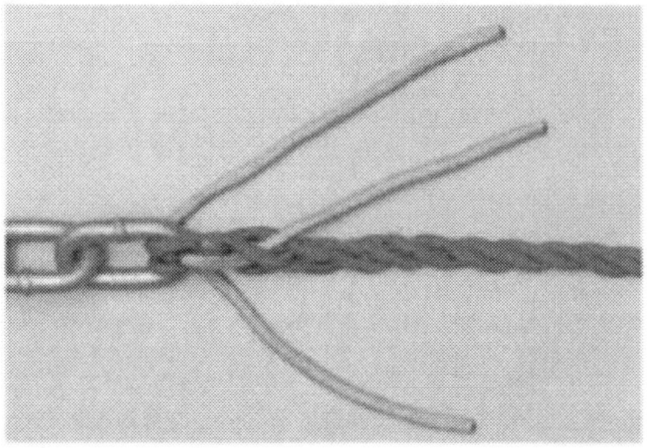

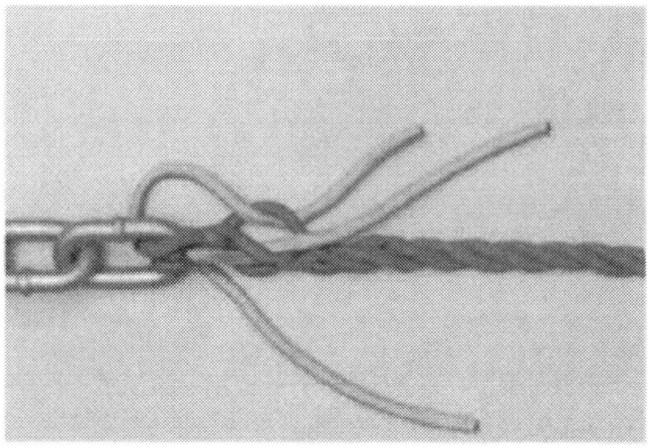

81

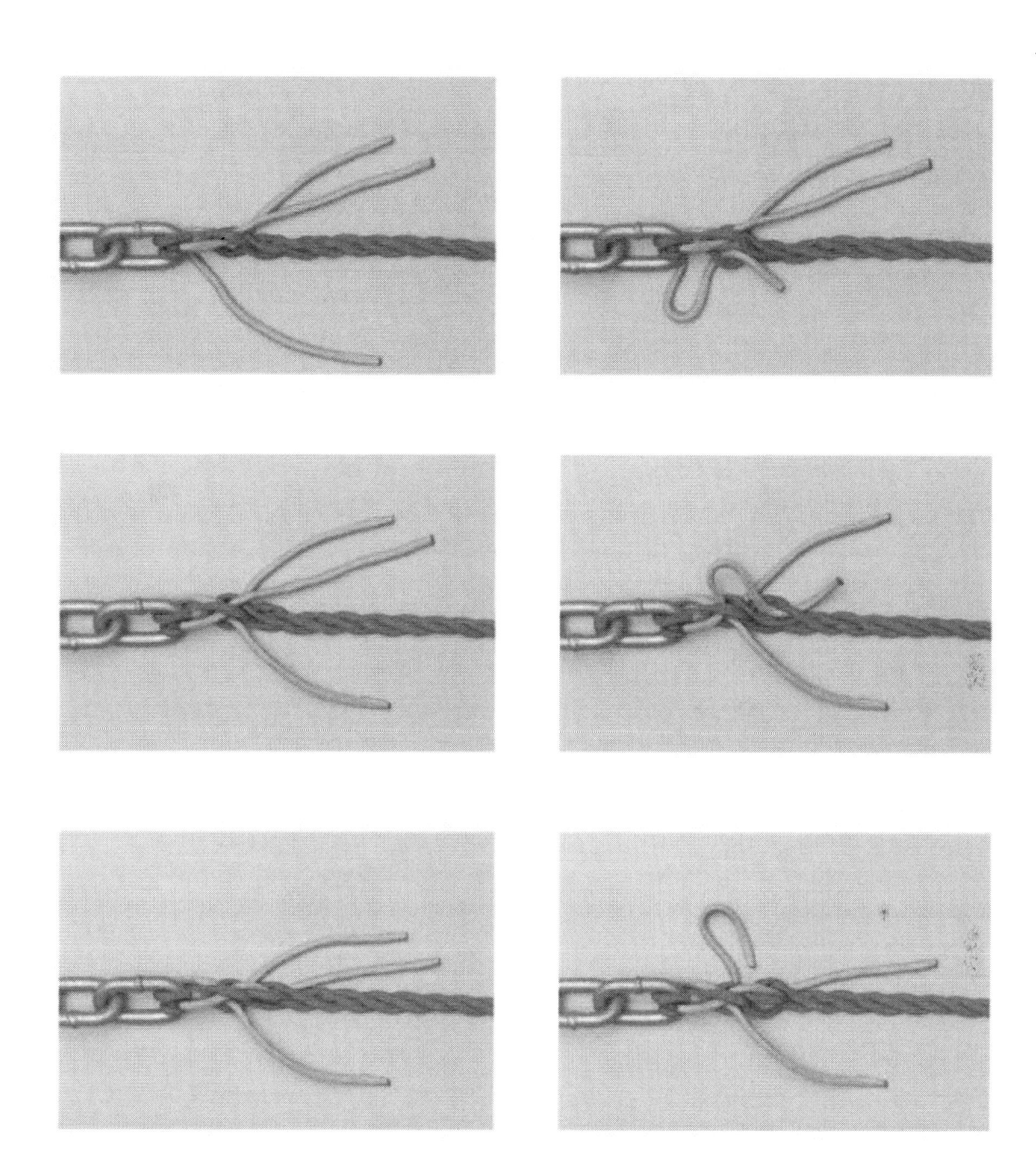

Tape rope. Unravel enough for 5 - 7 tucks. Pass the strands into the chain - one strand one way through the chain and two strands the other way. Splice each strand back into the standing end of the rope. Repeat for the second set of tucks, and the third and fourth. Use five to seven sets of tucks for security.

Uses: It is particularly useful when rope followed by chain passes over a windlass and descends into a chain locker.

Note: for photography, only five sets of tucks were completed. **Seven complete sets of tucks are recommended.**

Preparation: To prevent chaos, burn the three ends and wrap the rope at the correct length. For seven tucks, measure at least 21 times the rope's diameter and wrap the rope with tape or a Constrictor Knot tied in twine. Unravel the strands back to the tape or twine.

Making the Chain Splice: Pass two strands together through the end of the chain and pass the third strand in the reverse direction. It is neatest when the single strand passes between the other two. Lay the three tails down beside the rope and thread them through adjacent standing strands as close to the chain as possible. Complete the remainder of the splice by tucking each tail over and under the standing strands.

Practical aspects: As when making the Eye Splice, keep each end as neat and tightly wound as possible – at least for the first three tucks. After the first tuck is completed for all three stands, the wrapping tape (or the constrictor) should be removed so that the splice can be tightened against the chain. For neatness, remember to twist each tail tightly before pulling on it!

Durability: By its nature, a Chain Splice may be subject to heavy load and chafing. It should be inspected if used frequently and a worn splice should be cut off and remade a few inches further up the rope. However, in many yachts where the anchor is only used occasionally, the chain may rust and become untrustworthy long before the splice shows significant wear!

Cleat Hitch (Dock Line)

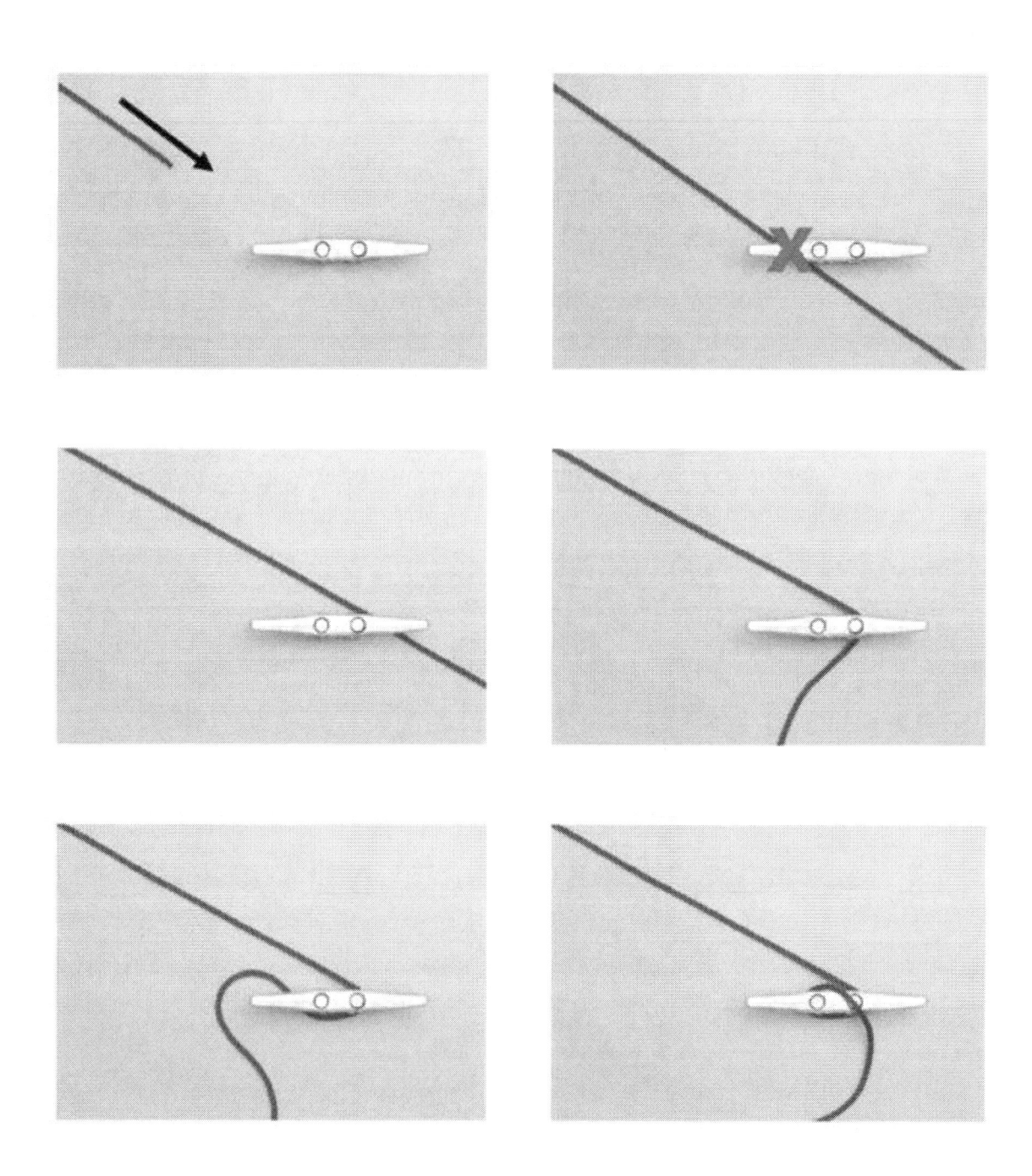

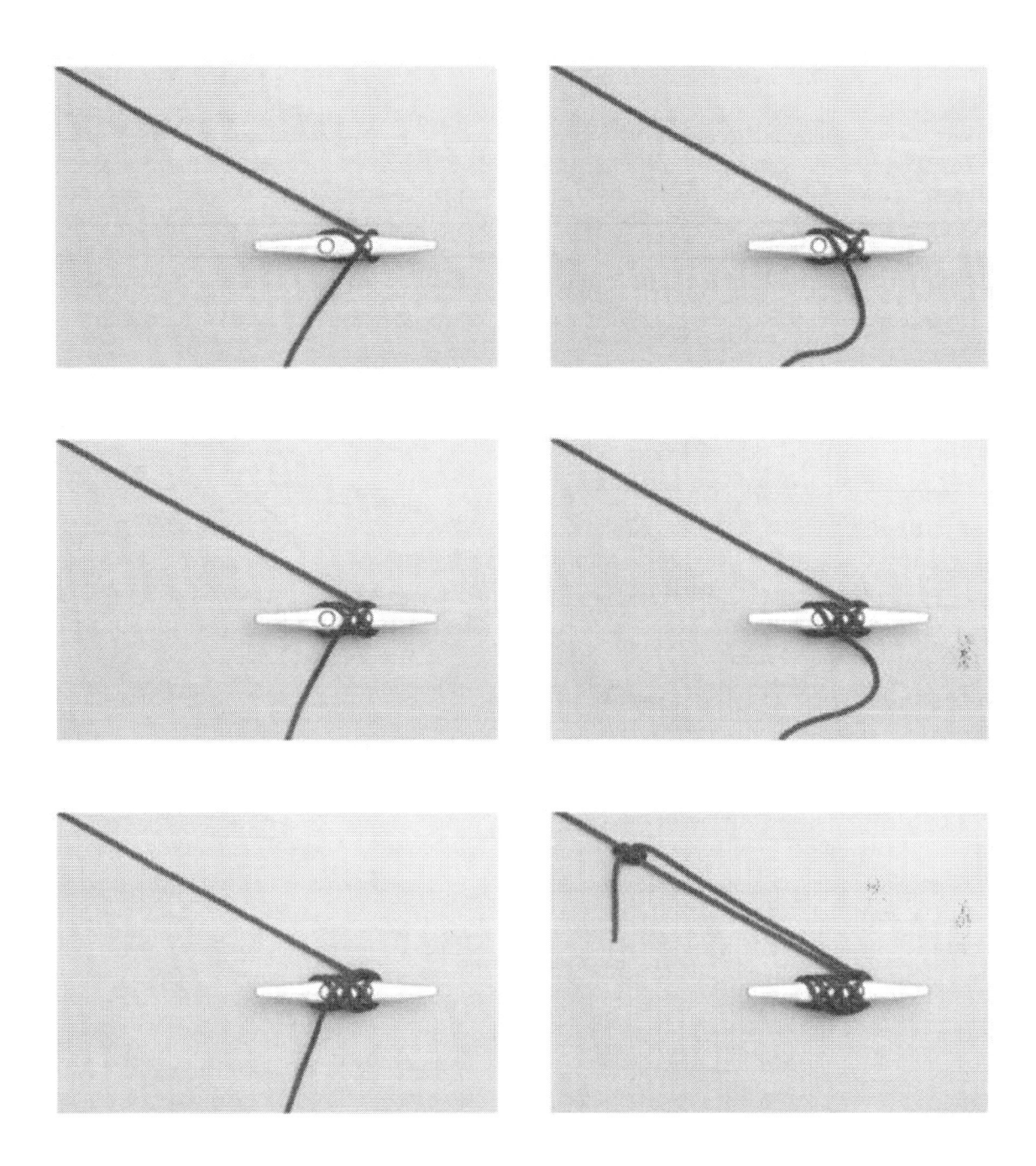

Do not bring the line around the near horn. Go around the far horn, then around the other, and back across the middle. Continue making several more figure 8 turns around each horn. There is often spare rope left unused. Coiling the rope as a Flemish Flake is a common option. However, it collects dirt and eventually leaves a spiral stain on the deck. A better solution is to use the tail to tie a Rolling Hitch around the Standing End. This is secure and keeps the deck clear.

Uses: The Cleat Hitch secures a rope to a cleat. It is deceptively simple and an unwary skipper who invites visitors to cleat a mooring line may be astonished and dismayed by the unsatisfactory results.

First Horn: Initially the rope must be led round the most distant horn of the cleat followed by a turn in the same direction round the other horn. Starting round the wrong horn increases the risk of a Cleat Hitch jamming.

No Round Turn: After passing the rope around two horns of the cleat, always cross over and make figure 8 turns afterwards. This is because the Figure 8 Turns lift the rope up against the horns and out of the way of the first turn. Jamming is a risk if the initial turn continues around and under the first horn a second time (making a complete round turn). Now if a towline briefly becomes slack, the initial turn can separate away from the cleat and then clamp down on top of the second turn making it impossible to release the rope while there is load on the towline.

Name: Some contributor's protest that the name "Hitch" is wrongly applied because there is no final Half Hitch. However, Cleat Hitch describes the purpose well – the rope is hitched to a cleat – and there are other "Hitches" that are sometimes used without a final Half Hitch, e.g., Tensionless Hitch and The Lighterman's, or Tugboat, Hitch.

Cleat Hitch (Halyard)

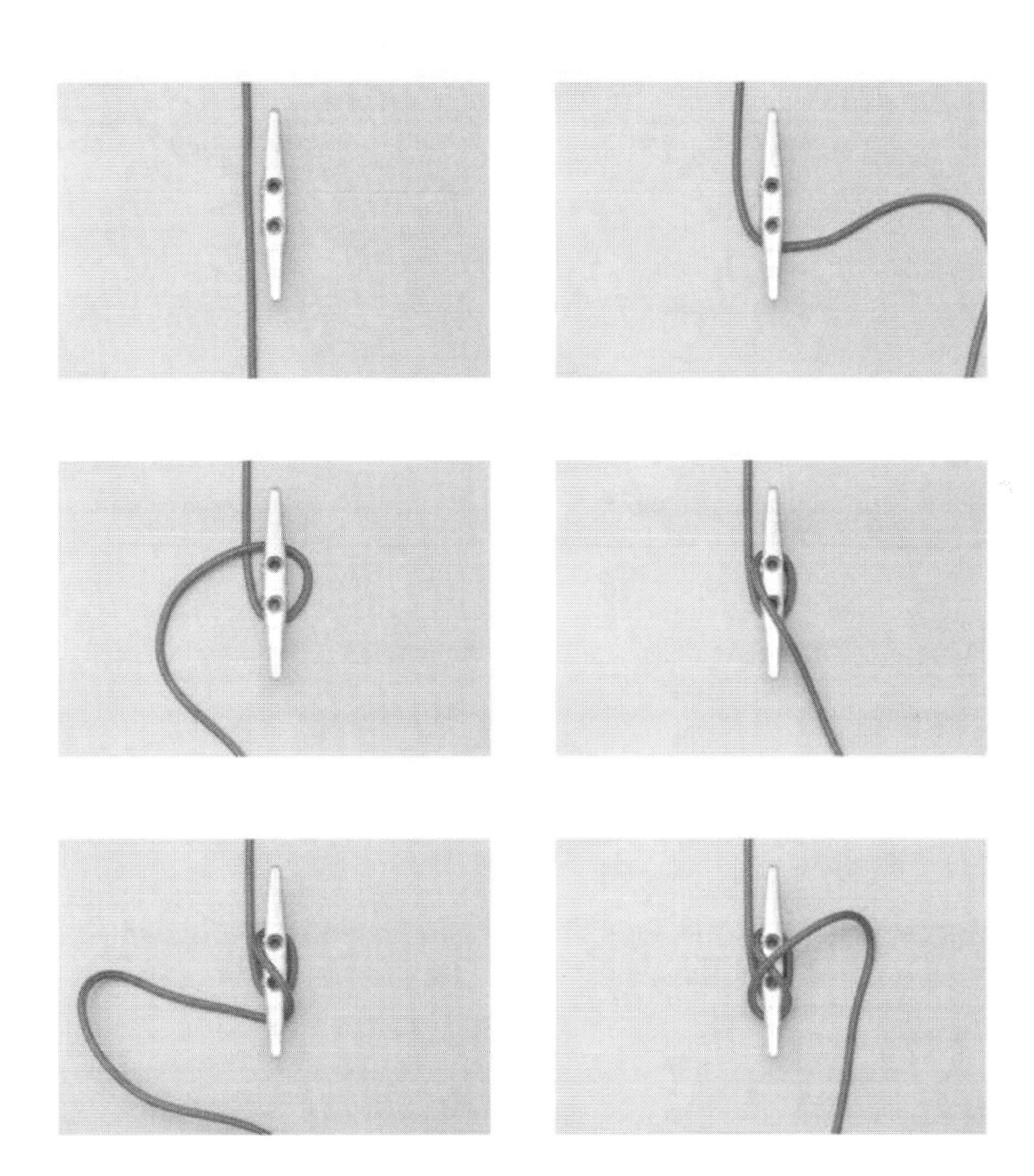

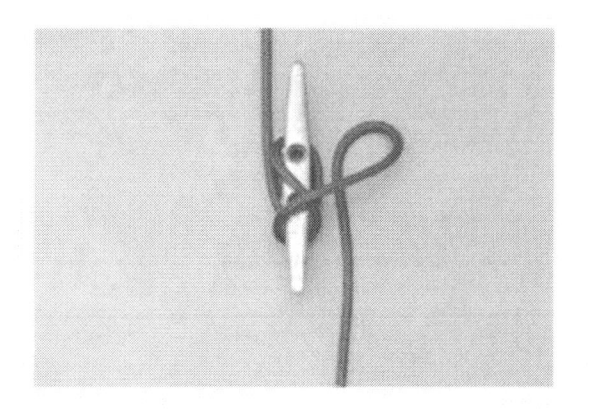

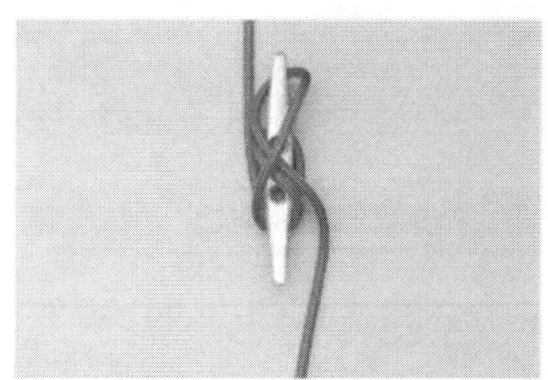

Pass the rope around the base horn and on around preposterous. Proceed down across the center and afterward up across once more. Wind a circle in the rope and snare it on the projection as a Half Hitch.

Uses: The Cleat Hitch ties down a rope to a fitting. It is misleadingly straightforward, and an unwary captain who welcomes guests to get a halyard might be shocked and unnerved by the inadmissible outcomes.

First Horn: A securing rope arrives at a deck projection at a point and should be driven around the most far-off horn of the fitting first. On the other hand, a halyard typically falls generally corresponding to the projection and circumvents the lower horn first. The bearing picked is frequently subjective.

No Round Turn: As displayed in the Cleat Hitch movement, the rope similarly passes around the initial two horns. There may be little mischief in proceeding in a similar course around the lower horn once more for a halyard. Be that as it may, for wellbeing, a uniform strategy is suggested. When Mooring, Towing, and Cleating a sheet: consistently cross the middle after the initial two horns. In this manner, do likewise for a halyard Cleat Hitch.

No Locking Turn: This movement shows the last locking turn – because it is customary in little boats. Never utilize a Locking Turn on a halyard on an enormous ship – utilize additional cross-overs. The fundamental necessity is the capacity to deliver rapidly. Additionally, the halyard ought to be wound where it will run out without any problem.

Fixing a Halyard: A halyard might be dependent upon an extensive burden. On more seasoned cruising boats, there may not be a winch. After the rope has passed around the base and top horns, one individual holds the tail and takes up slack while another swings sideways on the rope above to acquire the leeway.

History: "Belaying a rope" signifies getting it or making it quick. Before expected spikes, a rope used to be brought to an upward pin in a wooden bar called, obviously, a "Belaying Pin."

Number of Turns: The liveliness shows just a solitary hybrid before the hybrid with the Half Hitch. An excessive burden might send pressure to the Half Hitch and make discharge off-kilter. Consequently, extra hybrid turns are generally utilized.

Clove Hitch - End Rope

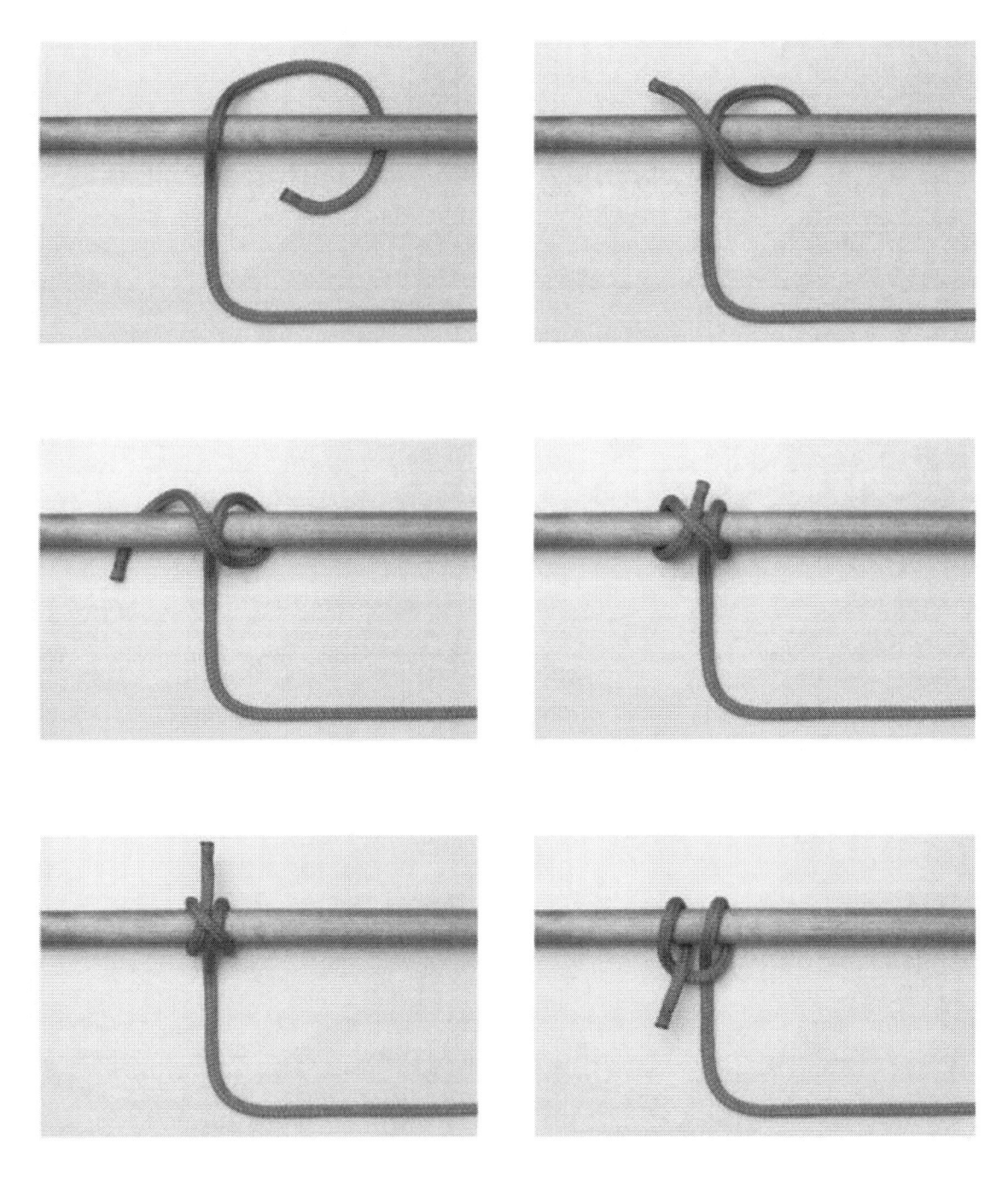

Pass the end of the rope around the post. Proceed over the standing end and around the post a subsequent time. String the end under itself and pull tight to frame the clove hitch.

Alert: The Clove Hitch was, initially, included here determined to denounce it. It has two monster deficiencies: it slips and, perplexingly, can likewise bind. It ought to be profoundly questioned when utilized by itself.

Uses: However, the Clove Hitch can be extremely valuable:

- **Theater Scenery**: Thanks to Curtis Mortimore of Ball State University for giving this model; when changing stage draperies swinging from a bar, a Clove Hitch around the bar permits the stature of the bar to be changed up or somewhere around moving the bunch somewhat. At the correct tallness, two or three Half Hitches round the standing end give security.

- **Boat Fenders**: Similarly, while joining a boat's bumper to a railing, the bumper's line can be at first gotten with a Clove Hitch and afterward, when changed, got with two Half Hitches round the standing end.

Risks: As expressed over, the Clove Hitch's issues are slipping and restricting. The Clove Hitch isn't a bunch to be utilized alone.

Constrictor Knot (Twisting Method)

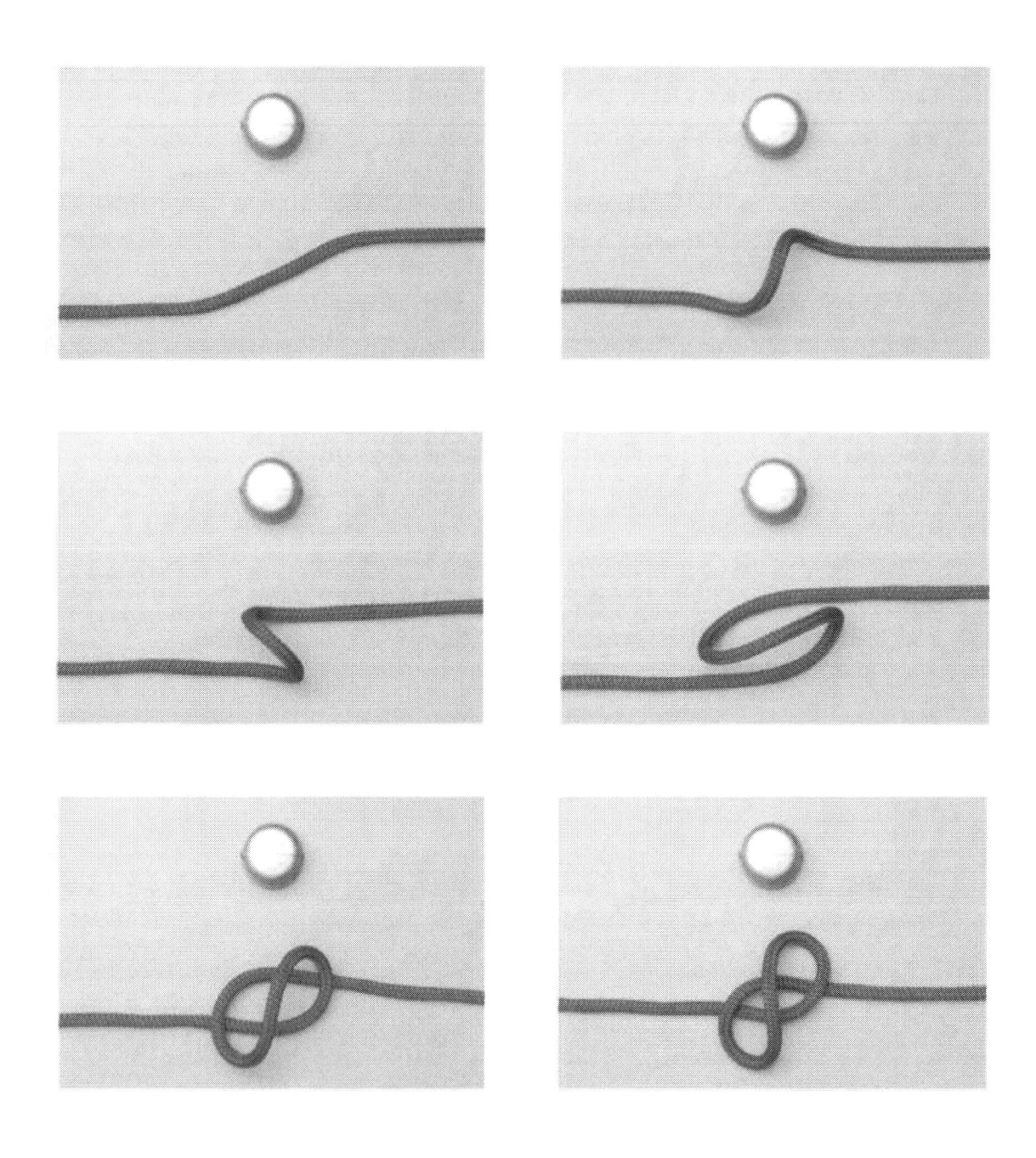

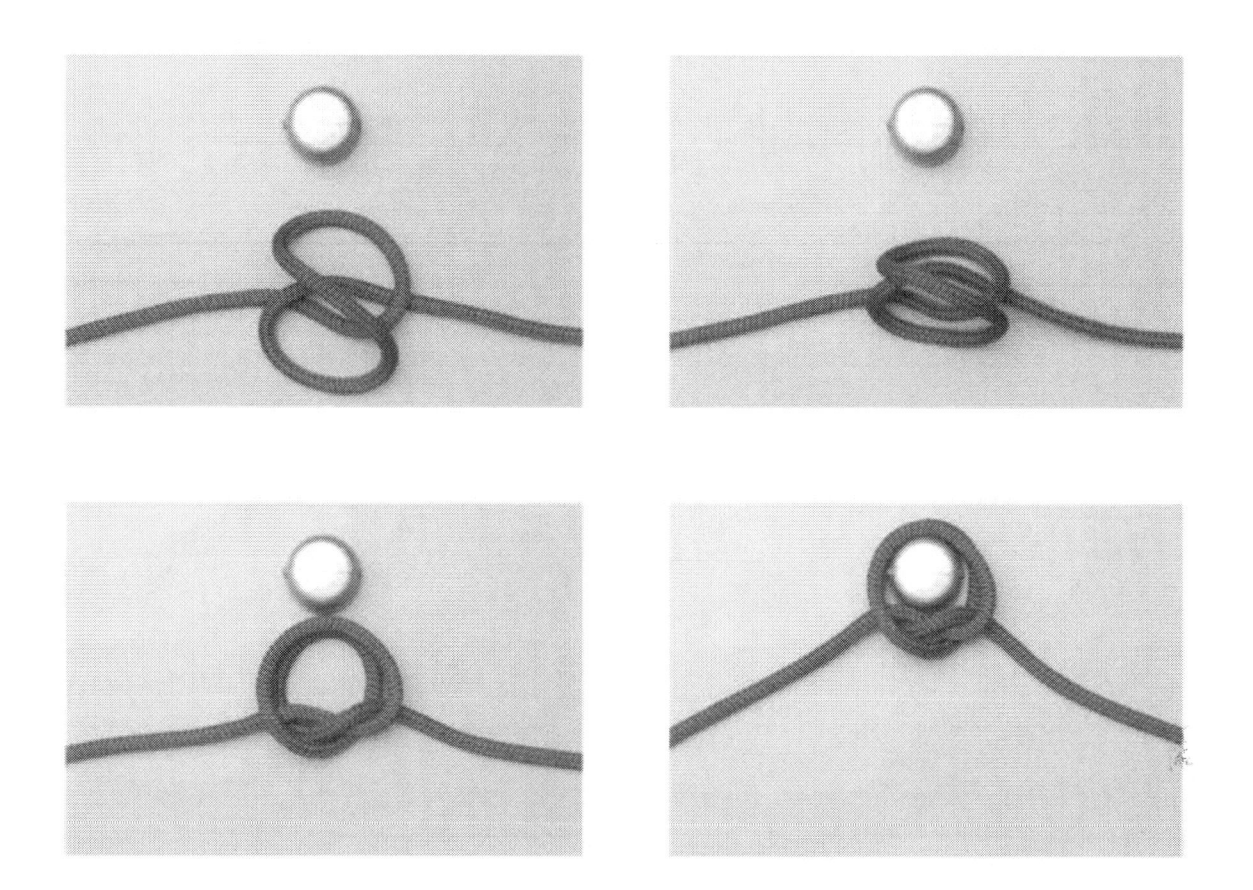

Bend the rope to shape a free figure 8. Overlay the circles down around the middle to shape the Constrictor Knot.

Uses: The Constrictor Knot has the right to be significantly more generally known and utilized. It is a superb fast brief whipping for a fraying rope's end and can be used to keep a rope's end together while it is being whipped. It safely ties the neck of a sack or pack; it has been utilized as a brief hose clasp, and it tends to be used to hold things together for sticking.

Impediments: When tied against a level surface, the Constrictor Knot bombs require a bent surface for the limiting goes to grasp the Half Hitch.

Delivery: The Constrictor Knot can be exceptionally difficult to fix – cutting the bunch can be the primary choice. When this is important, the limiting strand ought to be cut over the other constrictor strands, utilizing them to secure your rope.

Rope Size: The photos here show the rope tied in enormous breadth rope. This is just for the photography. The Constrictor Knot is regularly tied in twine or another little breadth line.

Double Overhand Stopper

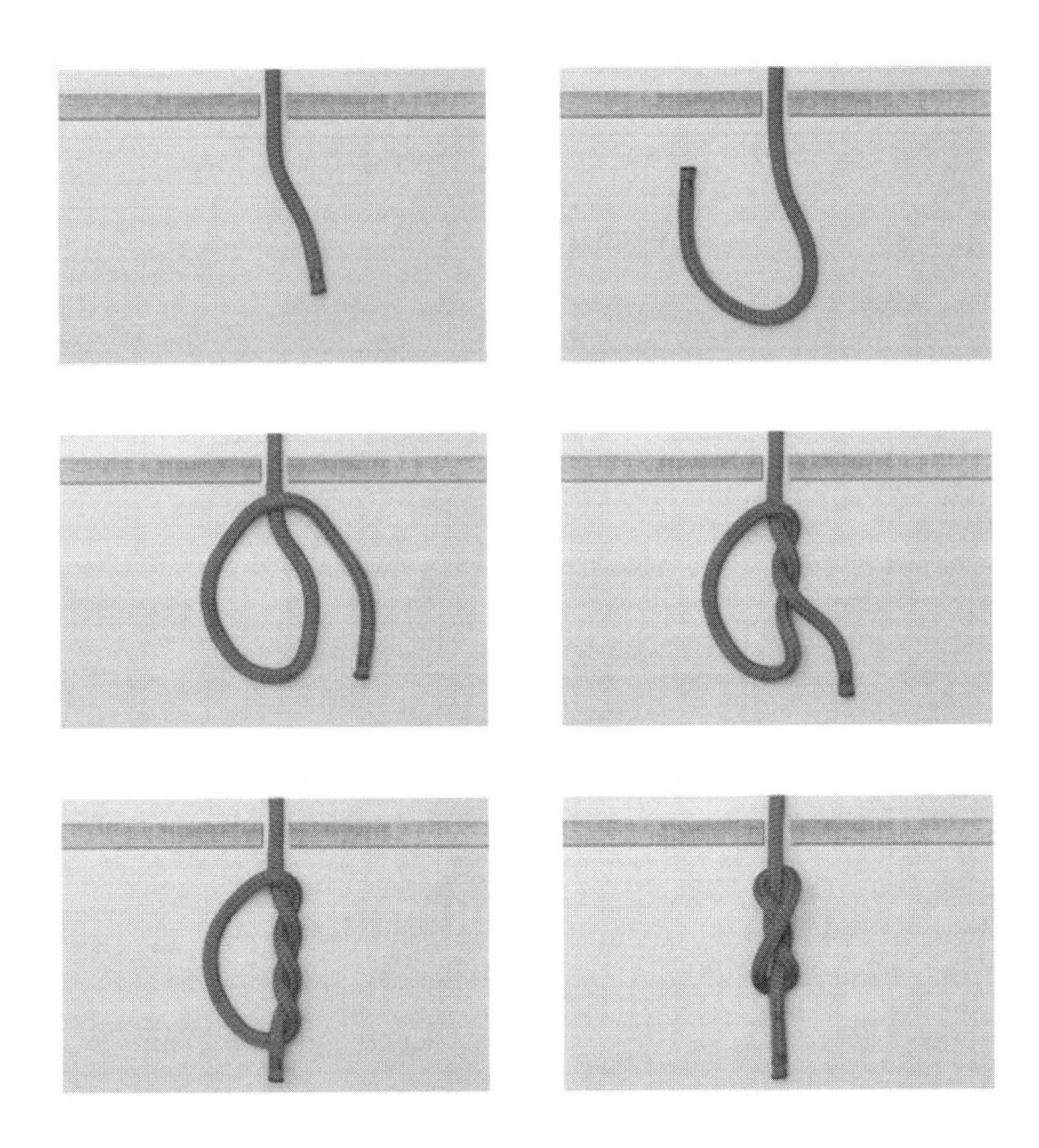

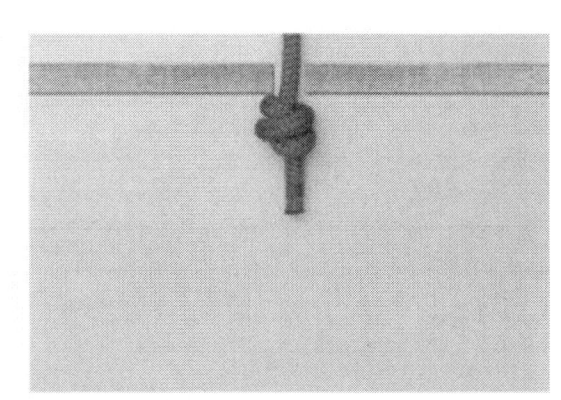

Structure a circle in the rope. Pass the end through it. Pass the end through the loop once more. Tighten the knot to make a solid plug tie.

Uses: The Double Overhand Stopper Knot depends on the Overhand Knot with one extra turn, making a dependable, modestly enormous plug hitch.

Utilizations with Other Knots: as well as going about as a Stopper Knot toward the end of a rope, the Double Overhand Stopper Knot has another utilization; it can likewise be utilized to build the security of another bunch.

eStar Stopper Knot

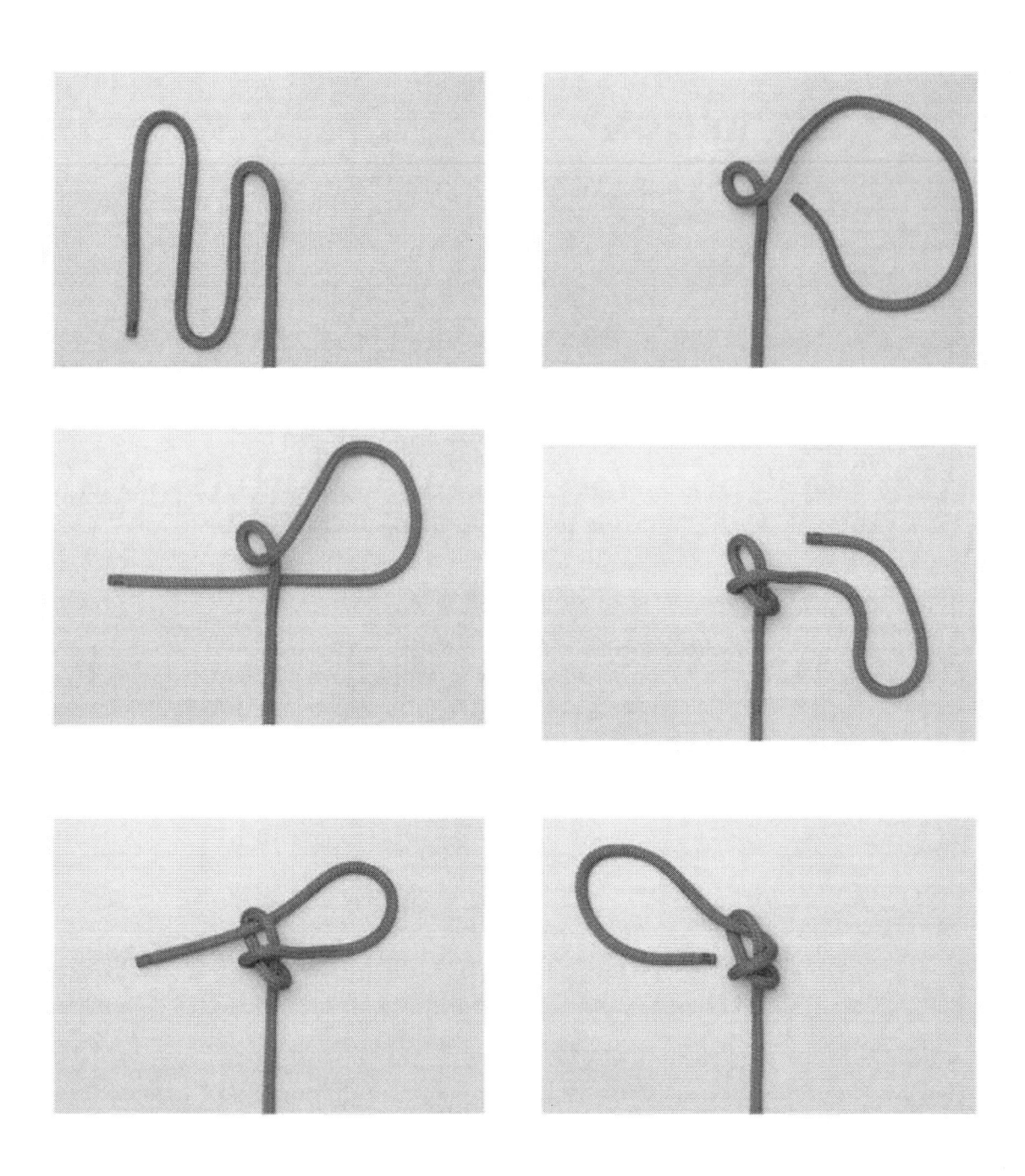

97

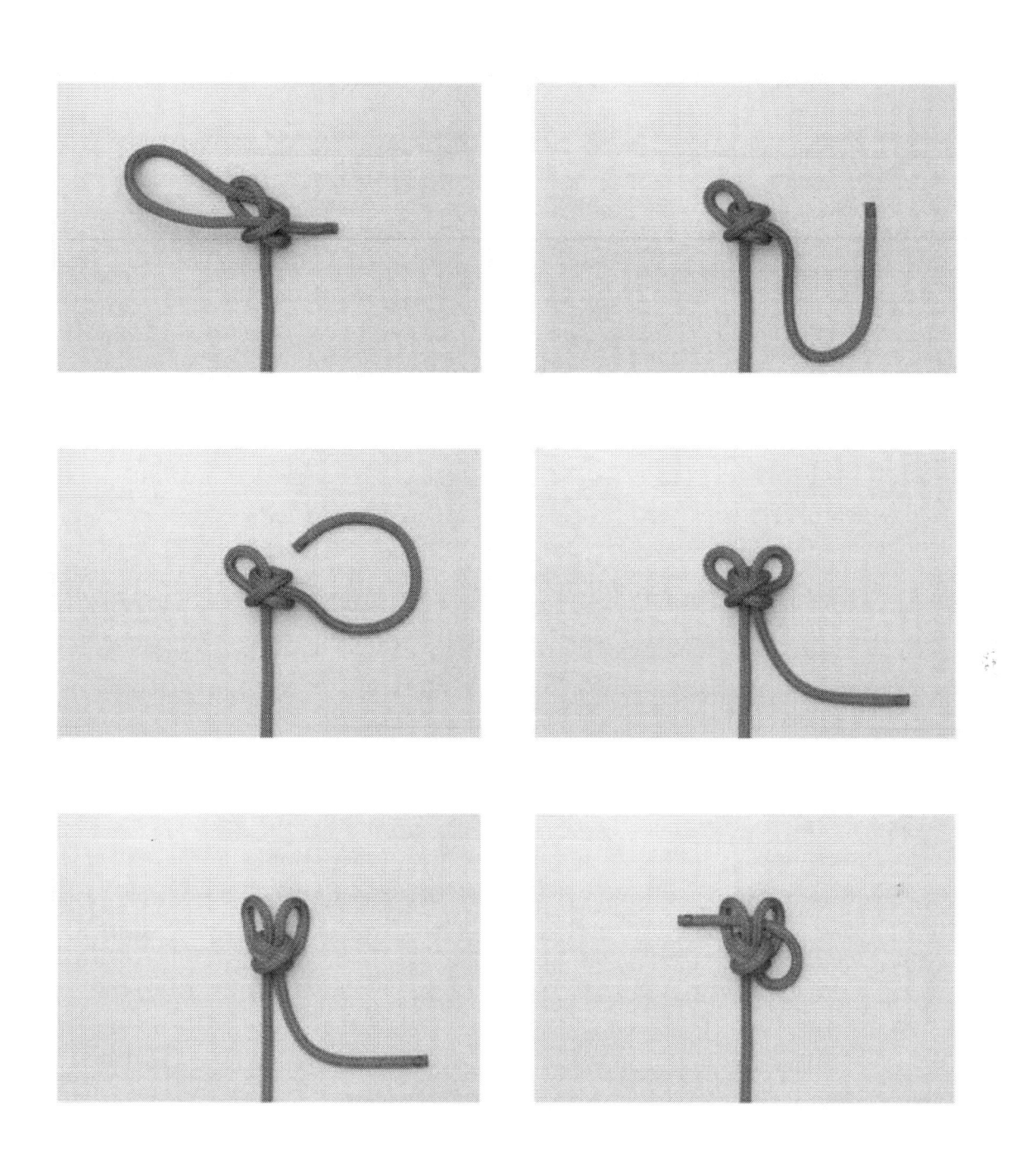

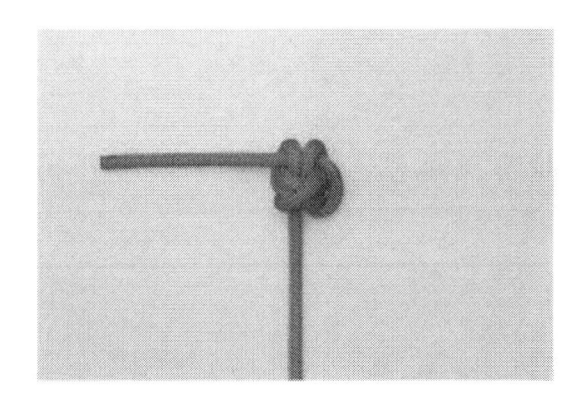

Fold the Tail End over the Standing End and on around itself. Proceed around the Standing End and afterward under itself to make a Buntline Hitch. Pass the Tail End through the Buntline Hitch and afterward across through the two circles that made. Fix the Buntline, the Standing End, and, at last, the Tail End.

Uses: The EStar Stopper Knot was portrayed by Evans Starzinger. He tried it against a few bunches planned for use as Stoppers and discovered it was the one in particular that didn't sneak through Dyneema.

Similitude to EStar Hitch: The EStar Stopper Knot begins as a Buntline Hitch Knot. Then, at that point, the Tail End is gone down through the Buntline so that any slipping makes the Standing End and Tail End move against one another in inverse ways. At long last, the Tail End goes through the circles that would pass around the bar in an EStar Hitch Knot. The EStar Hitch Knot grasps the Tail End, and the Buntline holds the Tail End and the Standing End against one another: the more grounded the strain, the more firmly the two are constrained against one another.

Benefits: The EStar Stopper Knot is sensibly simple to tie and stays secure in Dyneema.

Weaknesses: The EStar Stopper Knot is somewhat uneven and can't be loosened after weighty stacking.

Eye Splice

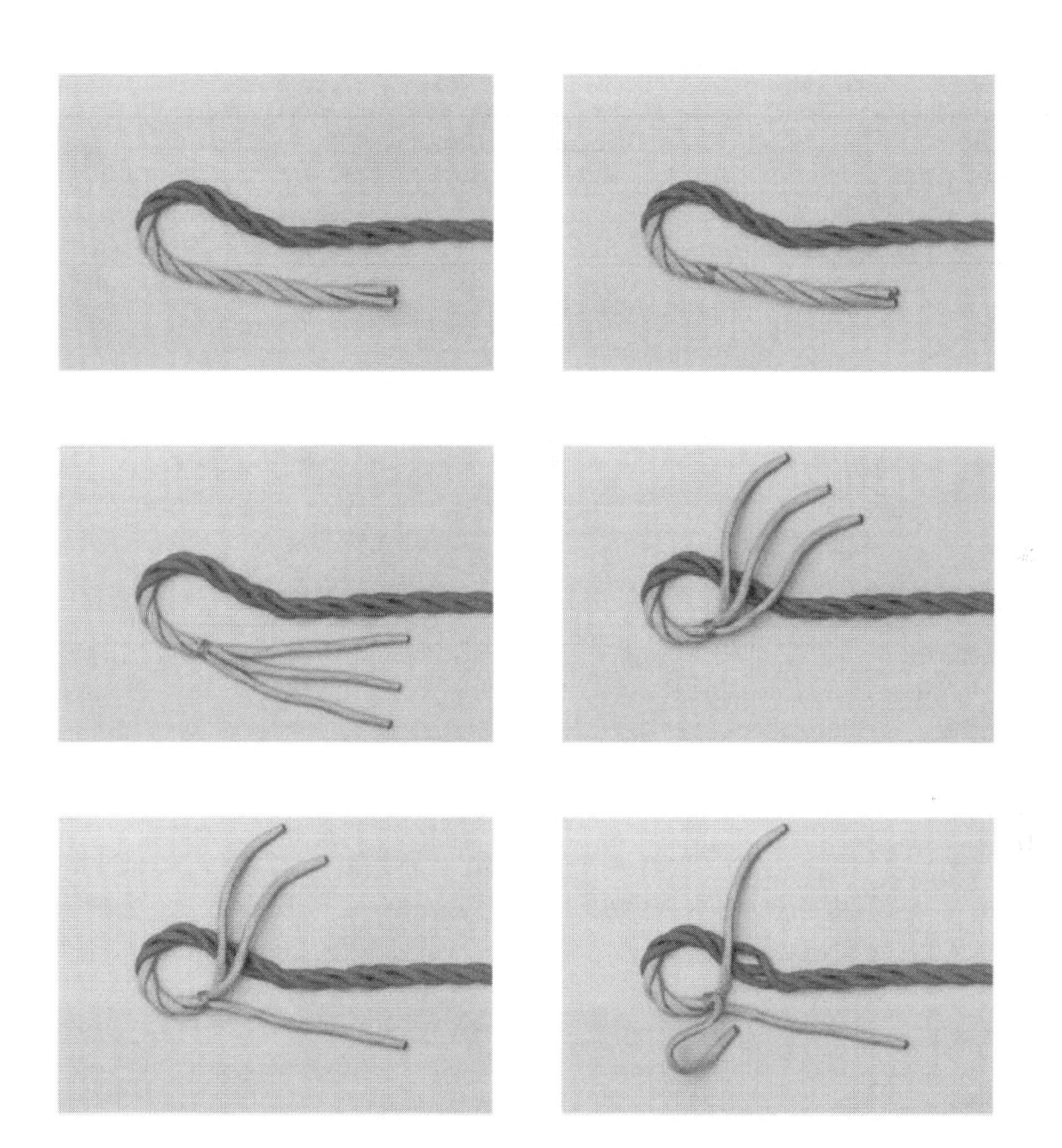

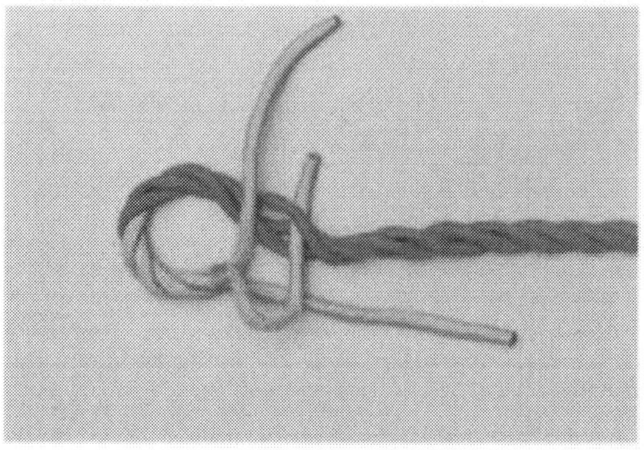

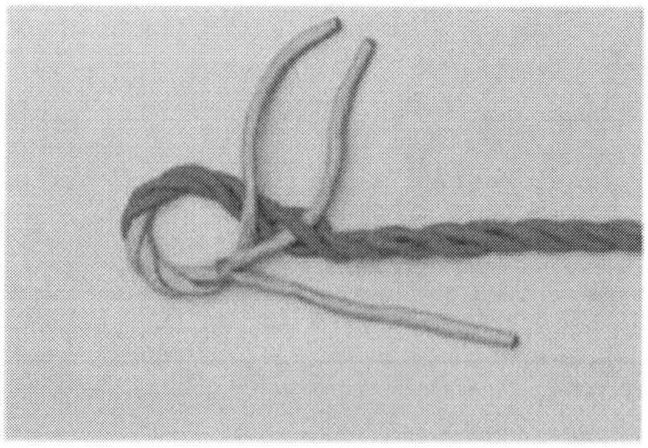

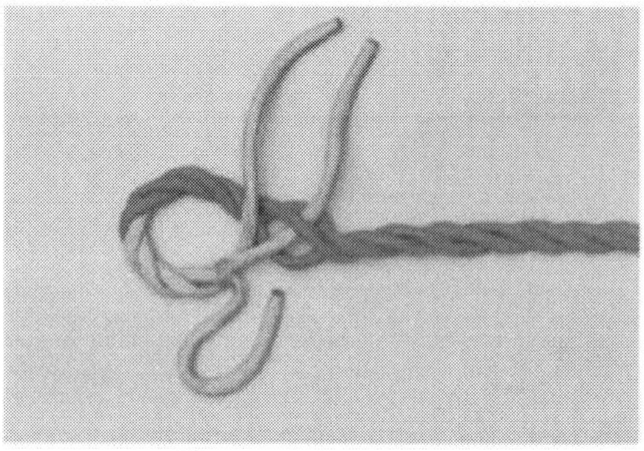

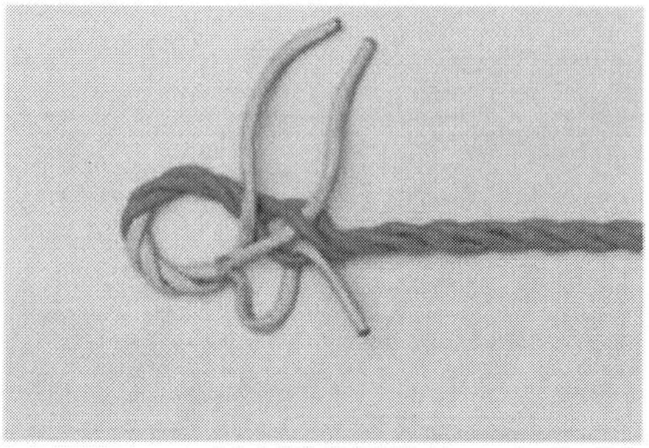

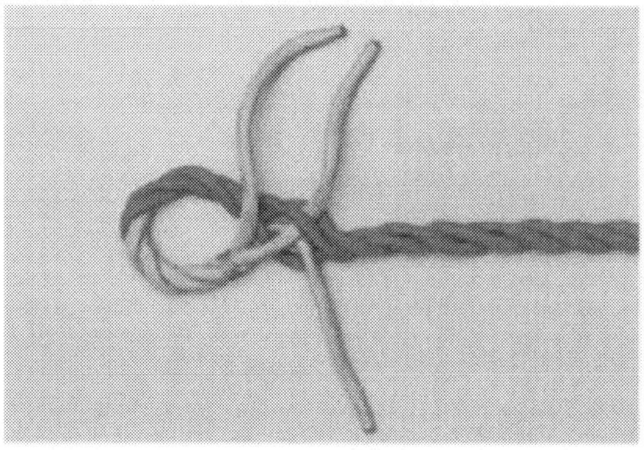

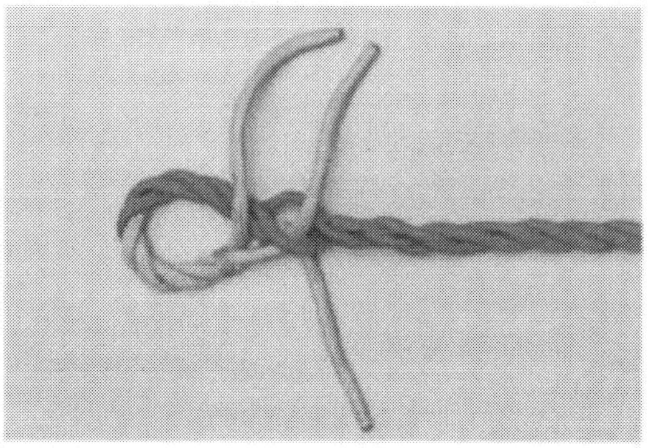

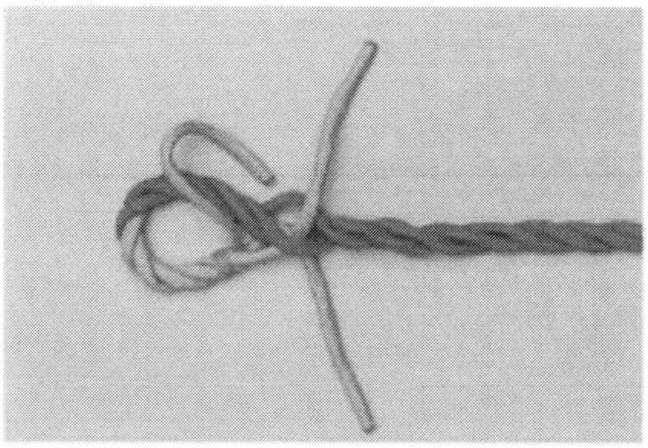
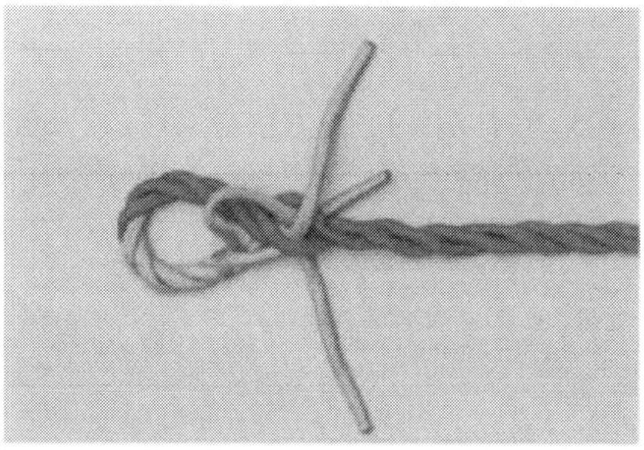
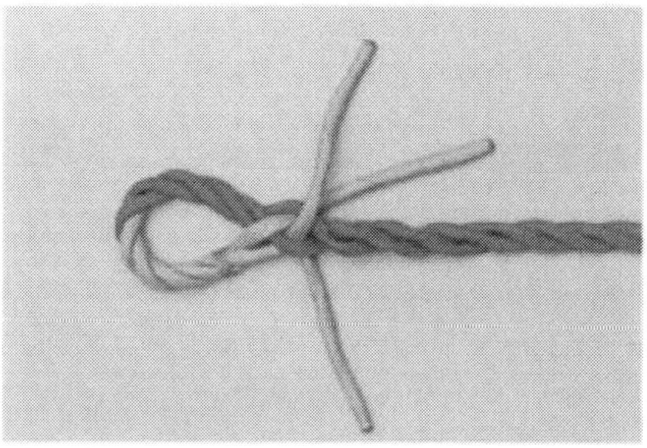
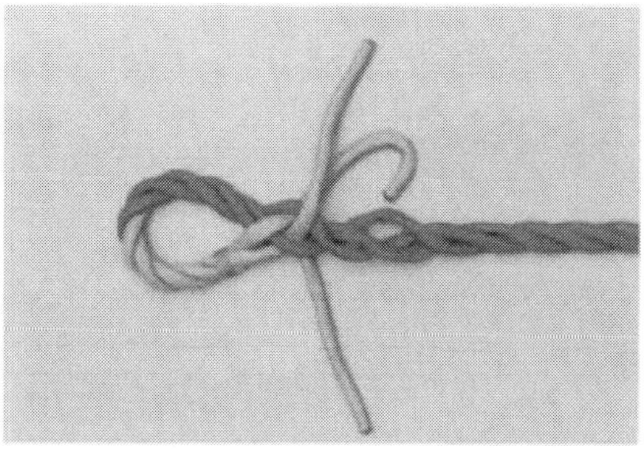
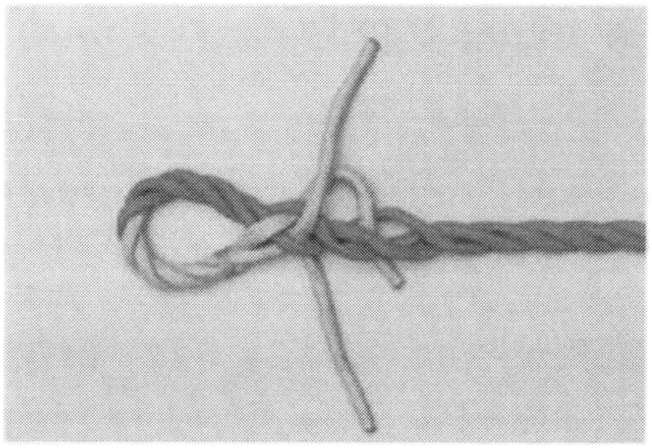
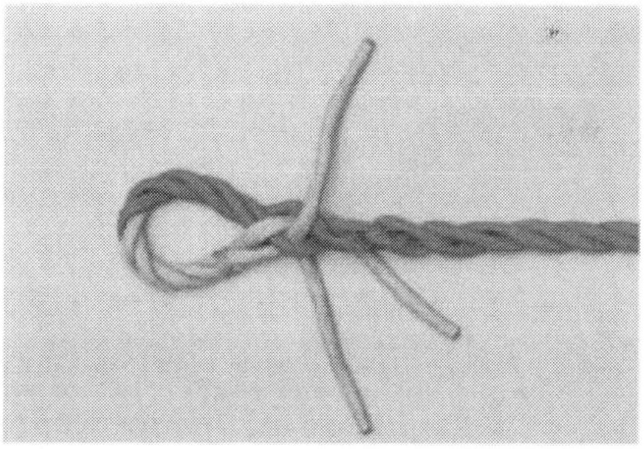

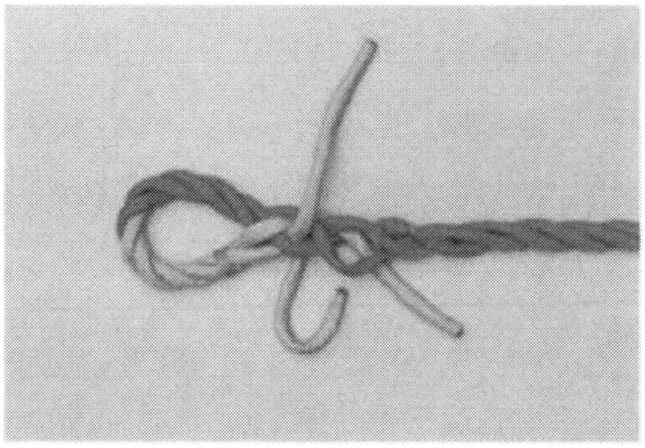

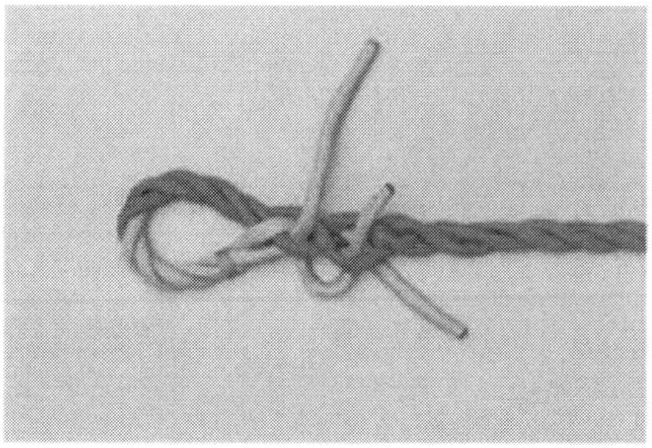

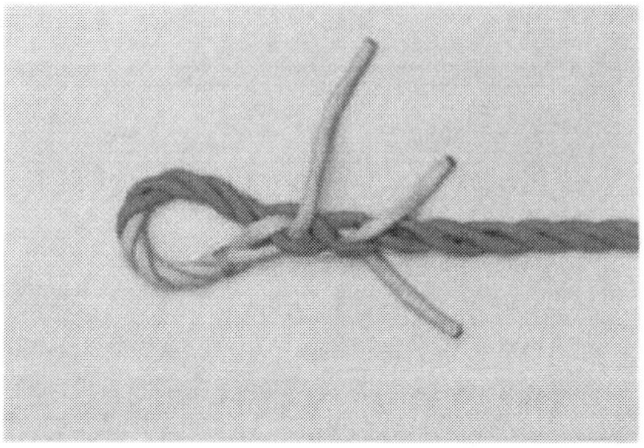

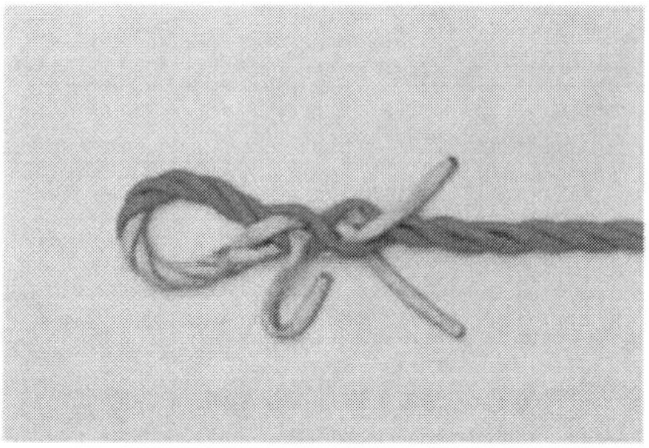

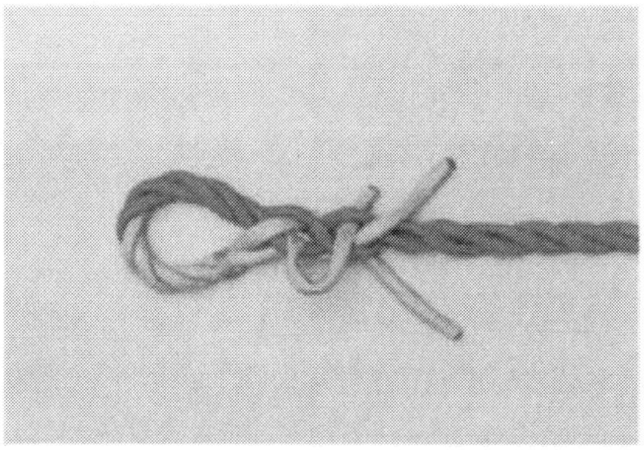

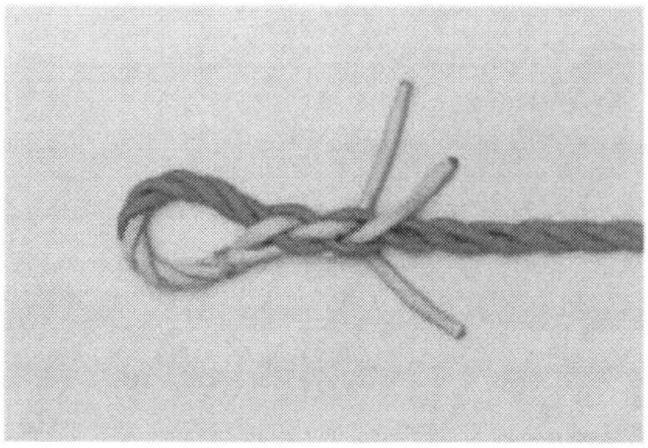

Tape rope. Unwind enough for five tucks (4 displayed here)—mastermind strands. Pass center one under a vertical strand. Pass lower one under lower adjoining standing strand. Pass the upper strand under the upper adjacent standing strand. Rehash the interaction for the excess arrangements of tucks. Eliminate the tape.

Significant: Modern manufactured materials will, in general, be dangerous and, presently, at least five complete "tucks" are required. For securing, towlines and other long-haul or basic applications, seven tucks are suggested. The activity shows the stringing of two complete tucks, with the last picture showing four tucks completed and fixed.

Fundamental Preparation: Secure the end of each strand by warmth, tape, or whipping twine. Measure the length to be unwound and secure the rope at that length with tape or string. The right size to disentangle is multiple times the width per "fold," i.e., for five wraps up half-inch distance across the rope, leave the free strands essentially 7.5 inches long; and for seven tucks, basically 10.5 inches. Make the necessary size of the circle and imprint the rope. In the movement, the imprint would be the place where the top fold of the Eye Splice is to be strung.

Procedure: In firmly laid or enormous measurement rope, it very well might be troublesome or difficult to pass each strand under the vertical strand without a reasonable device. The accompanying has all worked for me under various conditions:

Tape: One of the least complex techniques is to only enclose each end by concealing tape. This can give you a short "spike" to assist feed with each abandoning under the standing end.

Spike: Alternatively, go through a reasonable spike to open a vertical strand, and it might remain open long enough for the strand to be strung. I have utilized various ends, including marlinspikes, pencils, pens, and needle-nosed forceps.

Fid: The best apparatus is without a doubt a fid, a spiked aluminum bar with an open end, which opens up the vertical strand. You then, at that point, push the strand through embedded in the tail of the fid.

Construction: As in weaving, every one of the strands is passed first under and afterward over substitute standing strands. Simultaneously, the free ends will, in general, untwist and become messy. Handle each strand with care to hold its unique wind. After each strand is strung, it is helpful to wind it to keep its unique structure. Notwithstanding, after the prior arrangement of tucks, the strands ought to be permitted to spread and fit the type of the vertical strands.

Holding the Rope: Having arranged the ends and picked which strand to string where it is then all-around straightforward to get perplexed after it is strung. Grasp the other two tails, one on each side of the rope; they will then, at that point, be in the right spot when you need to pick the following end to string.

Completing the Splice: We will spend them in the graft if the ends have been sliced to the correct length. If they are excessively long, it is typically undeniably less challenging to make one more fold than to cut them and yet again consume them to stop them from disentangling. The consumed closes generally are somewhat more significant than the strand, giving some extra security to the Eye Splice.

Tightening the tails: It used to be famous to bit by bit thin the strands for few extra bucks. In tarred hemp, this made an extremely exquisite tightened join. The current rope is tricky to imply that the tightened tails will generally get ousted and make the joint look exceptionally messy. Genuine tightening of individual strands is seldom done now and ought to presumably never be endeavored by beginner, periodic, join creators.

Elective Taper: After delicate tucks have been made for strength, cut and consume one strand and afterward proceed with the Eye Splice with the leftover two strands. Cut and finish one more and graft the excess strand before cutting and consuming it as well.

Halyard Hitch

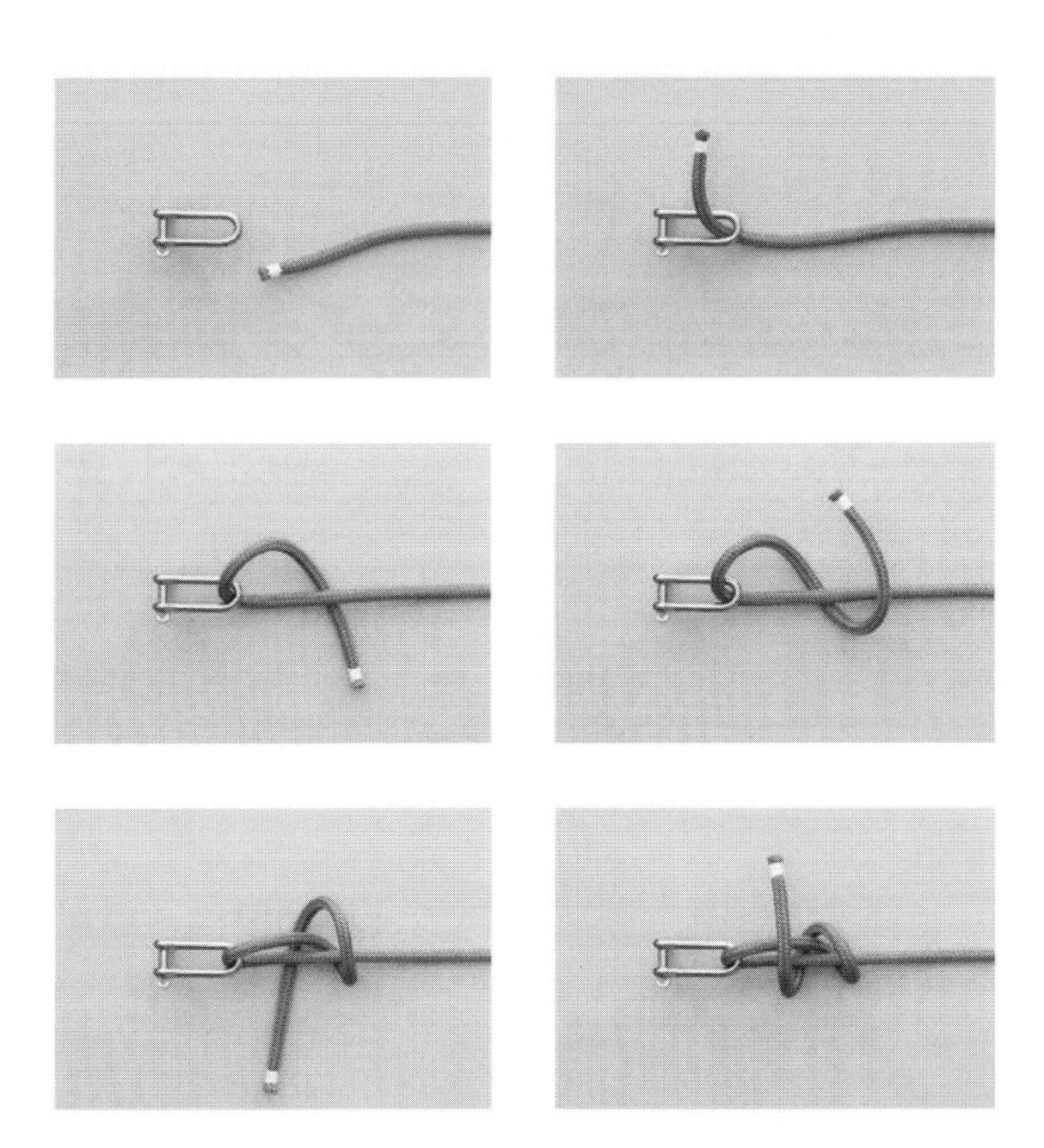

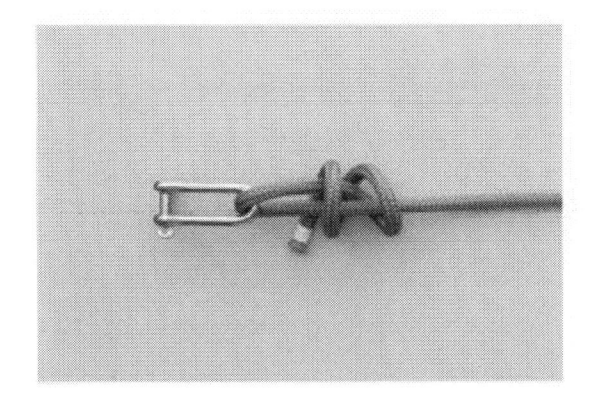

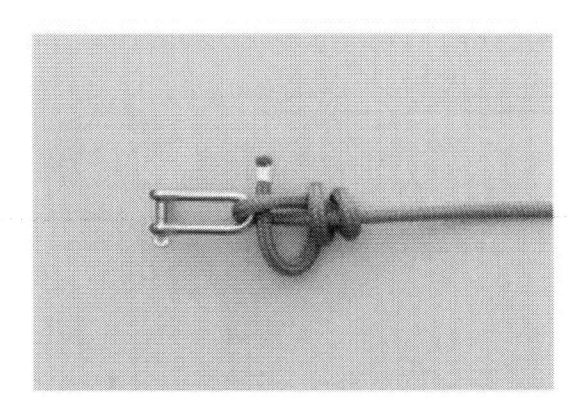

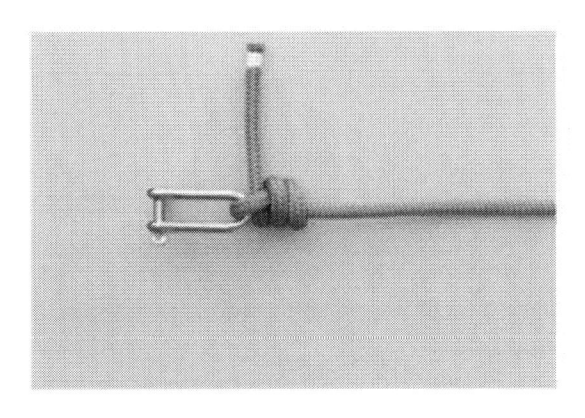

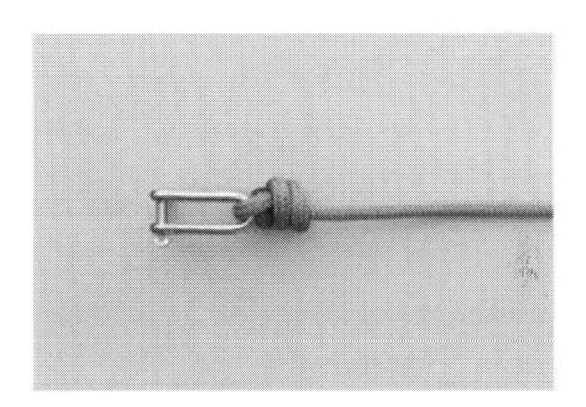

Pass the tail through the shackle and afterward twice around the standing end. Pass the end through the circle alongside the bond and pull highly close. Trim and heat-seal the end near the bunch.

Design: The Halyard Hitch Knot has a similar construction as the Stevedore Stopper however is appended to a shackle. When finished, the end exits neighboring the bind and is practically undetectable. By contrast, the end of Buntline Hitch escapes from the bond.

Alert: It is difficult to fix the Halyard Hitch Knot around a considerable distance across post or article; the hole between the shaft and the turns remains too huge even to consider giving a hold. The bunch looks slick when the end is stopped and liquefied by warming. Warmth treatment is unimaginable with present-day aramid strands, e.g., Kevlar®, Technora®, and Twaron®, and, with them, the bunch would be less appropriate. At the point when managed short, this bunch ought to never be utilized for primary burdens.

Benefits: The Halyard Hitch Knot is incredibly more minor, which makes a commendable decision for a halyard.

Hindrances: This Halyard Hitch Knot can't be tied or loosened under load and, after being vigorously stacked, it tends to be challenging to deliver.

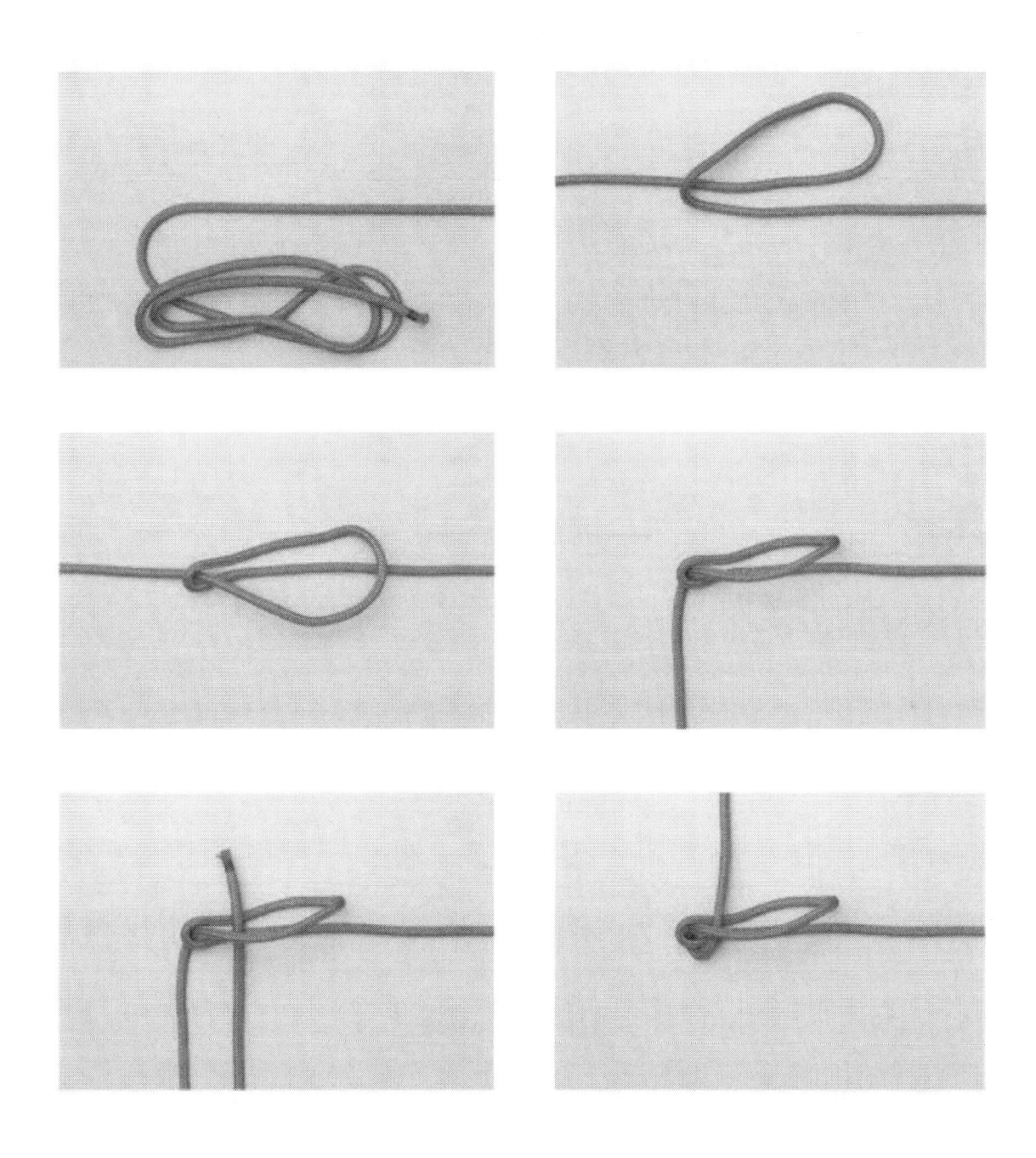

Heaving Line Knot

110

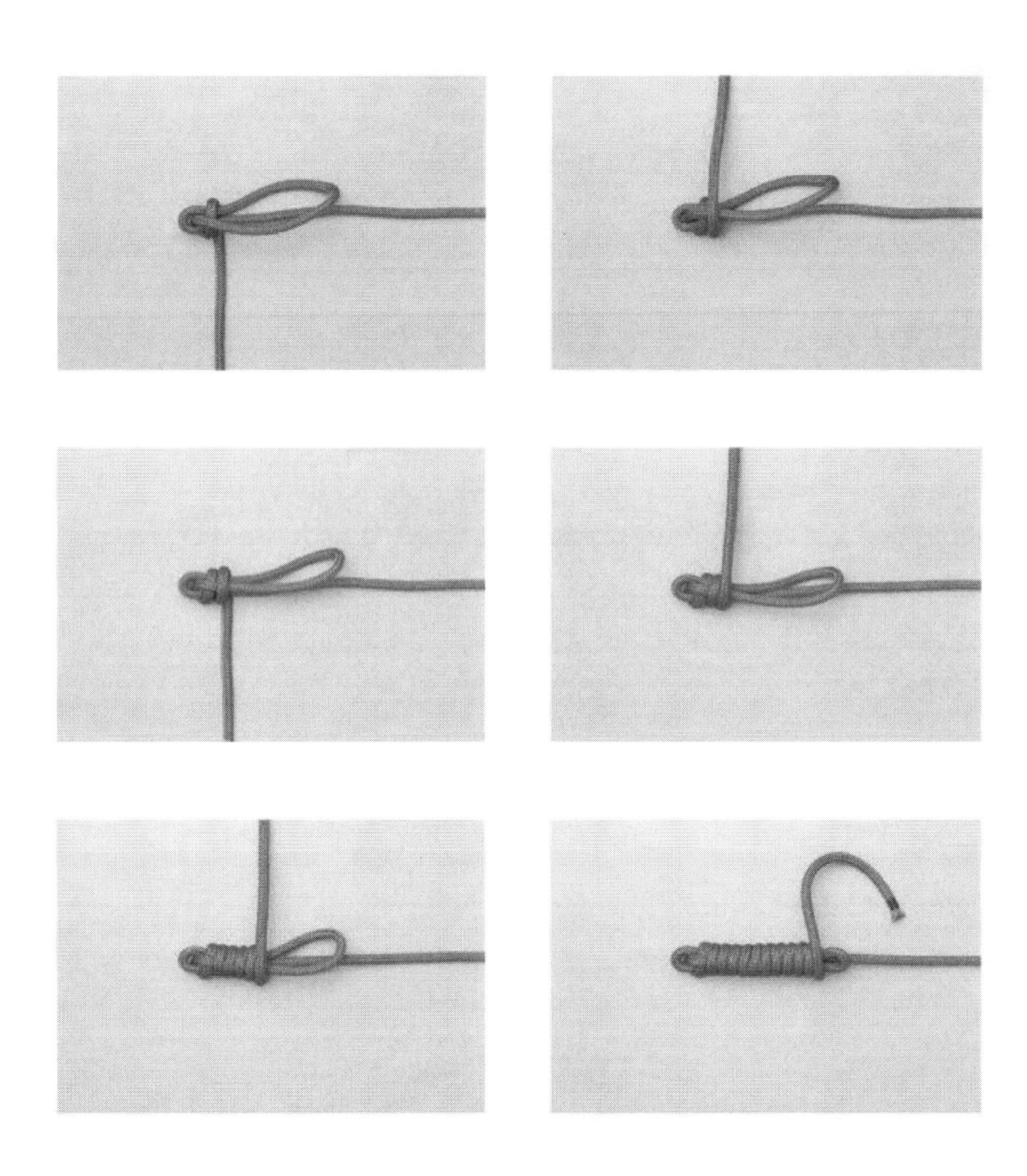

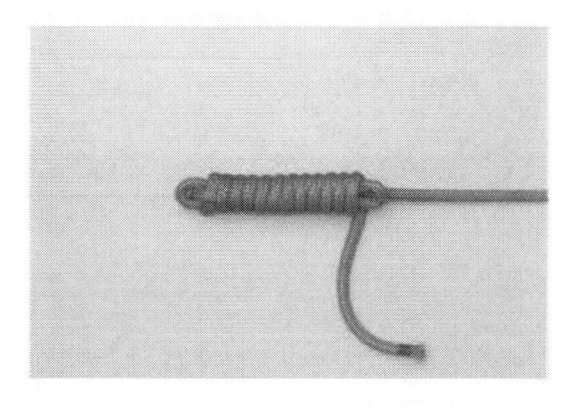

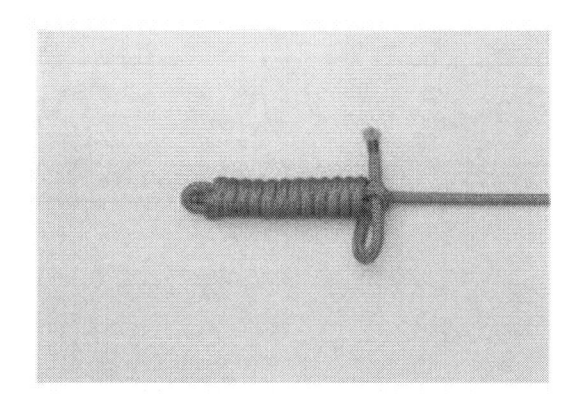

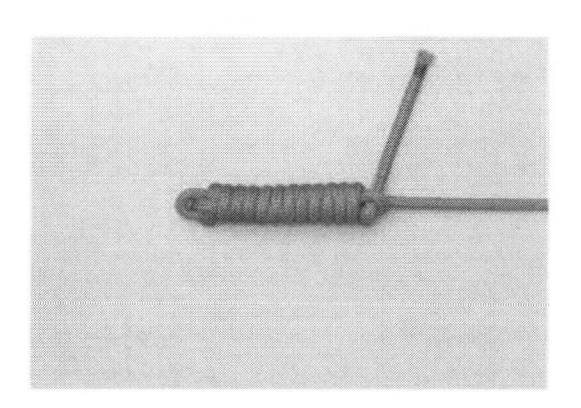

Plan sufficient rope. Make a bight and hold it with the goal that it encases the last part. Wrap the last piece at first around only two strands and afterward around every one of the three strands to go through the last part. Complete the bunch bypassing the last leg through the circle.

Uses: It makes a basic, respectably weighty, hurling tie.

Tying it: The movement shows the construction of the Heaving Line Knot. Nonetheless, by and by, it is desirable to leave a circle at each end during wrapping. When complete, pulling the end circle shrivels the other circle firmly around the short last part. Then, at that point, removing the standing end recoils the end circle.

Length Required: The quantity of turns utilized is discretionary and influences the length of rope required. The ten wraps here used around 3 ft of 1/4″ breadth rope (0.9 m of 6 mm distance across). To save speculating or squander, test an underlying fold over three strands.

A Heaving Line ought not to be joined straightforwardly to the fundamental hawser: it very well may be difficult to confine it when the hawser is stacked. It is suggested the utilization of a transitional short length of rope, and this permits the Heaving Line to be segregated from the middle of the road rope and reused.

Icicle Hitch (Loop Method)

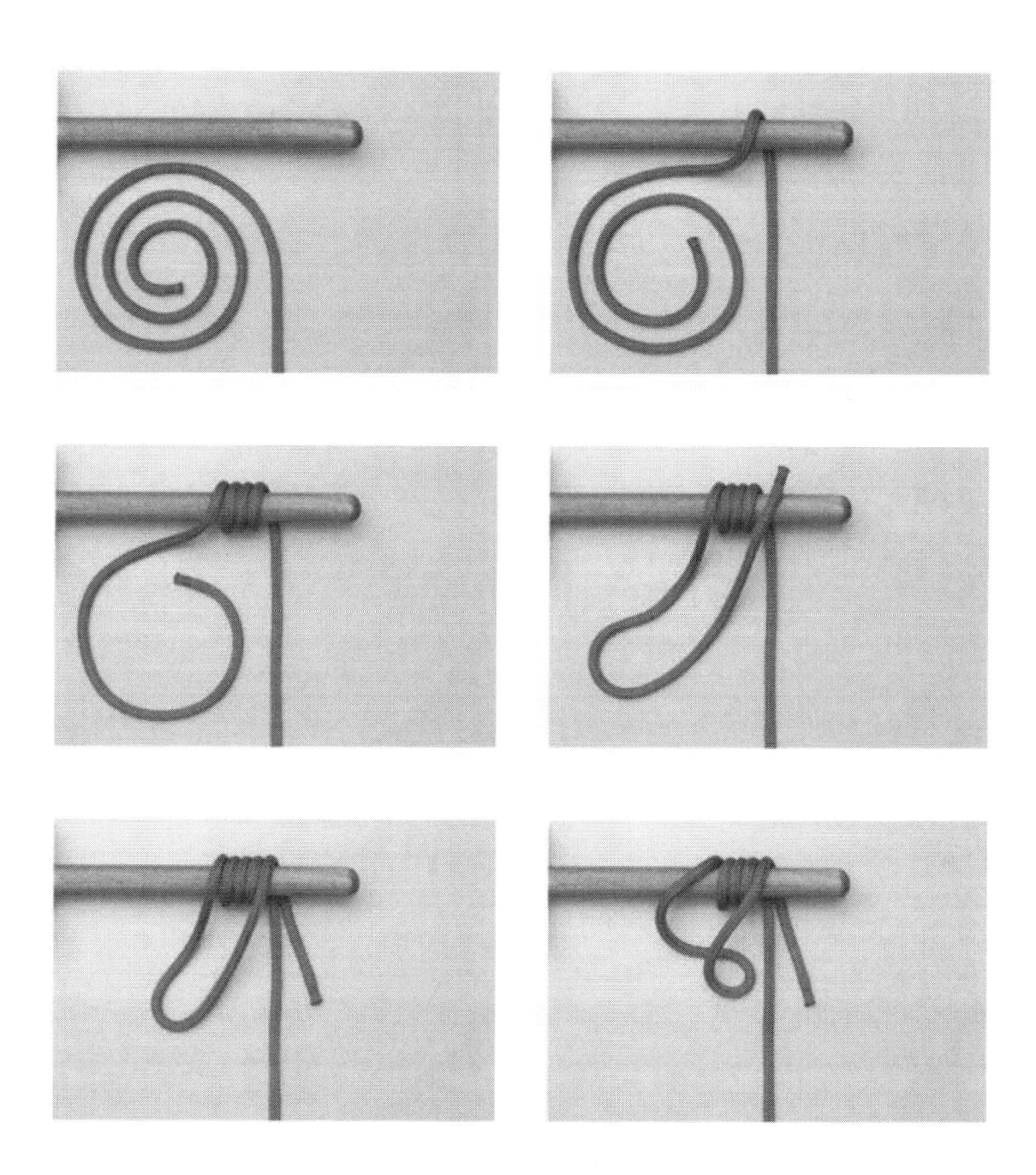

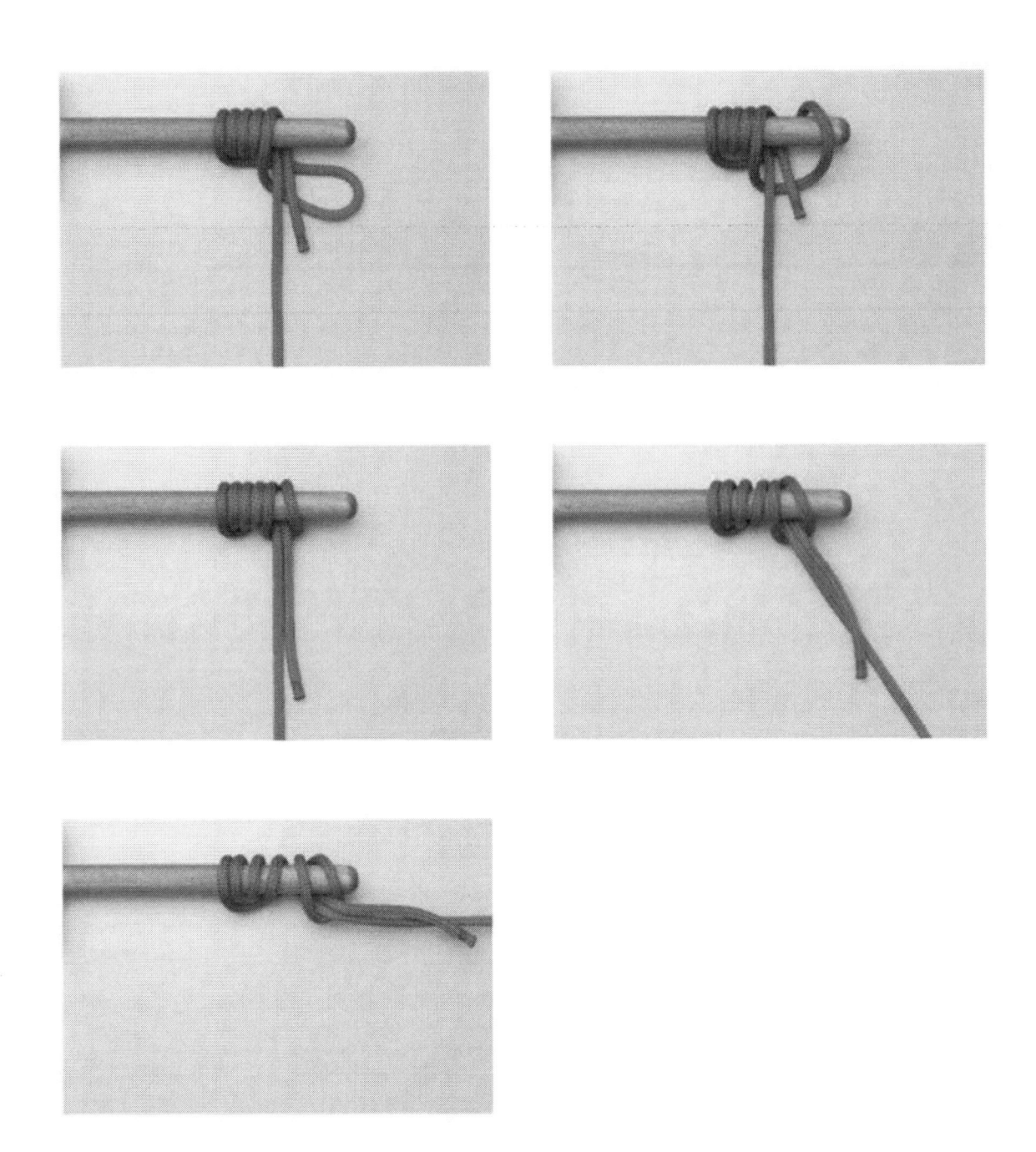

Fold the rope over the shaft multiple times, moving away from the post end. Leave a circle hanging and pass the end of the rope back over the shaft close by the standing end. Pass the circle behind the two closures and snare it over the post. Fix the bunch. The last burden ought to be corresponding to the shaft.

Uses: The Icicle Hitch Knot is utilized when power is applied corresponding to a post or shaft in just a single way. In August of 2009, I thoroughly investigated it in Practical Sailor, and they viewed it to be better than other slides and hold ties, including the Rolling Hitch.

Benefits: The Icicle Hitch Knot holds a smooth surface so well that it even chips away at a tightened surface like a marlinespike – henceforth its name.

Upsides and downsides: The Icicle Hitch Knot is somewhat simple to tie and can be utilized over a bar or toward the end of a shaft.

Lighterman's Hitch

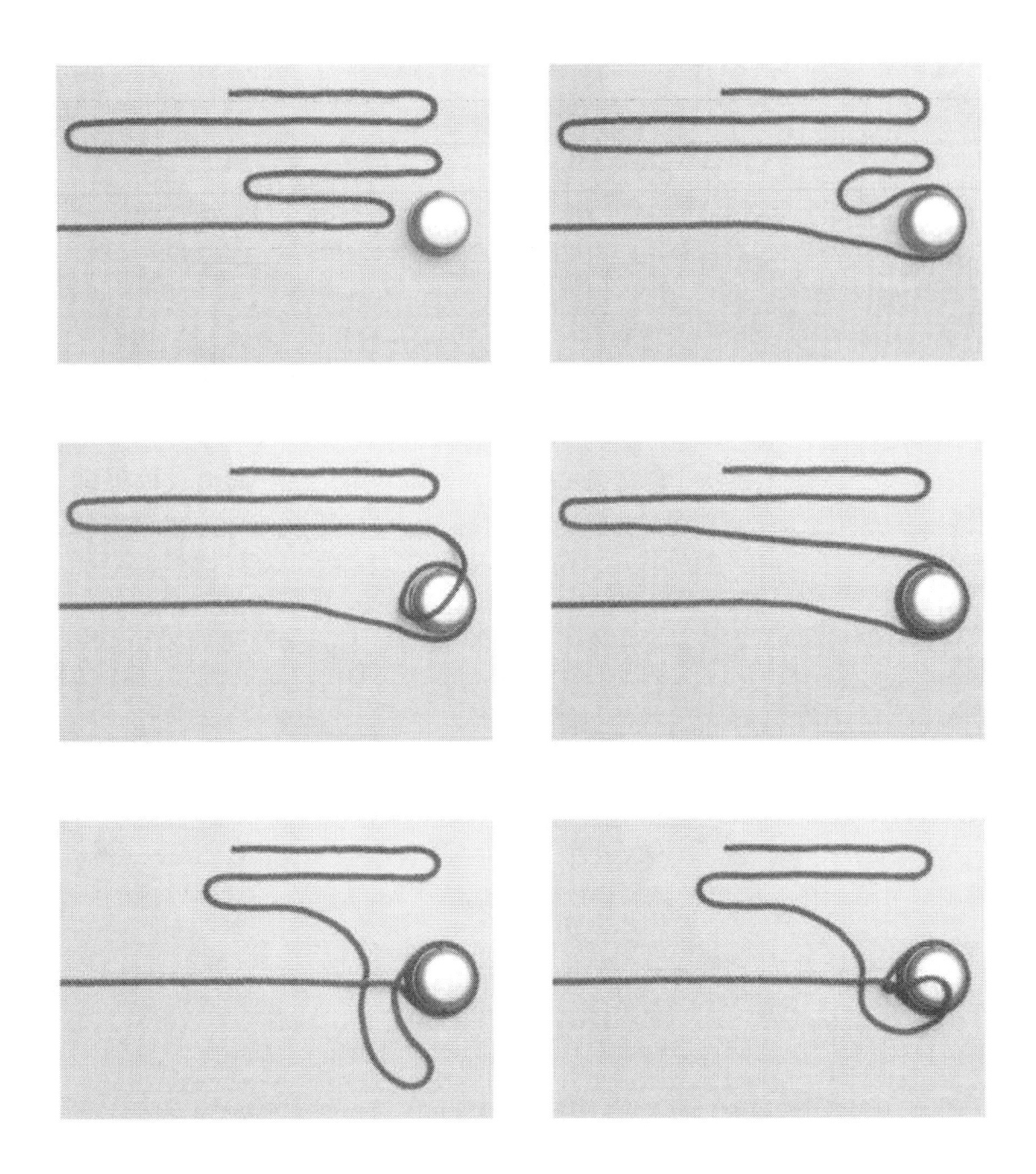

116

117

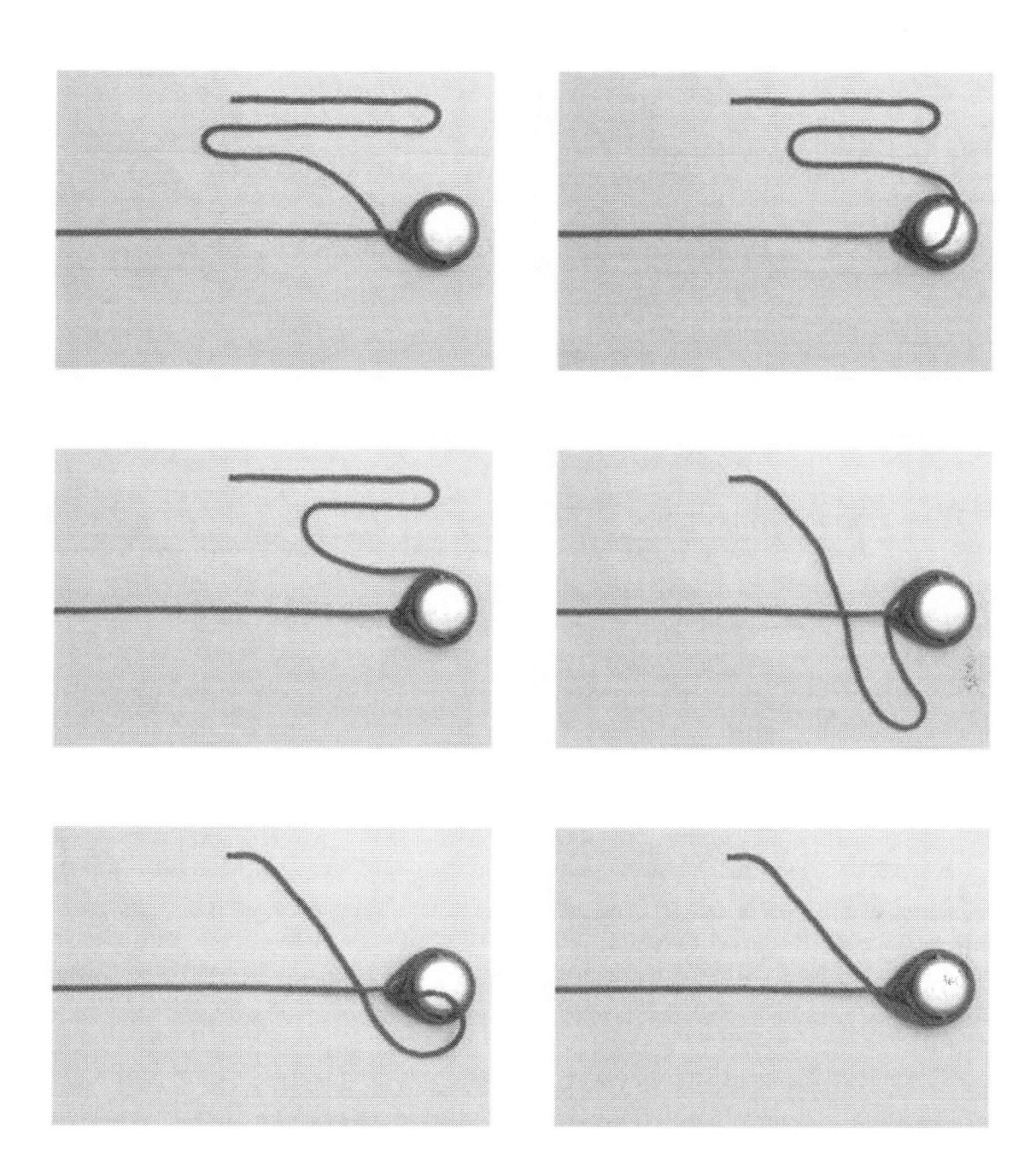

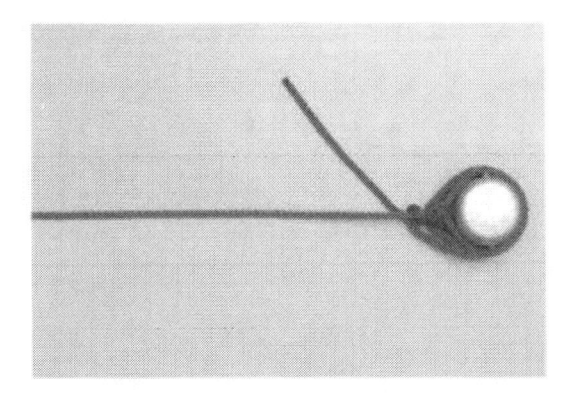

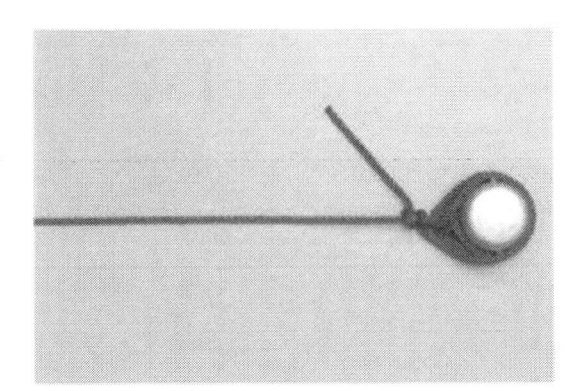

Fold the rope twice over the bollard. Pass a bight under the standing end and over the bollard. Fold an additional turn over the bollard. Pass a bight under the fixed end and over the bollard and keep adding more turns on a case-by-case basis. The Lighterman's Hitch is secure if adequate turns are utilized. Nonetheless, it is usually wrapped up with two Half Hitches around the standing end.

Uses: It is uncommon in its way to deal with taking a weighty burden. No bunch is tied – instead, the rope is passed around the standing end one way and afterward in the other – each time dropping a bight over the bollard.

Tying it: The Lighterman's Hitch Knot adaptation displayed here begins with two beginning turns (regularly called "a Round Turn"). This gives a reliable method of taking the underlying strain and is regularly enough to control a heap. At the same time, the hitch is being finished and take into account a more secure delivery later. For more considerable burdens can utilize an additional underlying turn.

Benefits: The excellence of the Lighterman's Hitch Knot lies in its straightforwardness and the simplicity with which it tends to be securely loosened and backed out. As each turn is eliminated, the tail can decide how simple it is to control the heap.

Midshipman's Hitch

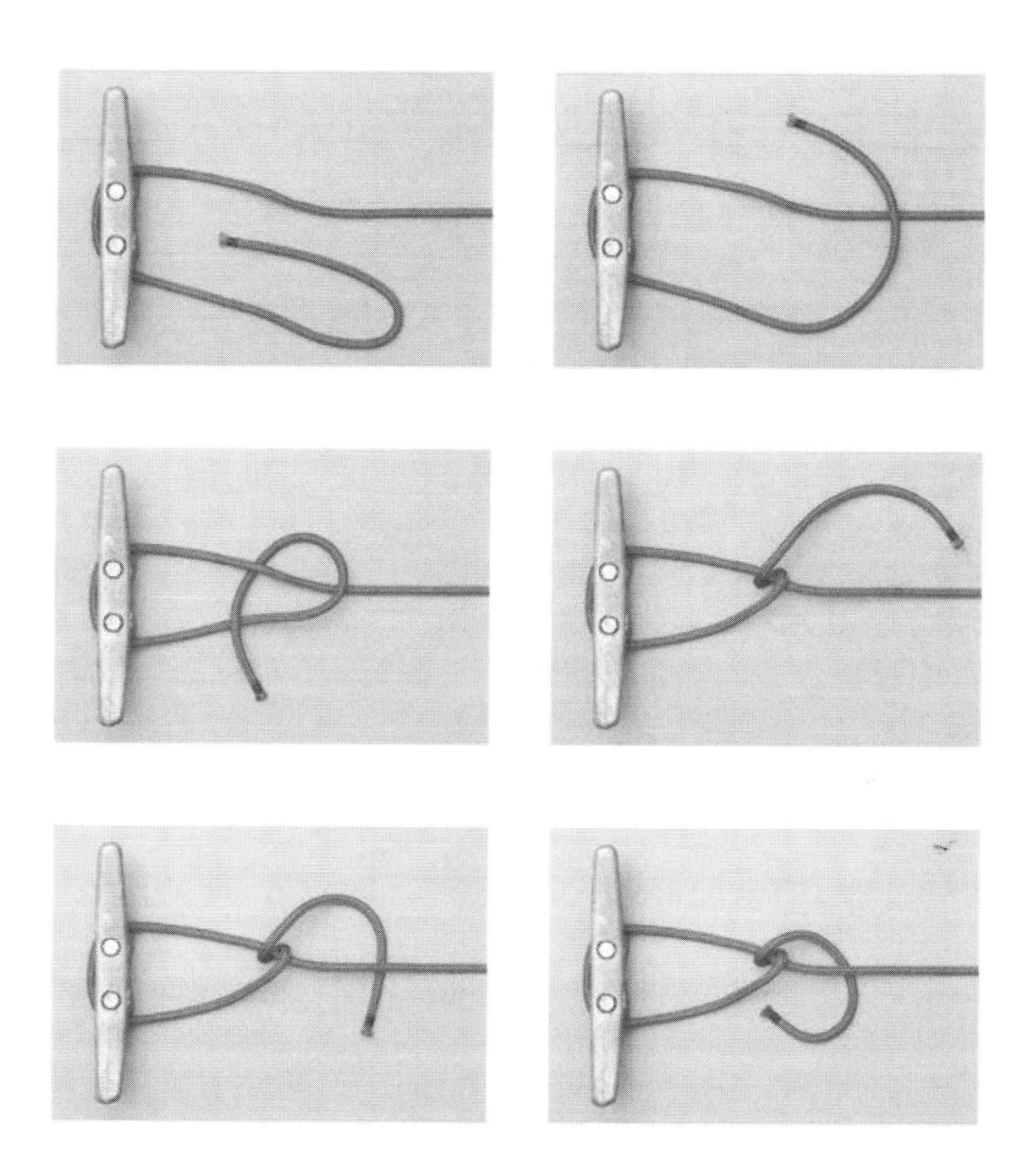

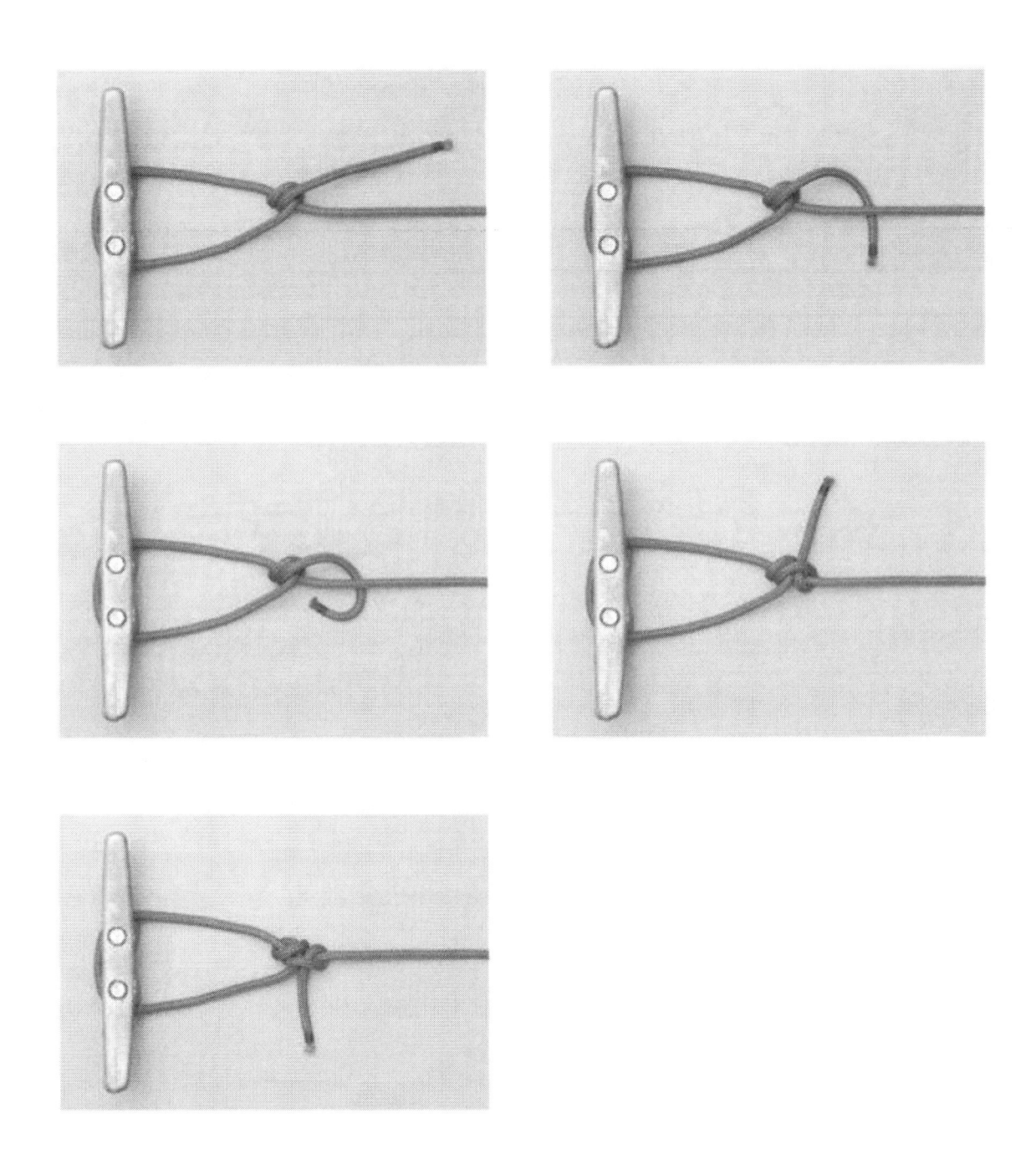

Pass the last part around the standing end. Pass it around once more. Wrap it up adjacent to the primary turn and pull it up close to frame an Awning Hitch. Proceed around and attach a Half hitch to make the Midshipman's Hitch. A Half Hitch the converse way makes an Adjustable Hitch.

Construction: The Midshipman's Hitch Knot makes a flexible circle toward the end of a rope. The bunch can be slid here and there the standing end, yet when fixed, hold safely.

Benefits: The Midshipman's Hitch Knot is moderately simple to tie or unfasten under load, and, even in the wake of being vigorously stacked, it is sensibly simple to deliver.

Overboard: it is the main bunch to tie in the following unlikely yet critical situation: you fall over the edge and seize the line you have wisely left, following toward the back and wind up holding tight with trouble. Before you tire, you figure out how to bring the dramatic end of the rope around your back. At that point, you need to attach an appropriate bunch to make a circle around you. You can't tie an anchor under load, and two Half Hitches will slide and constrict you. The Rolling Hitch is the appropriate response. Indeed, even as the subsequent turn is tucked "up" into the right spot, the significant strain is taken, and the last Half Hitch can be attached with less criticalness.

Pile Hitch

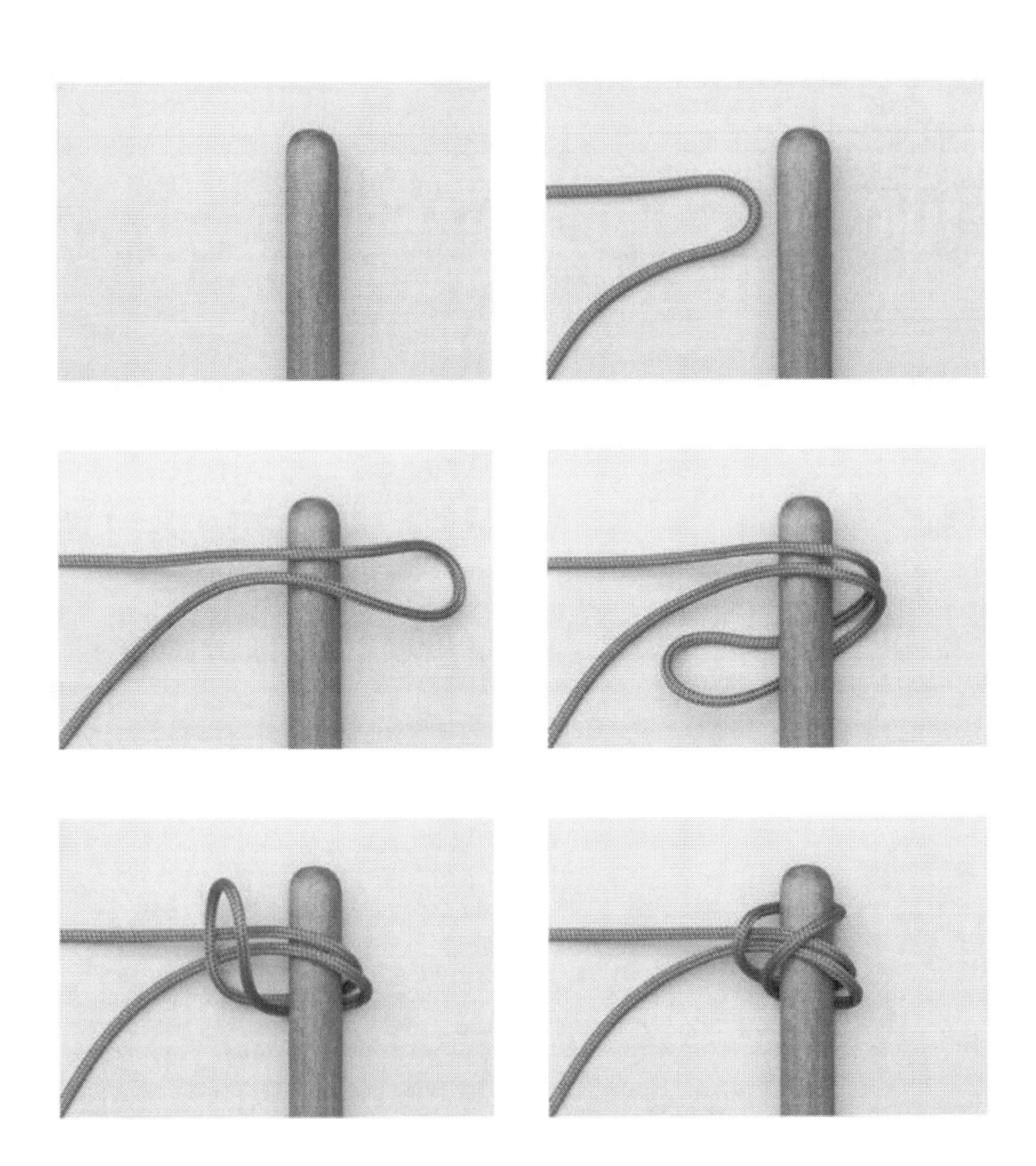

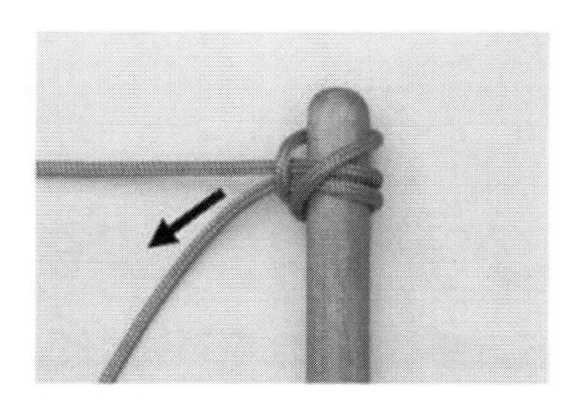

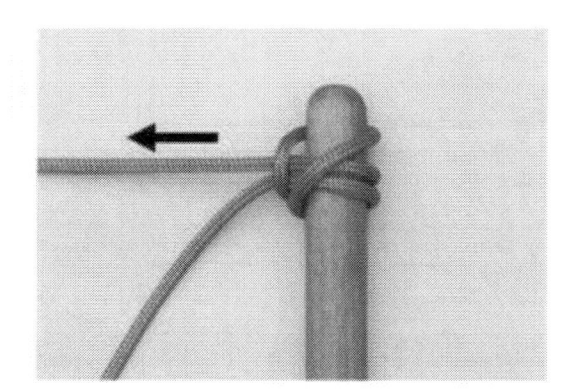

Pass a bight of the rope around the post and under the standing end. Drop the bight over the highest point of the post. Fix the hitch so the fixed end can take the heap.

Uses: A Pile Hitch gives a vital method to append a securing line to a dock post rapidly, and it is shockingly secure and quickly cast off. The Pile Hitch can't, notwithstanding, be suggested as a highly durable securing hitch. Can likewise utilize a progression ofPile Hitches to make a rope fence.

Rolling Hitch

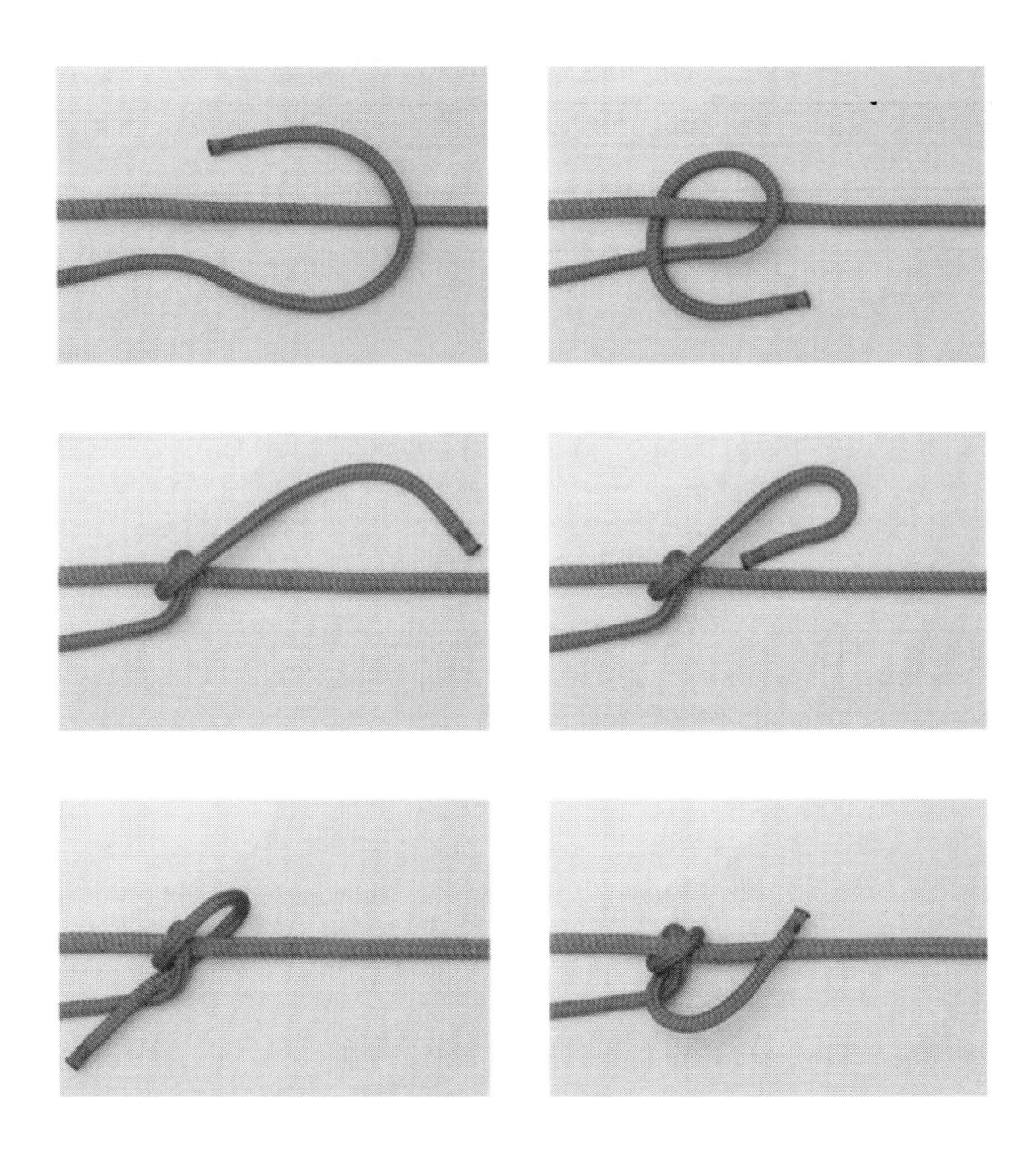

Pass the end around the fundamental rope to make a Half Hitch. Proceed around going over the primary turn. Fold the string between the standing end and the main arc. Fix to make it secure (this presents a little canine leg in the direct cord). Proceed around to add a last Half Hitch.

Uses: it joins a rope (generally more modest) to another (typically bigger) when the pull line is practically equal.

Caution: Some cutting-edge ropes are exceptionally elusive, e.g., Spectra®, Dyneema®, and Polypropylene. A Rolling Hitch won't hold at all in such materials.

Under Load: The Rolling Hitch is one of a handful of bunches that can be tied and unfastened with the load on. It doesn't bind and, when tied accurately, doesn't slip. Be that as it may, a few specialists prescribe utilizing the last part to attach a subsequent Rolling Hitch to back up the first in basic applications.

Variety Using a Bight: When there is a long last part, the Rolling Hitch can be tied utilizing a bight (circle) rather than the end. This is especially helpful when the Rolling Hitch is being used as a Spring Line. In any case, scrupulousness is fundamental. The initial segment of the bunch is tied using one strand of the circle. The other strand is kept far removed, yet the dramatic end isn't gotten through. When the initial segment of the bunch is secure and will take the strain, the bight can be utilized to tie at least one-Half Hitches.

Round Turn & Two Half Hitches

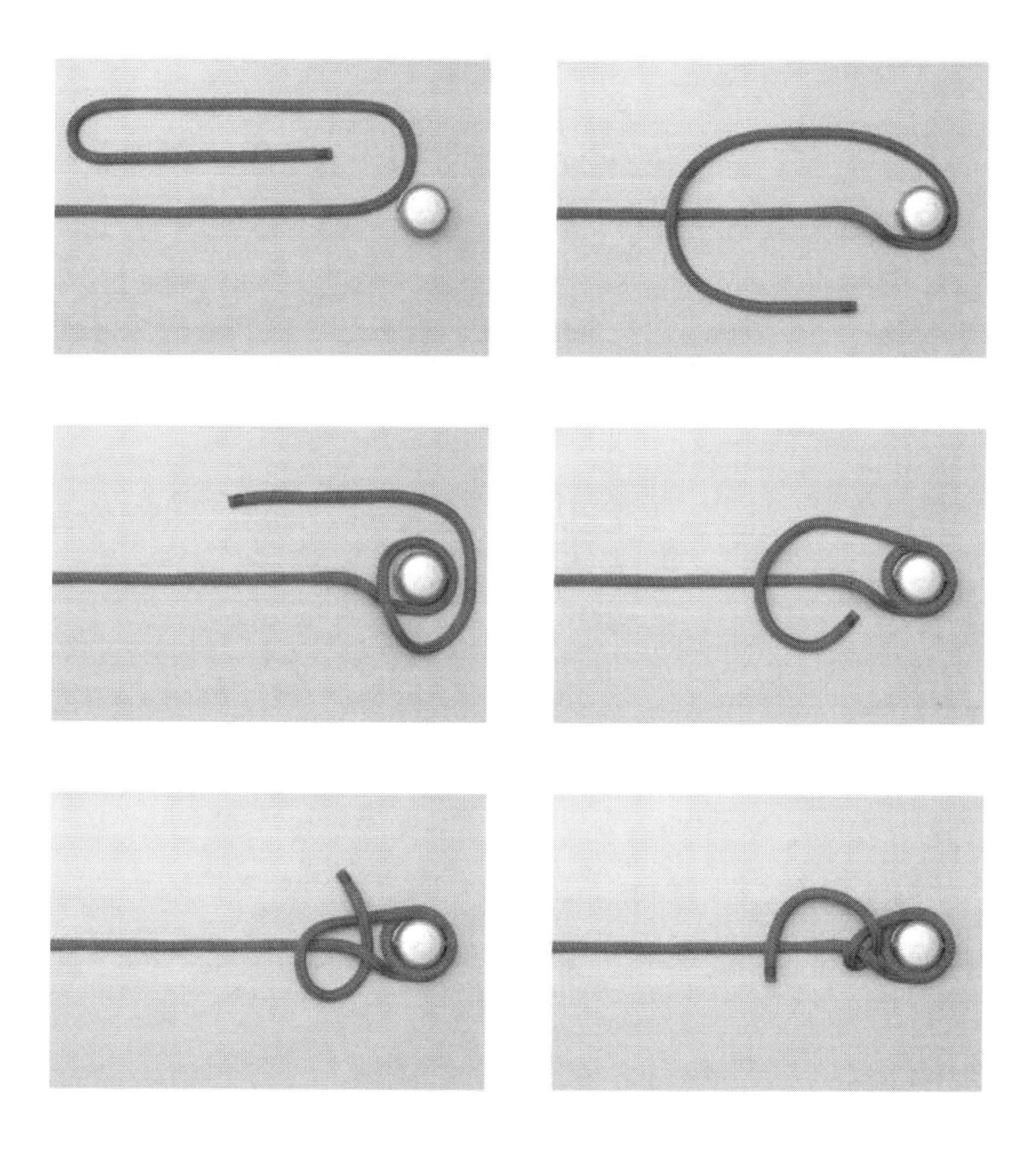

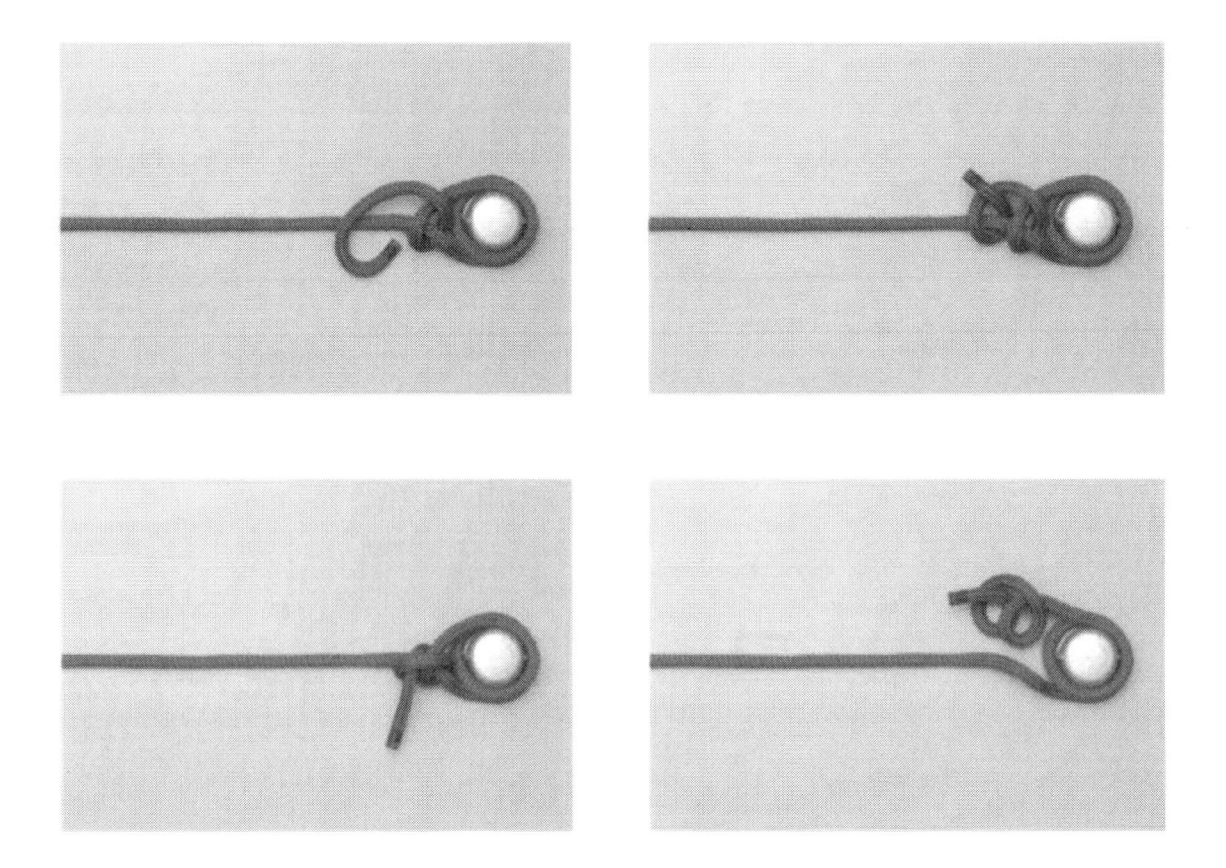

Pass the end around the post twice. This takes the strain while you seal the deal. Circumvent the standing end to make the main Half Hitch. Pull this tight. Proceed around a similar way to make the subsequent Half Hitch. Pull tight to finish the bunch.

The Round Turn and Two Half Hitches are attached back to the standing end with a clove hitch. It is like the anchor twist; however, the primary Half Hitch isn't passed under the underlying turn.

The Round Turn and (at least two) Half Hitches are extremely valuable for joining a rope to a ring, bar, shaft, or dock post, albeit likely less secure than the Anchor (Fisherman's) Hitch. As the name recommends, the Round Turn and Two Half Hitches is made out of two significant parts:

1. **Round Turn**: The underlying 'Round Turn' – two passes of the tail – should take the underlying strain while you complete the bunch. This might be basic when dealing with a securing line. An extra turn, or even two extra turns, should be added at first if you are taking care of a weighty burden, e.g., with a vast vessel or in a solid breeze. These turns permit you to control the heap while you add the:

2. **Two or More Half Hitches**. The two Half Hitches structure a clove hitch around the standing end. Notwithstanding, it is customary to see one extra or more Half Hitches to make the bunch safer or go through an overabundance line.

Sealing the deal: Learn to attach the Half Hitches with one hand! This permits you to utilize the other hand to take the strain of a vessel that may effortlessly pull with a power far more prominent than you could some way or another control. As underscored above, when managing such management, use however many turns on the post to control the strain.

Bearing: Always tie the Half Hitches the equivalent 'way.' If you start the main Half Hitch with the tail dying from you over the rope, then, at that point, do likewise with the following (and the following).

Variety Using a Bight: When there is a long tail, the Half Hitches can be tied utilizing a bight (circle) rather than the end, and this devours an abundance of rope that may somehow hang in the manner or require curling.

Running Bowline

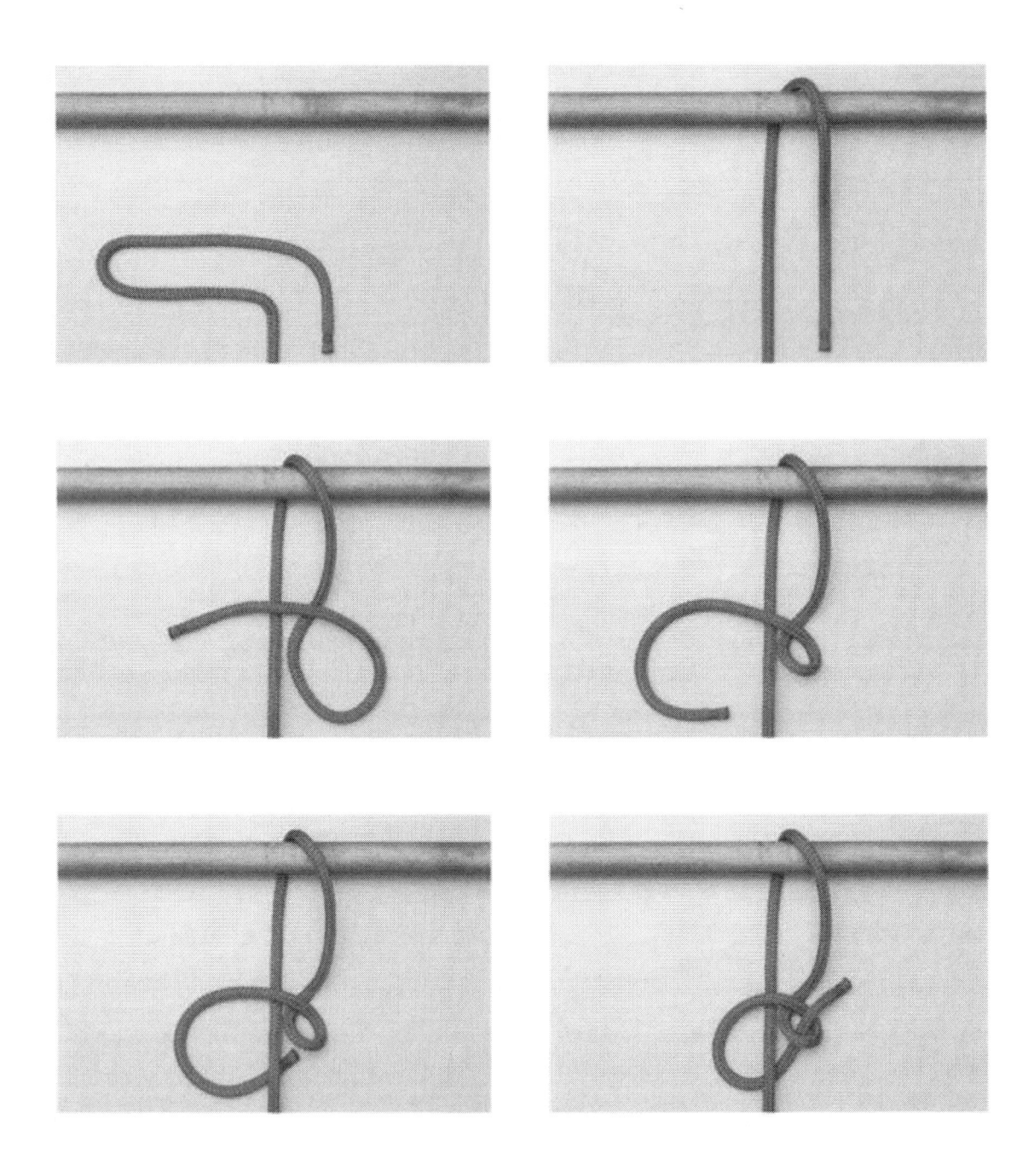

Pass the rope over the pole. Structure a circle in the tail. Pass the short end around the standing end, through the loop, around itself, and back through the loop to shape the anchor. Pull-on the upright end to run the anchor facing the post.

Uses: The Running Bowline is an essential method of tying a nose that won't connect and can be slid scattered without any problem. In drifting, it is suggested for use when recovering apparatus or wood which has fallen over the edge and in moving for recovering articles in spots like chasms. At home, it is helpful to hang a Child's Swing. The preliminary test is to track down an appropriate branch, and the second is to toss the rope over it effectively.

Choices: When the Standing End is free, it is frequently simpler to initially tie the Bowline and afterward string the Standing End through it.

Recovery: Once the Running Bowline is cozy facing the branch, recovery later can be an issue. The bunch might be twenty feet noticeable all around, and you have neither courageous rope climbers nor long stepping stools. Arrangement ahead of time gives choices: either a light recovery line can be connected to the Bowline, or the Bowline can be attached with an extremely long tail. Nonetheless, if the long end choice is thought of, the Alpine Butterfly Loop would be better because it requires no stringing of a long end to tie it.

Choices: A comparable running noose could be made with different circle hitches – including the actual Noose. The benefit of utilizing a bunch like an anchor is that it will not quit for the day tie on the standing end. Since the rope is under strain, the Running Bowline will grasp its heap – or the branch. When not stacked, it can effectively scatter the bunch.

Stevedore Stopper

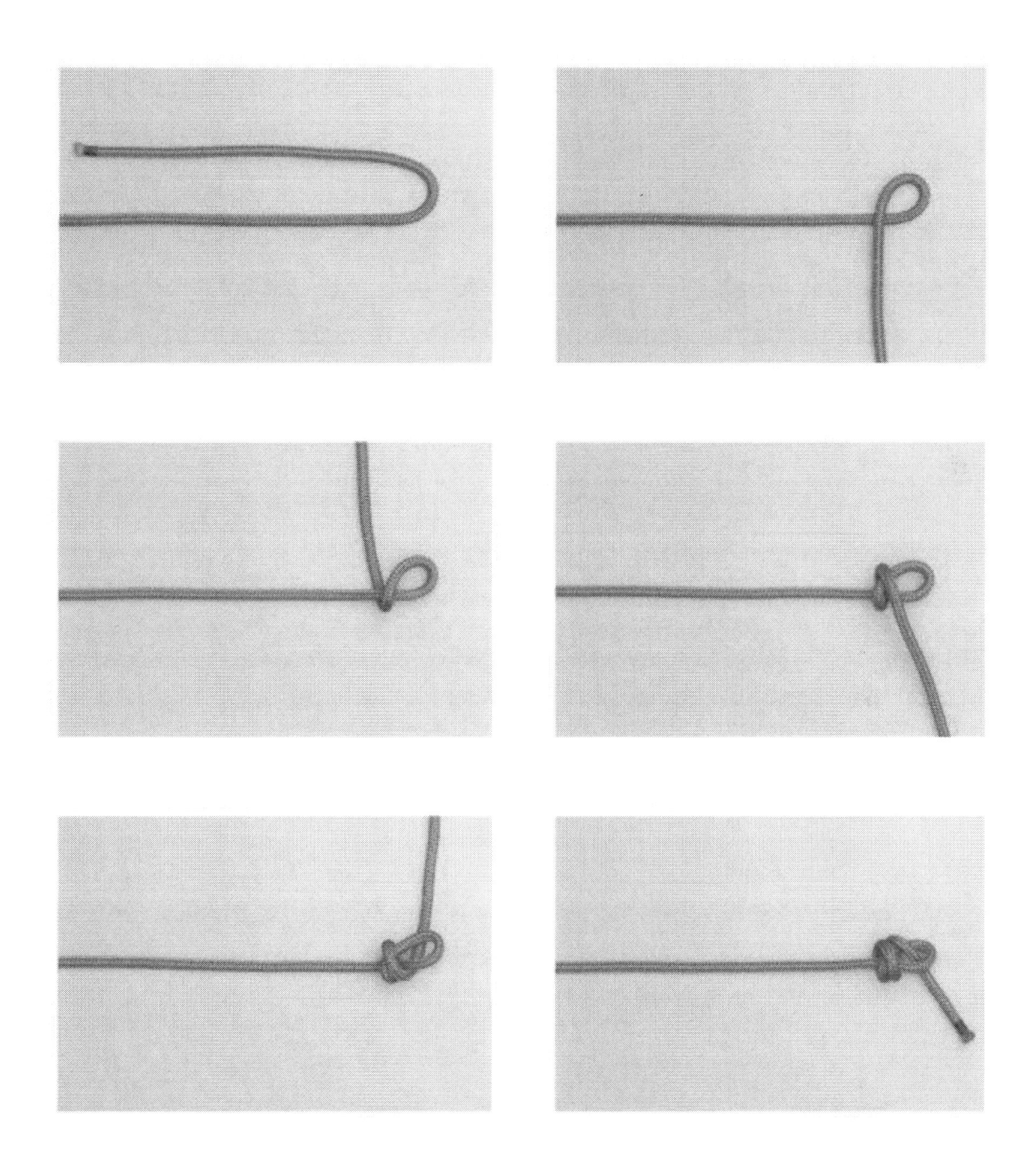

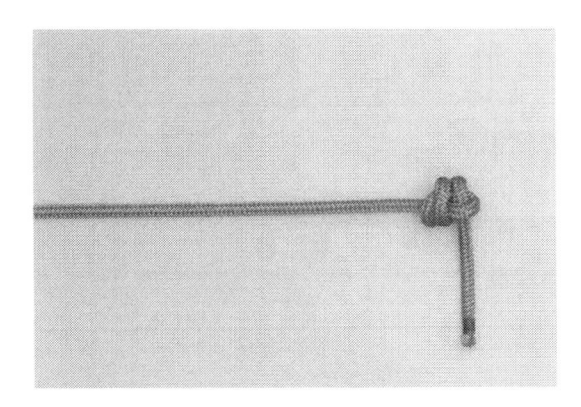

Structure a bight toward the end of the rope. Pass the last part across the standing end and proceed around to make two complete turns. Then, at that point, pass the end down through the bight and fix the turns. At last, pull on the standing end to grasp the last part.

Uses: The Stevedore Stopper Knot is a dependable, respectably cumbersome plug tie. It is a great bunch to utilize when setting a covering – it tends to be used to get an end that has been gone through a grommet.

Design: The Stevedore Stopper Knot begins like tying a Figure 8 Knot. Then, at that point, the Tail End is relaxed before going through the bight.

Benefits: The bunch is decently massive, is effectively tied, and is more straightforward to unfasten than a Figure 8 Knot even after weighty stacking.

Perfection Loop Knot

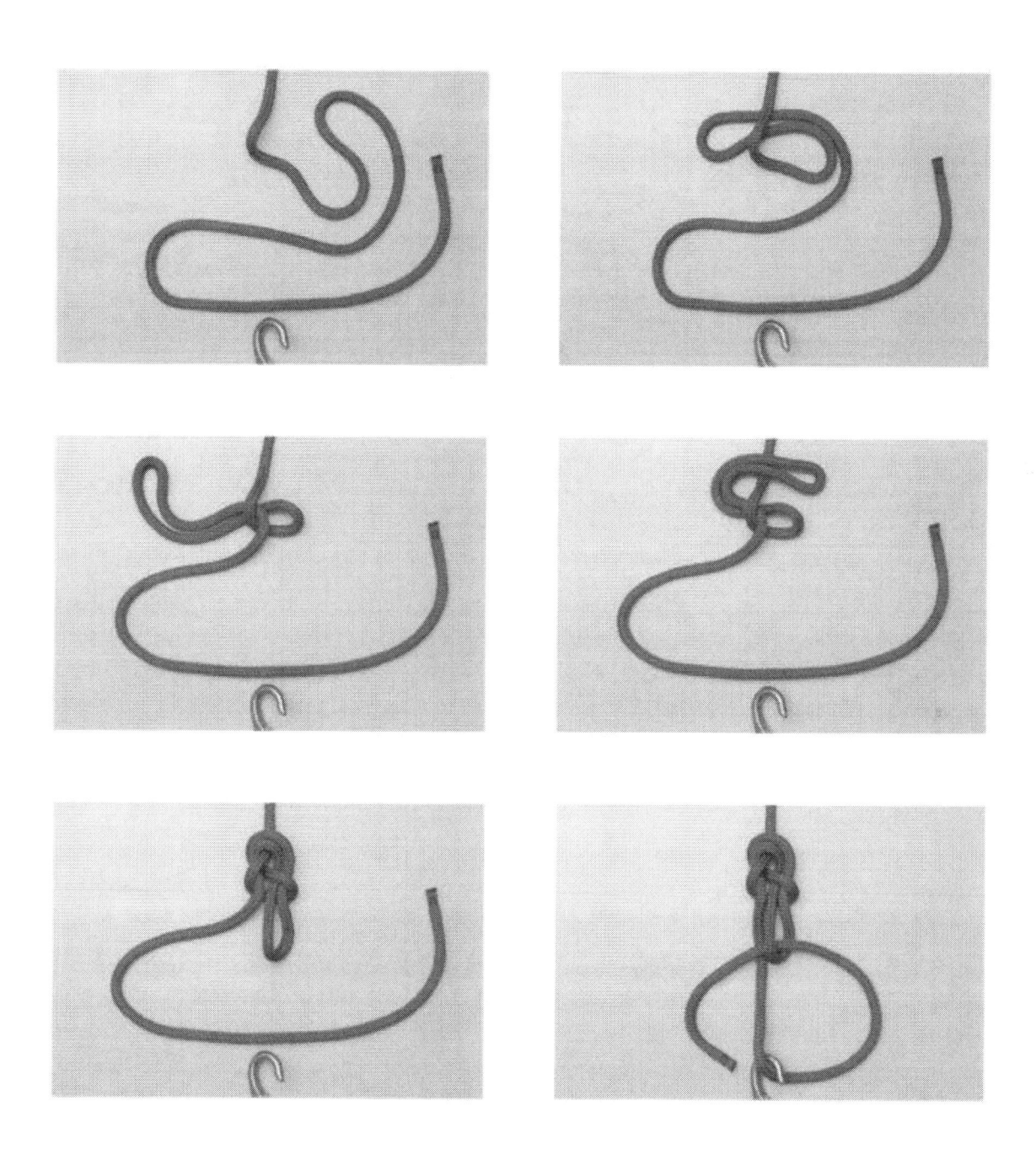

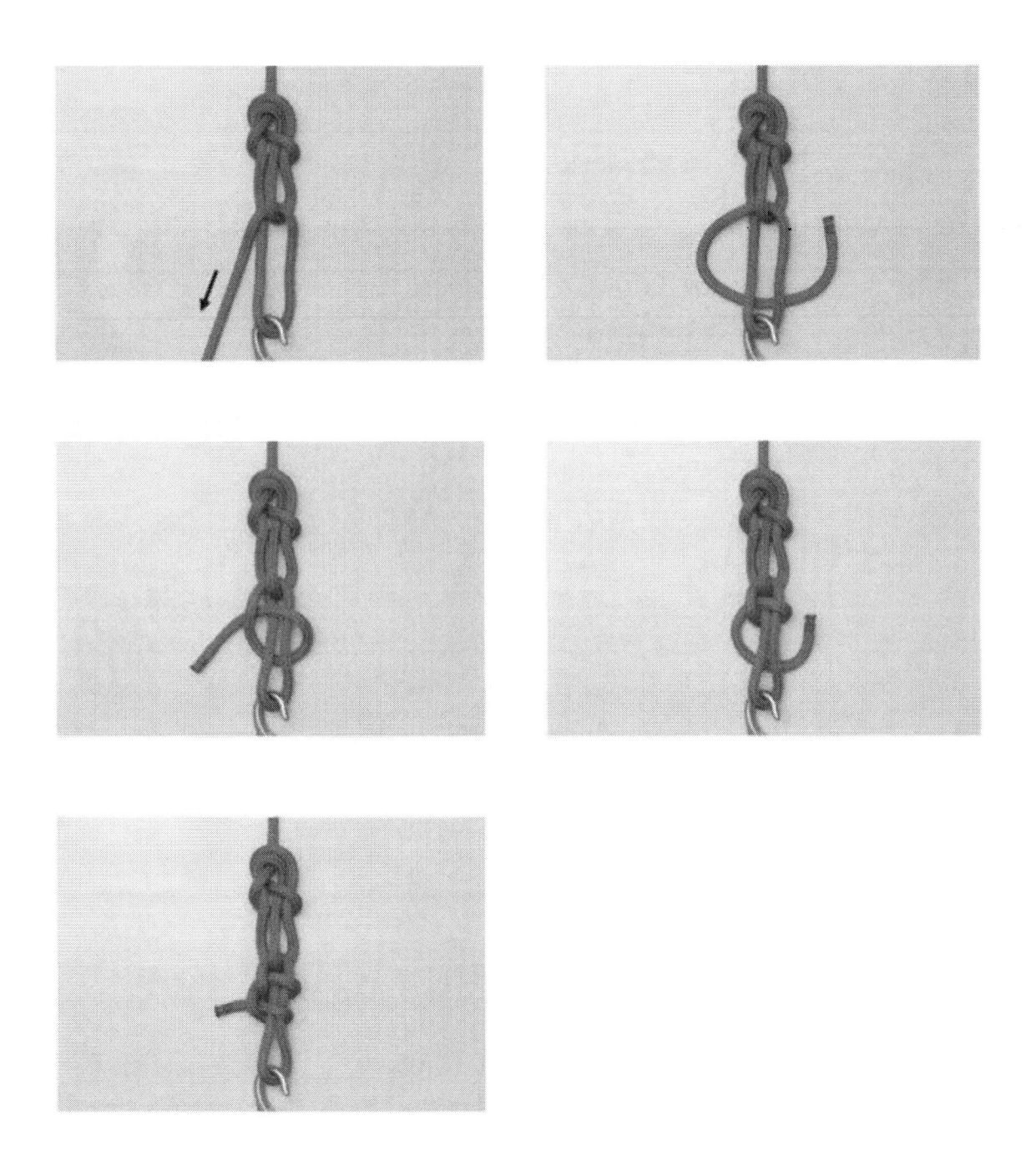

Structure a circle as far as it goes. Structure a subsequent circle and lay it on top of the first with the label end under the standing end. Pass the label end between the two processes. Get the top circle through the base circle. Grease up and fix by pulling on the fixed end and the new ring. Trim the end.

Uses: The simplest method is to make a little circle toward the end of a pioneer or scarf that will lie totally by the standing end. It is generally used to join a Perfection Loop to end a fly line to a Perfection circle in a Leader utilizing a "Circle to Loop" association.

Tying it: The Perfection Loop Knot is most effectively tied in the hand. Hold the immediate circle among fingers and thumb. Wrap the subsequent turn round the finger and thumb and afterward between the two processes. Fold the second turn through the primary, making sure that the circle crosses and traps the end.

Elective: It can likewise be tied through a fly or bait by passing the free end along the way displayed in Frame 7 of the activity.

Benefits: The Perfection Loop Knot makes a steady circle that lines up flawlessly with the standing end. Utilizing a "Circle to Loop" association, The Perfection Loop Knot considers speedy and helpful pioneer changes.

Zeppelin Bend

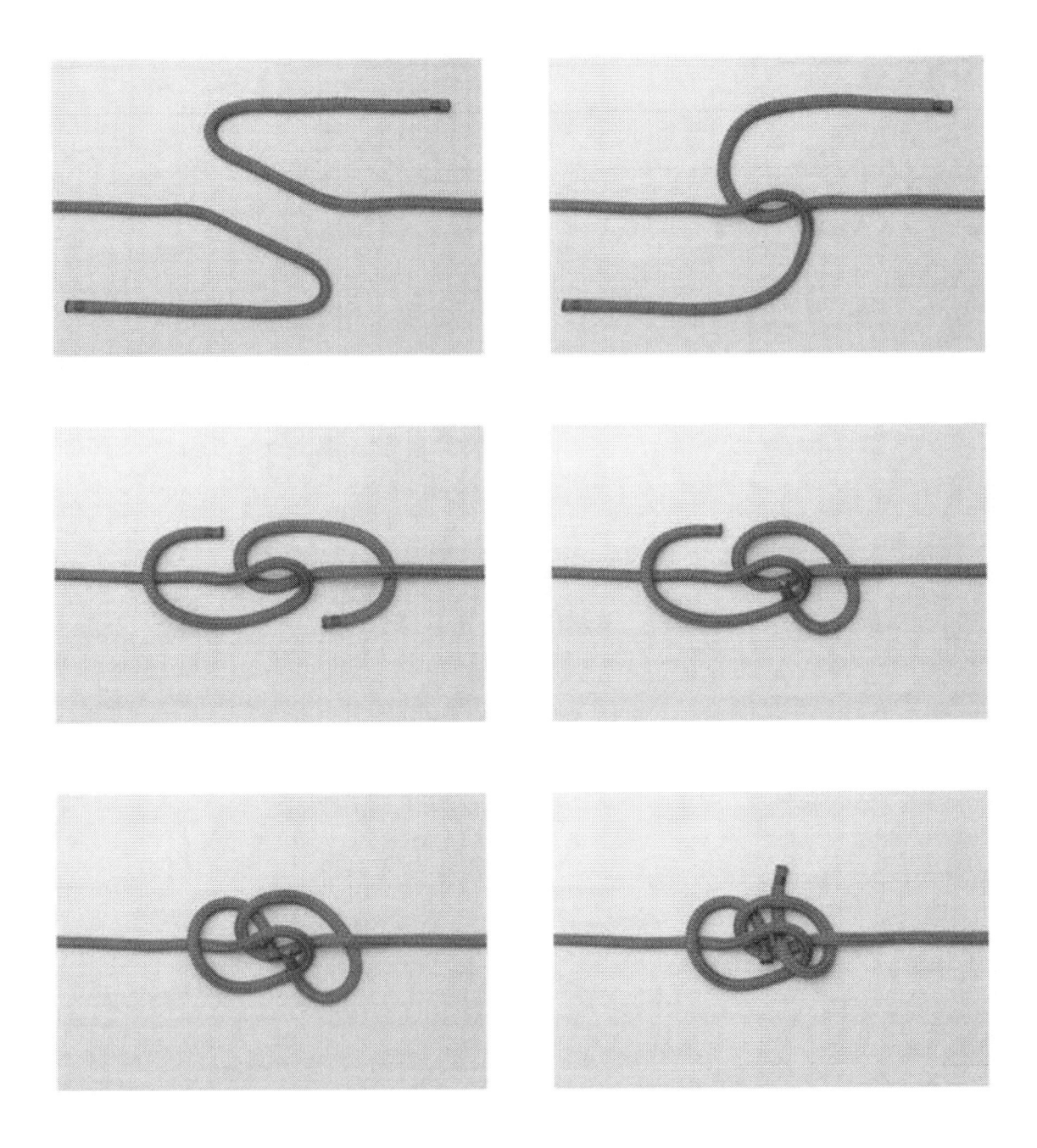

Structure a bight in the two ropes and cross over them. Pass each end around across itself - going over for the top bight and under for the base bight. String the two closures past one another through the center. Fix to frame the Zeppelin Bend. Back see.

Uses: The Zeppelin Bend is one of the curves utilizing interlocking overhand bunches. A solid twist can be unfastened even in the wake of being intensely stacked yet not, nonetheless, while still under load. It is a phenomenal option in contrast to the more broadly utilized Double Fisherman's since it wipes out the danger of sticking.

Caution: For the Animation, the closures were left short. For primary burdens, e.g., when Climbing, the closures should be left significantly longer.

Airship Stories: Although exceptionally far-fetched, the Zeppelin Bend has been depicted as being utilized to get Airships. To be sure, terrible habit Admiral Charles Rosendahl, Commanding Officer of the American Zeppelin (Los Angeles/ZR3), was even expected to have demanded that the Zeppelin Bend be utilized to secure his aircraft. These accounts currently appear exceptionally far-fetched. Giles Camplin, Editor of Airship Heritage Trust's Journal Dirigible, detailed the accompanying in Issue No. 60, Summer 2010:

1. The docking method commonly utilized shackling two wires together.

2. In later life, Rosendahl asserted the obliviousness of the bunch.

3. Can't loosen the Zeppelin tie under load.

4. Using a twist to join two ropes would be an off-kilter approach to secure anything.

5. A rigger who flew on the R100 revealed they generally utilized a Rolling Hitch.

Tying it: The interlocking circles' game plan and how they finish through the middle are basic. Albeit the Zeppelin Bend is getting and can be loosened effectively, its likeness to different curves utilizing interlocking overhand bunches chances disarray – and ruins. Therefore, we likewise suggest the Alpine Butterfly Bend tied using a similar strategy used for the Alpine Butterfly Loop. The system is essential because Roo stresses the danger of making an Evil Impostor when misconnected.

Benefits: The Zeppelin Bend is dependable with very little propensity to slip or tie. It is extraordinarily secure and shake-safe in all materials.

Hindrances: Attention to tying it effectively is essential. After it is connected, it very well may not be easy to recognize it from the less good Hunter's Bend.

Slim Beauty Knot

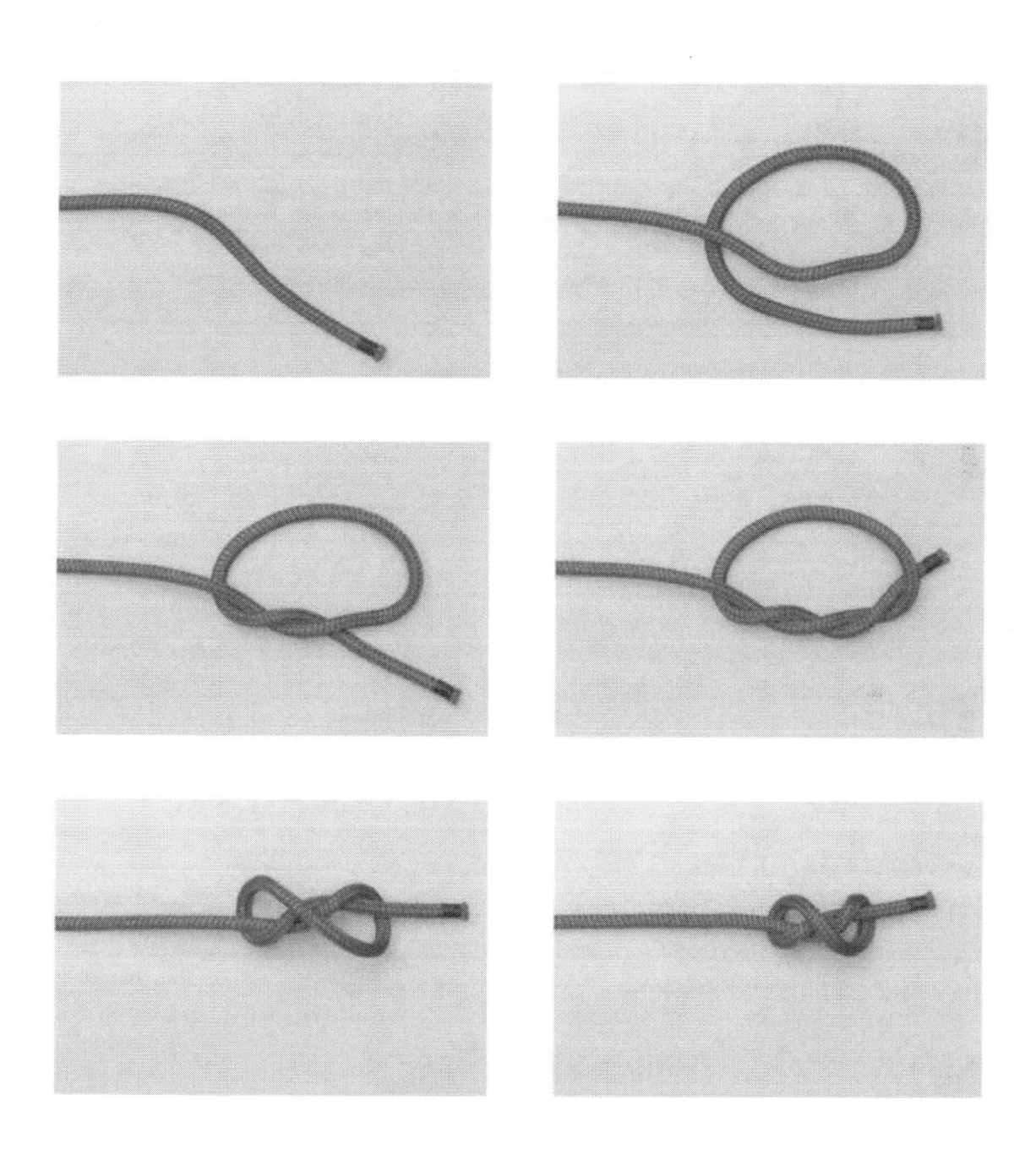

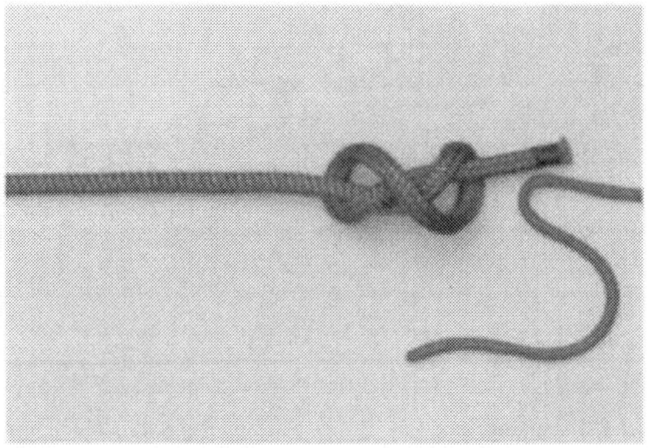

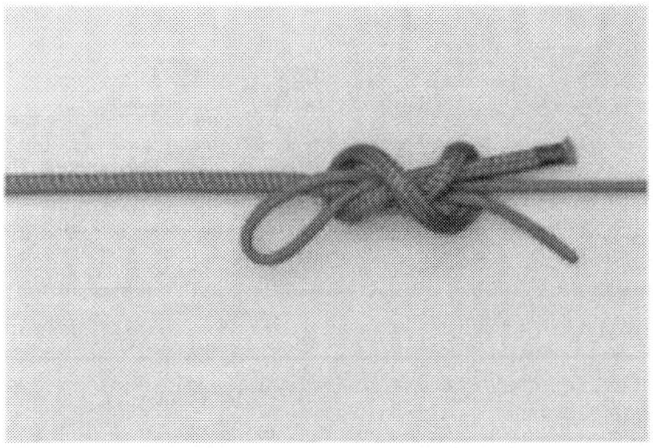

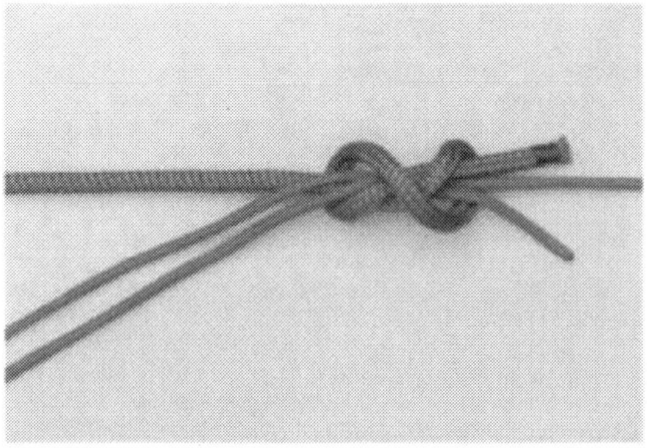

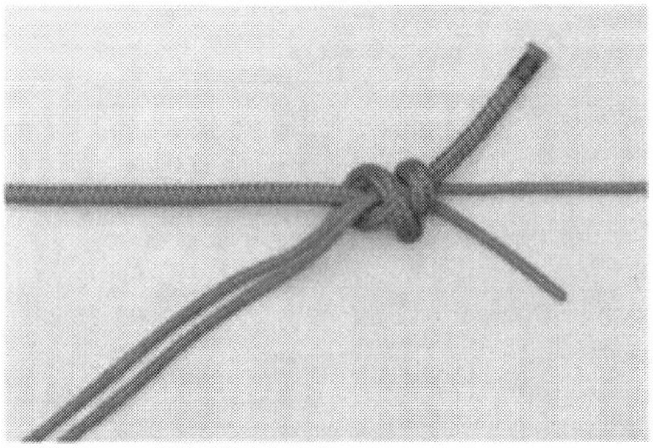

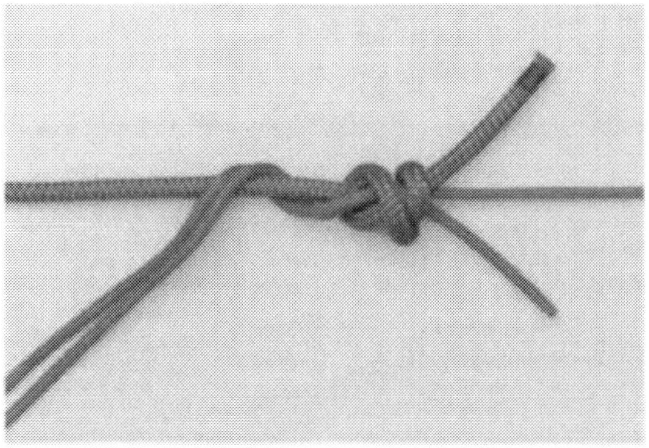

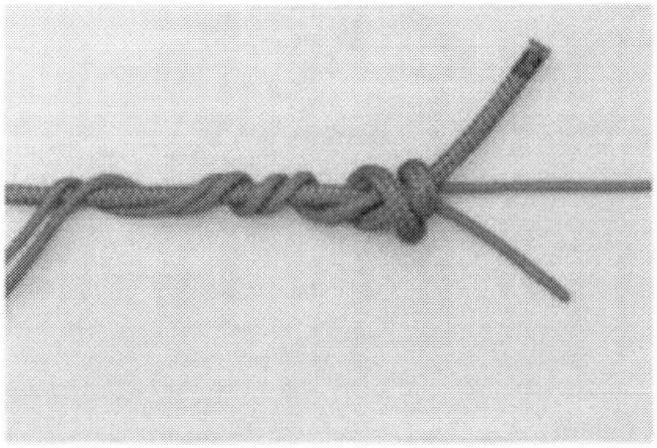

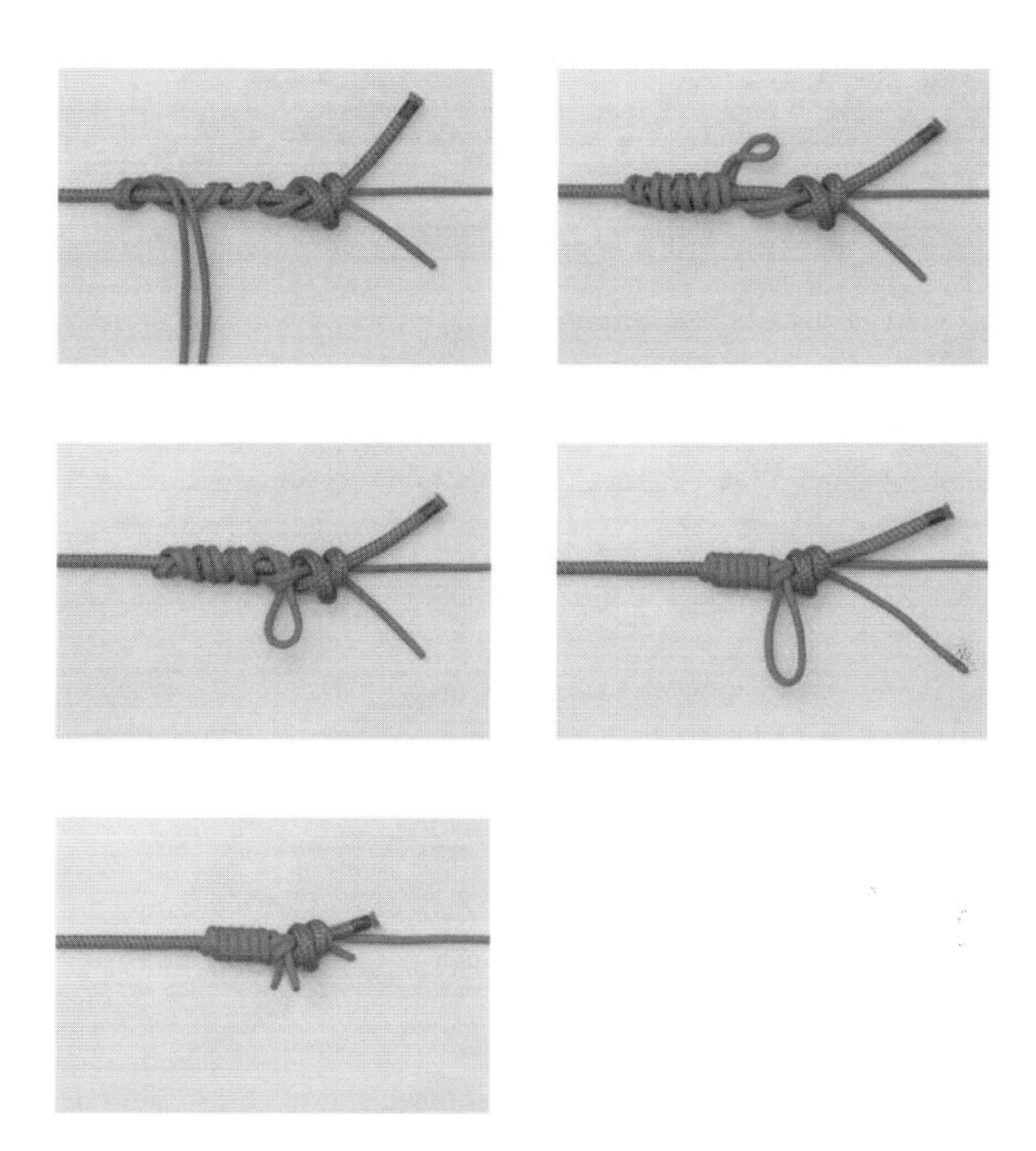

Tie a Double Overhand bunch in the Tippet and fix it structure two circles. Pass a bight of the entire line through the two circles. Fold the bight four turns over the Tippet and afterward one more four turns outside the initial four turns. Fold the bight under itself. Grease up, pull tight, and trim the closures.

Uses: The Slim Beauty Knot is a magnificent bunch for joining various measurements and various materials. As displayed in the activity, it is valuable when it binds an enormous Tippet to the Main Line. Tarpon anglers use this because it is solid and simple to tie, and many individuals use it as a more practical option than a Bimini Twist.

Tying it: The suggested number of turns utilized for the Slim Beauty Knot shifts, and Simon Becker depicts using as not many as three turns outwards and two turns returning. Different scholars express operating around ten turns toward every path.

Benefits: The Slim Beauty Knot is utilized to join interlaced to mono just as little breadths to huge distances across. It is an adaptable bunch that is somewhat simple to learn and recall, and it is likewise conservative and straight when finished.

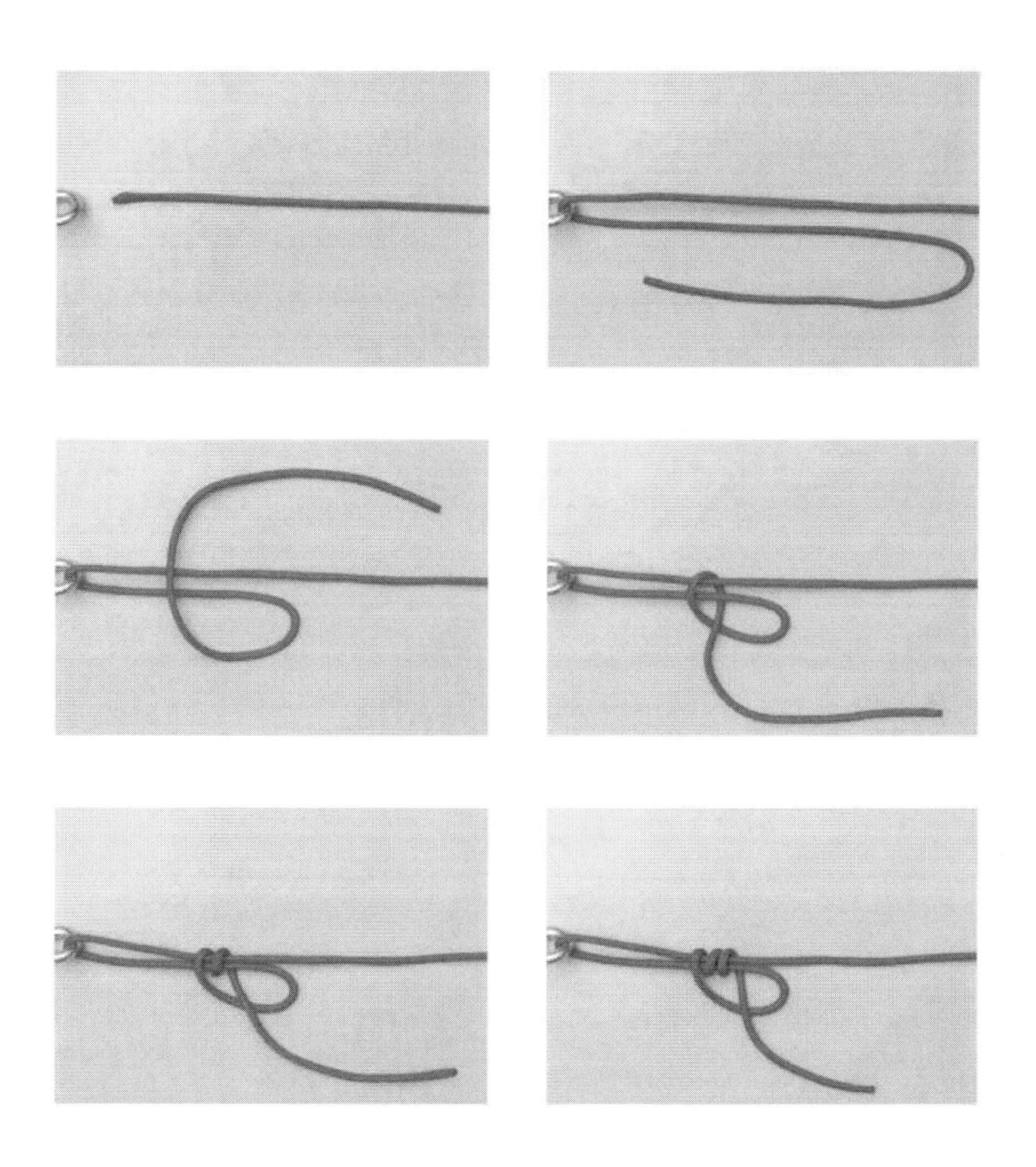

Uni Knot

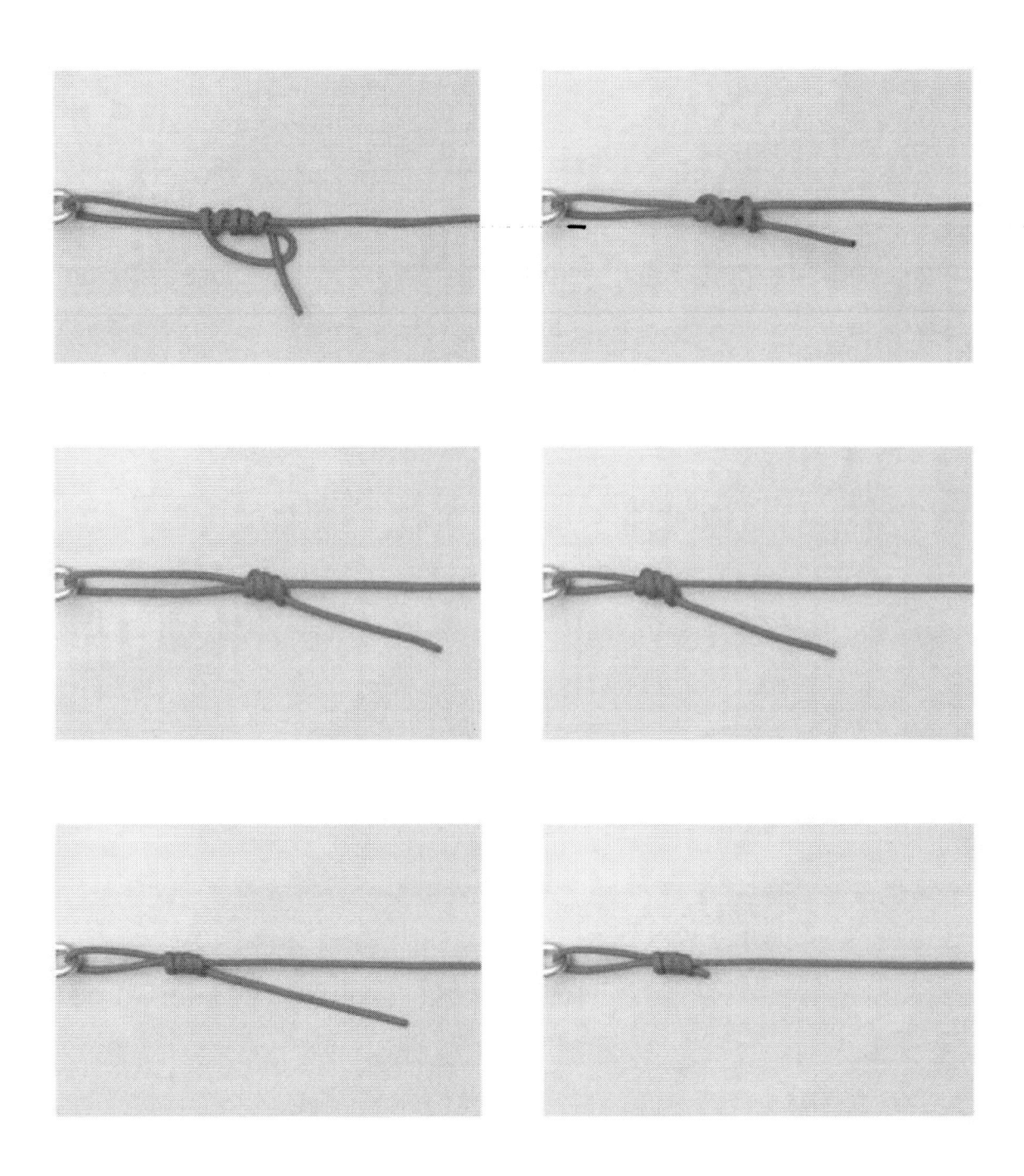

Pass the end through the eye. Structure a full circle close by the vertical line. Working inside the ring, fold the end over the two lines multiple times. Grease up, fix the circle twistings, and slide the bunch to the ideal circle size, with the circle on a post draw on the label end and less hard on the fixed-line. Trim the end.

Names: The Uni Knot was imagined by Norman Duncan and is otherwise called the Duncan Knot. It was additionally distributed later under the name Uni Knot by Vic

Dunaway, similar to an adaptable bunch with numerous applications. It is otherwise called a Grinner Knot and has a similar appearance as a Hangman's Noose, although diverse inside. When used to join two lines, it is known as a Double Grinner or a Double Uni Knot.

Trasformation: The Uni Knot goes through a transition as it is fixed, and the outer wraps become inward and the other way around.

Tying it: The animation shows that the Uni Knot at first structures a movable circle. When at long last fixed, the bunch ties and turns into a fixed concerning the level of improvement. When utilized for joining two lines (as in the Uni Knot framework), each bunch is tied around the other's standing end.

Trilene Knot

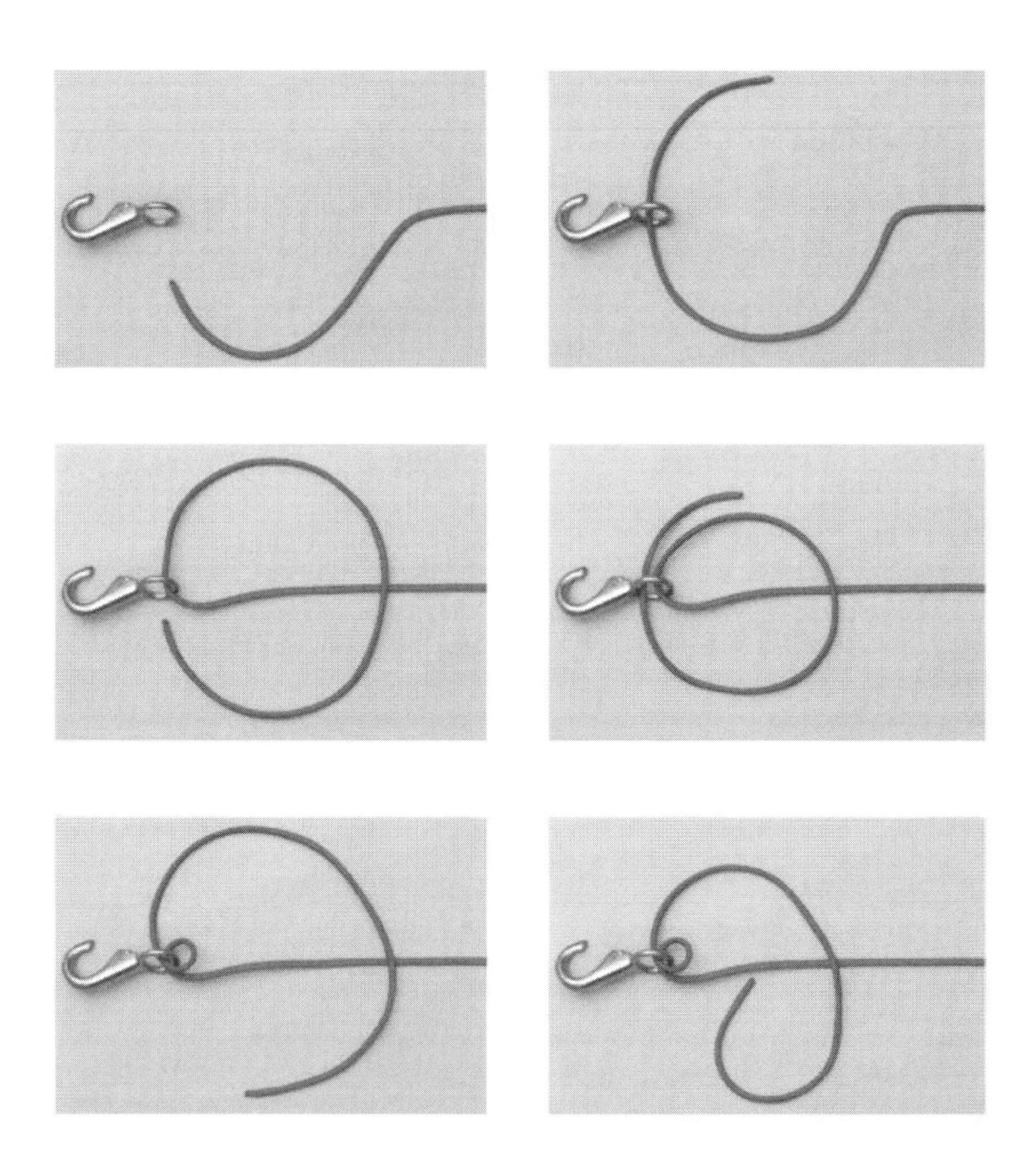

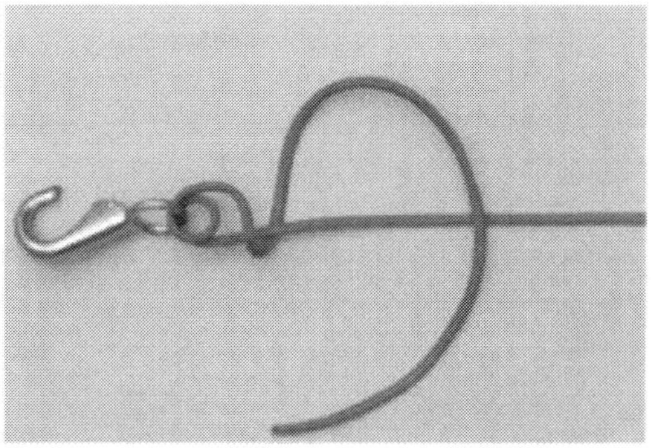
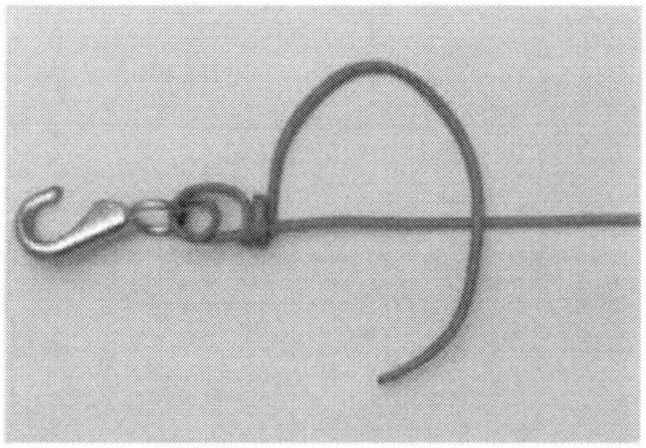
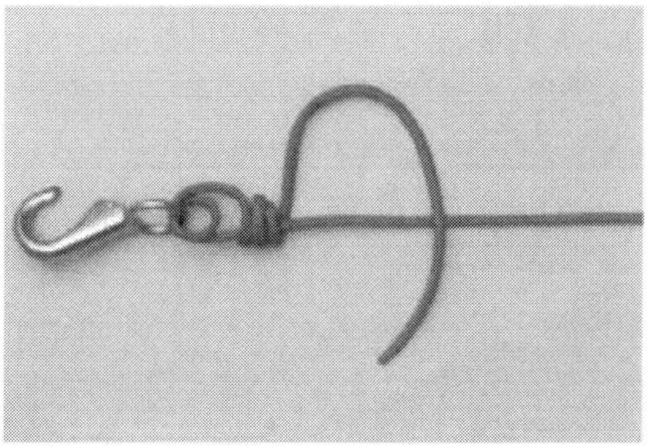
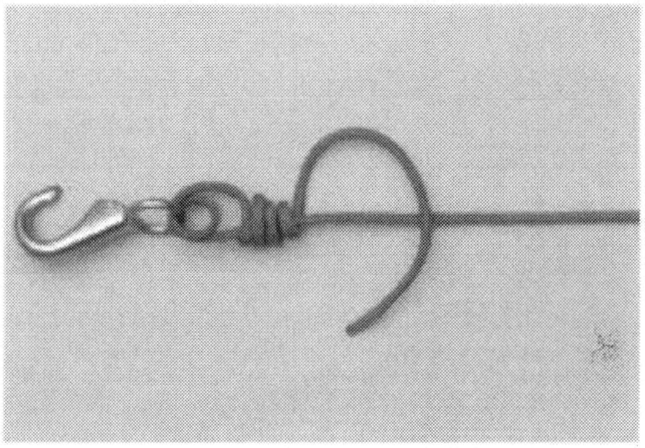
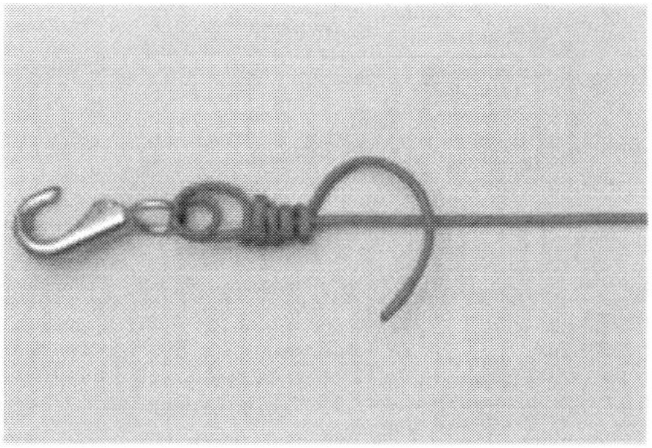
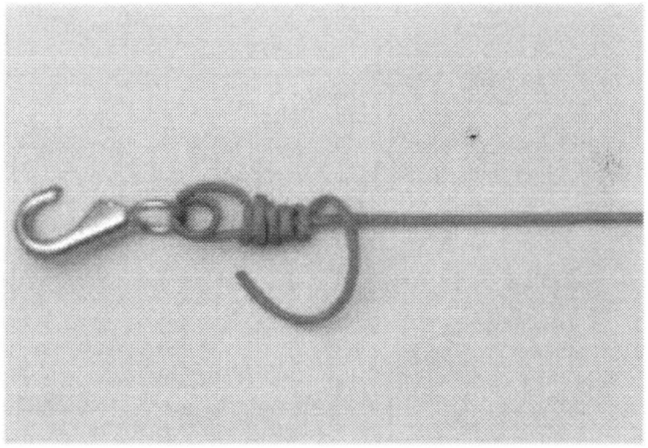

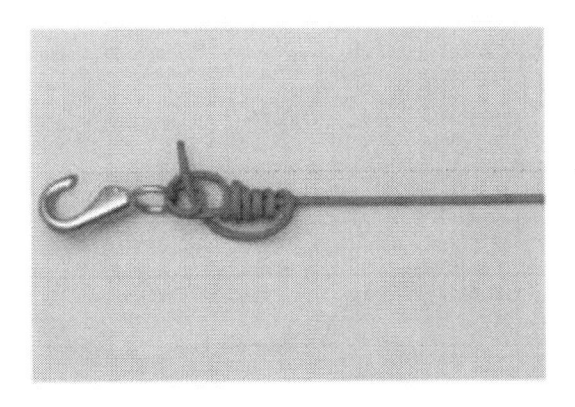

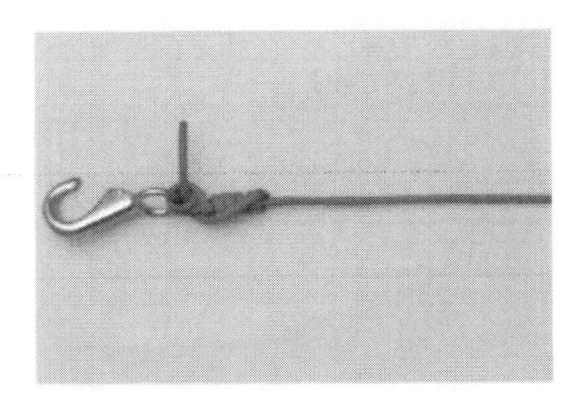

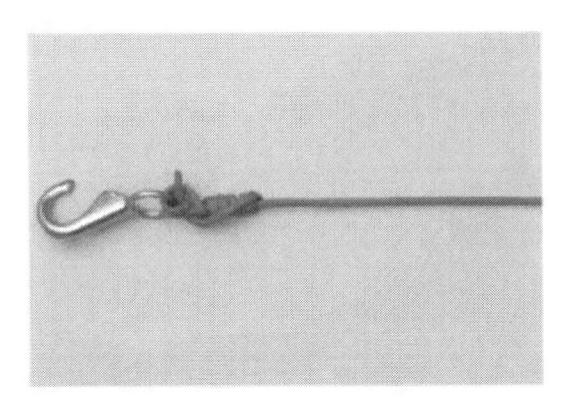

Pass the label stopping point through the eye twice. Fold it over the standing end five or multiple times. String the end through the first circle close to the eye. Grease up and pull the bunch tight. Trim the end, yet not very short.

Uses: The Trilene Knot is a solid and dependable bunch to join monofilament lines to snares, turns, and draws. It opposes slippage and disappointments and is an incredible and more grounded option compared to the Clinch Knot.

Tying it: When managing the label end of the Trilene tie, leave about an eighth of an inch for security.

Benefits: The twofold wrap of a line through the eye takes a portion of the strain and might be liable for claims that the Trilene tie holds a great extent of superior line strength. This is almost certain when the thickness of the eye is more noteworthy than the line distance across.

Surgeon's Join Knot

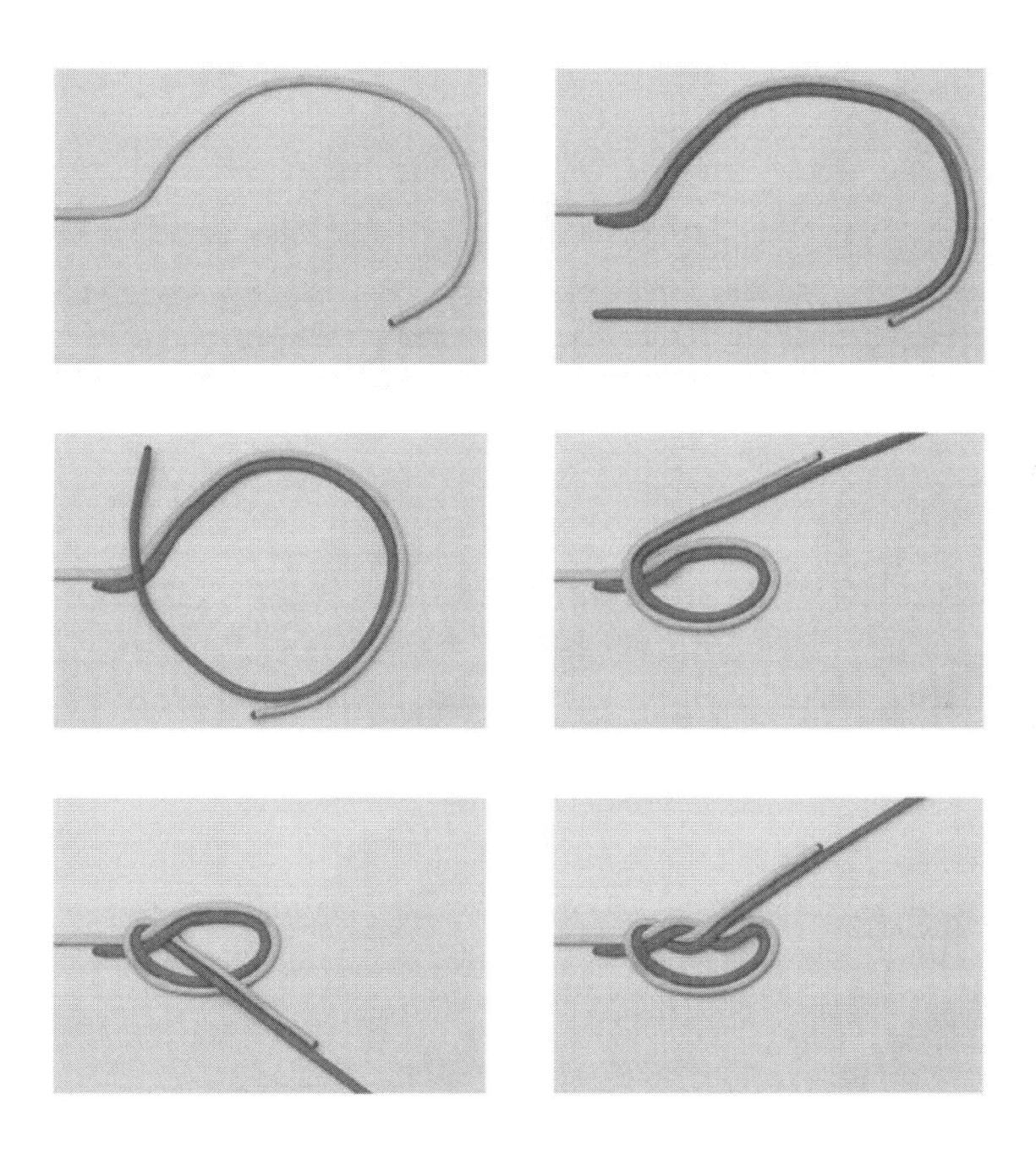

151

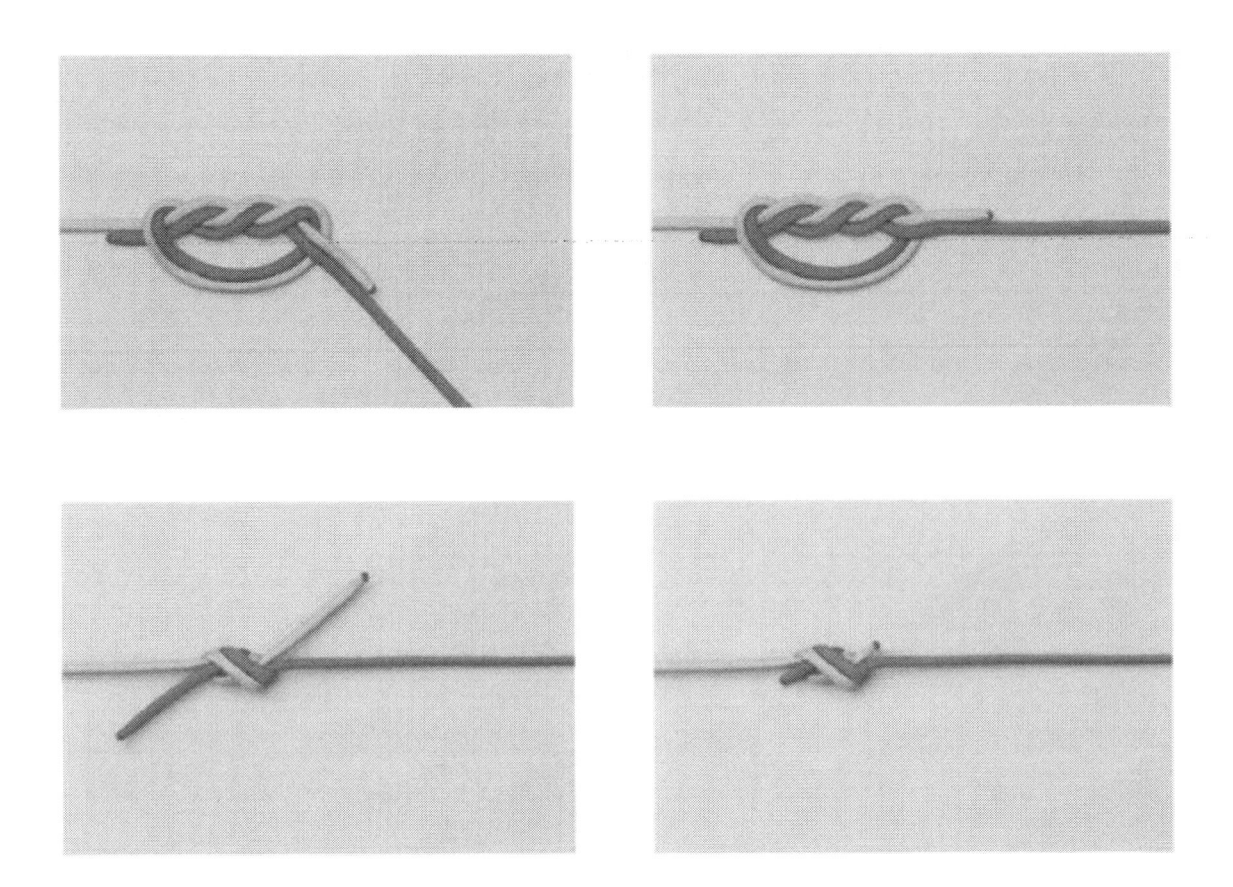

Spot the pioneer and the scarf next to each other. Utilize the two lines to shape a circle with an excellent cross-over to tie a twofold overhand bunch. Get the two ends through the loop and afterward during a time. Grease up the bunch and pull it tight. Trim the closures.

Uses: The Surgeon's Knot, or Surgeon's Join, is not difficult to tie and is helpful to join two fishing lines of decently varying size, e.g., a scarf to a pioneer. It is connected as a Double Overhand Knot – which most likely clarifies why it is here and there known as the Double Surgeon's Knot – excess since "Specialist's Knot" infers the utilization of the two turns.

The Surgeon's Knot permits you, with a similar pioneer, to choose the size of a scarf to suit the size of the fly. It is generally used to join two bits of monofilament.

Tying it: The Surgeon's Knot must be attached with a scarf because the typical strategy for connecting it requires the whole length of the scarf to be gone through the overhand bunch twice. In the wake of shaping the bunch, painstakingly set the bunch by pulling on each of the four ends.

152

Alternative: As an alternative, the two lines can be gone through the overhand bunch; a third is an ideal opportunity to frame the Triple Surgeon's bunch.

Benefits: The Surgeon's Knot is perhaps the most straightforward bunch to learn and is a great bunch to join two lines of respectably varying size.

Disadvantages: It is preferably bulkier over the Blood Knot and makes a slight point in the line.

Snell Knot

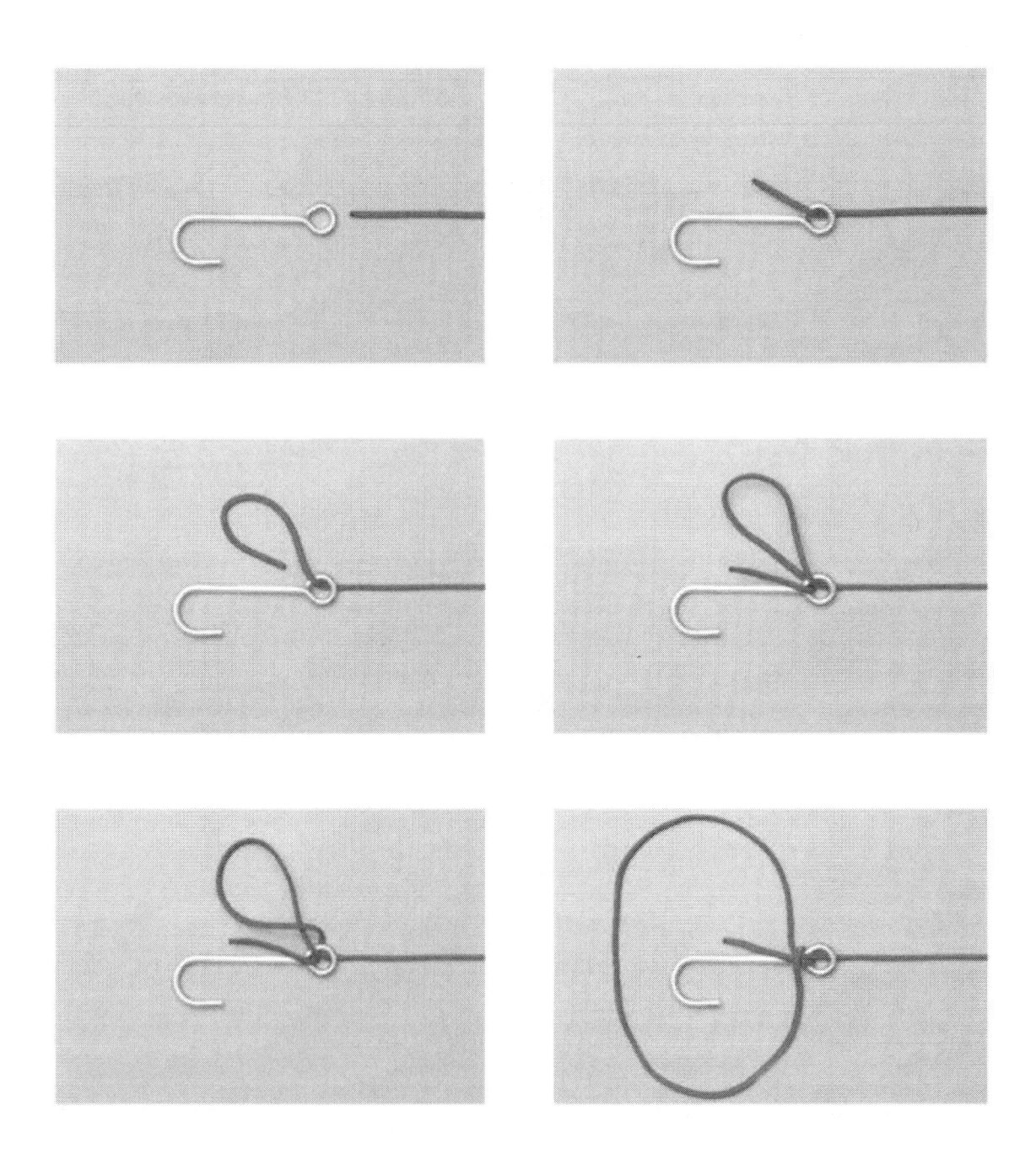

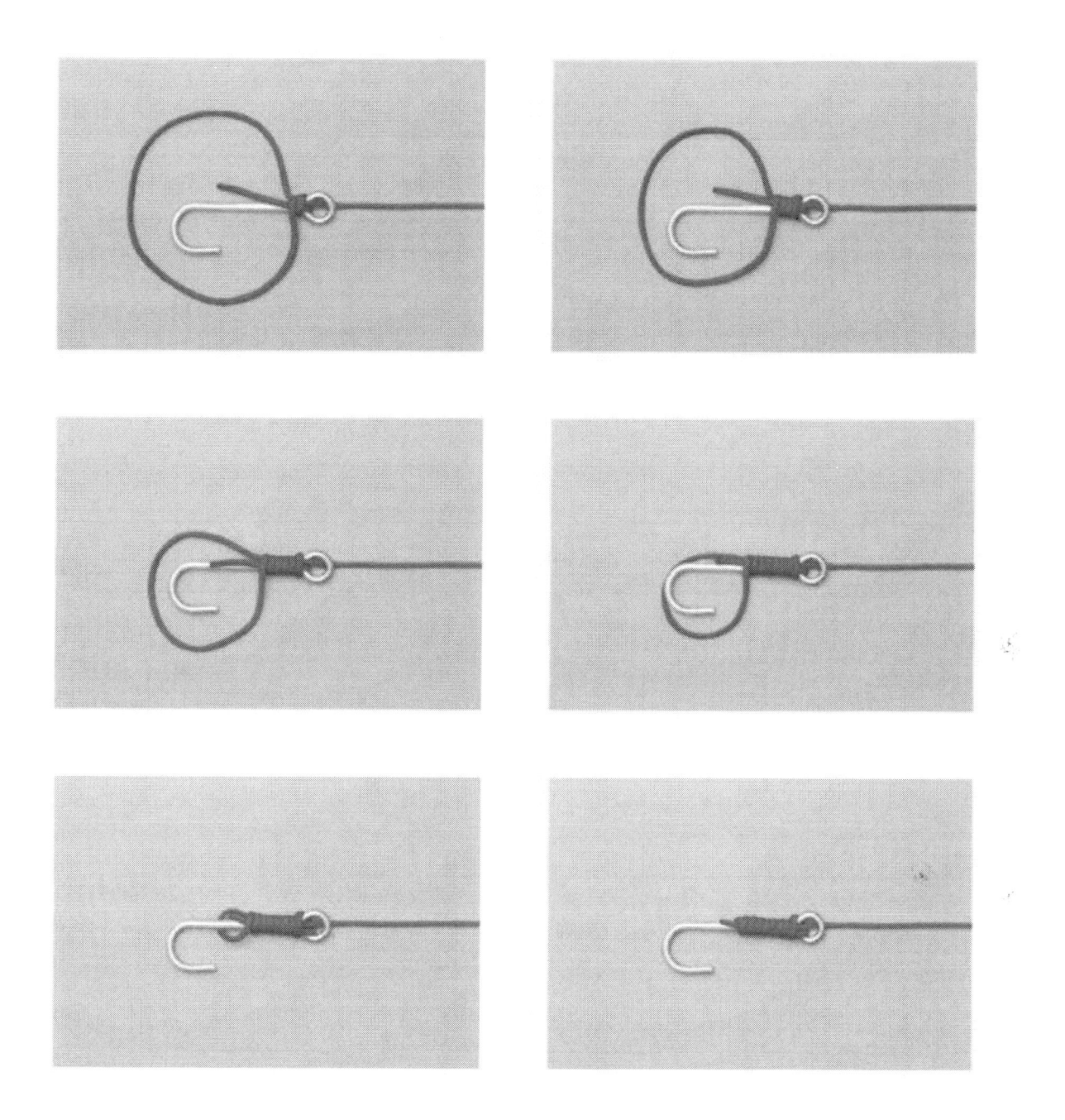

Pass the end of the pioneer through the eye and afterward through again a similar way. Hold the look and the two pieces of the line. Fold the circle over the knife of the snare seven or multiple times. Psychologist the loop by pulling on the standing end. Grease up and remove the two closures to fix the bunch and trim the end.

Uses: The Snell Knot permits the pioneer, or scarf, to be straightforwardly attached to a teased snare. Initially developed this fishing tie with eyeless pitfalls; however, it is still broadly utilized today. The Snell Knot adjusts the fishing line or pioneer to the knife of the snare.

Tying it: The Snell hitch requires folding a circle over the fishing snare. When fixing the bunch, hold the turns under your fingers to guarantee they cozy down flawlessly.

Benefits: The Snell Knot is one of the more established fishing ties and is professed to give a solid association that saves the strength of the fishing line – especially if the thickness of the eye is more noteworthy than the line breadth.

San Diego Jam Knot

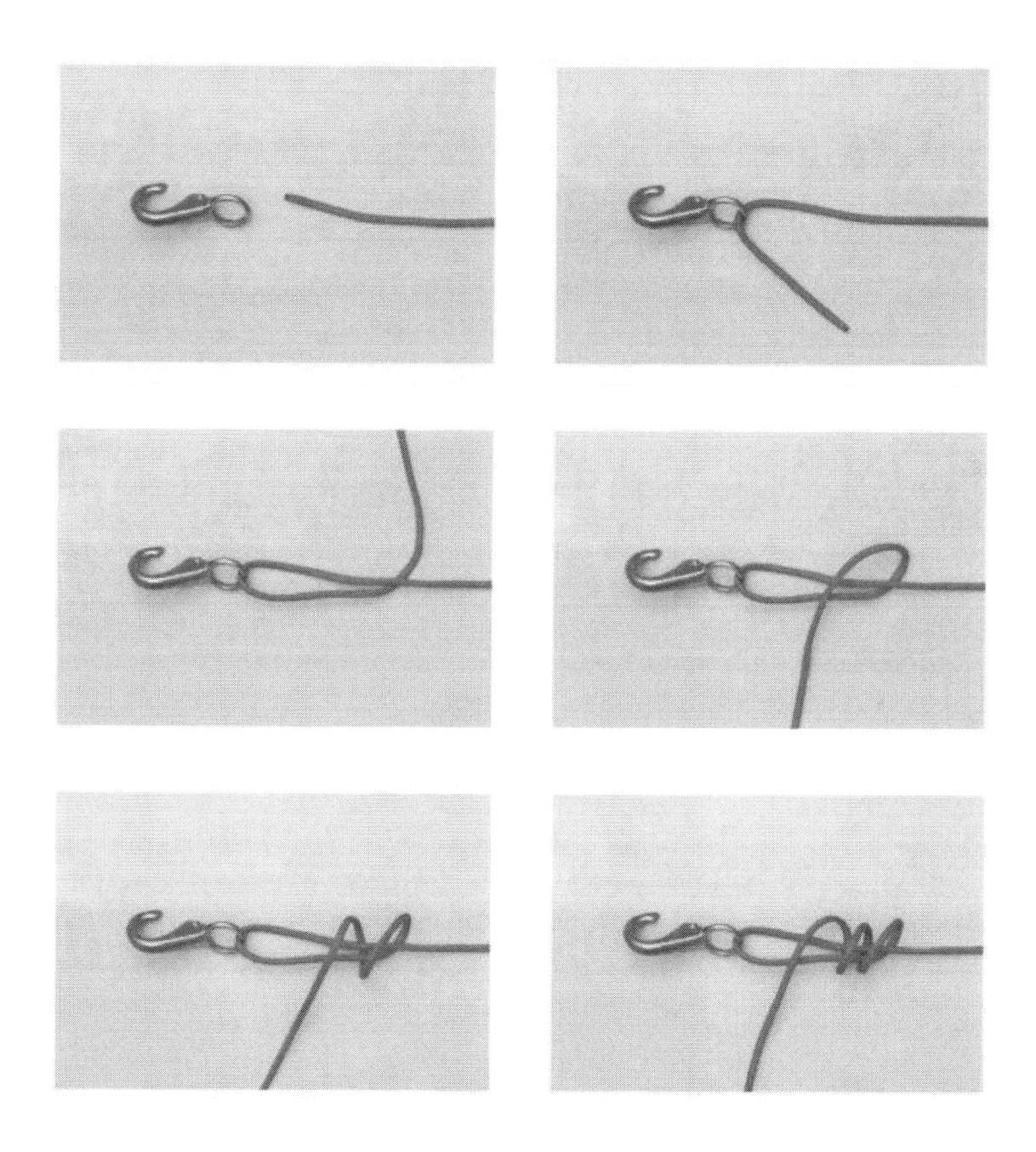

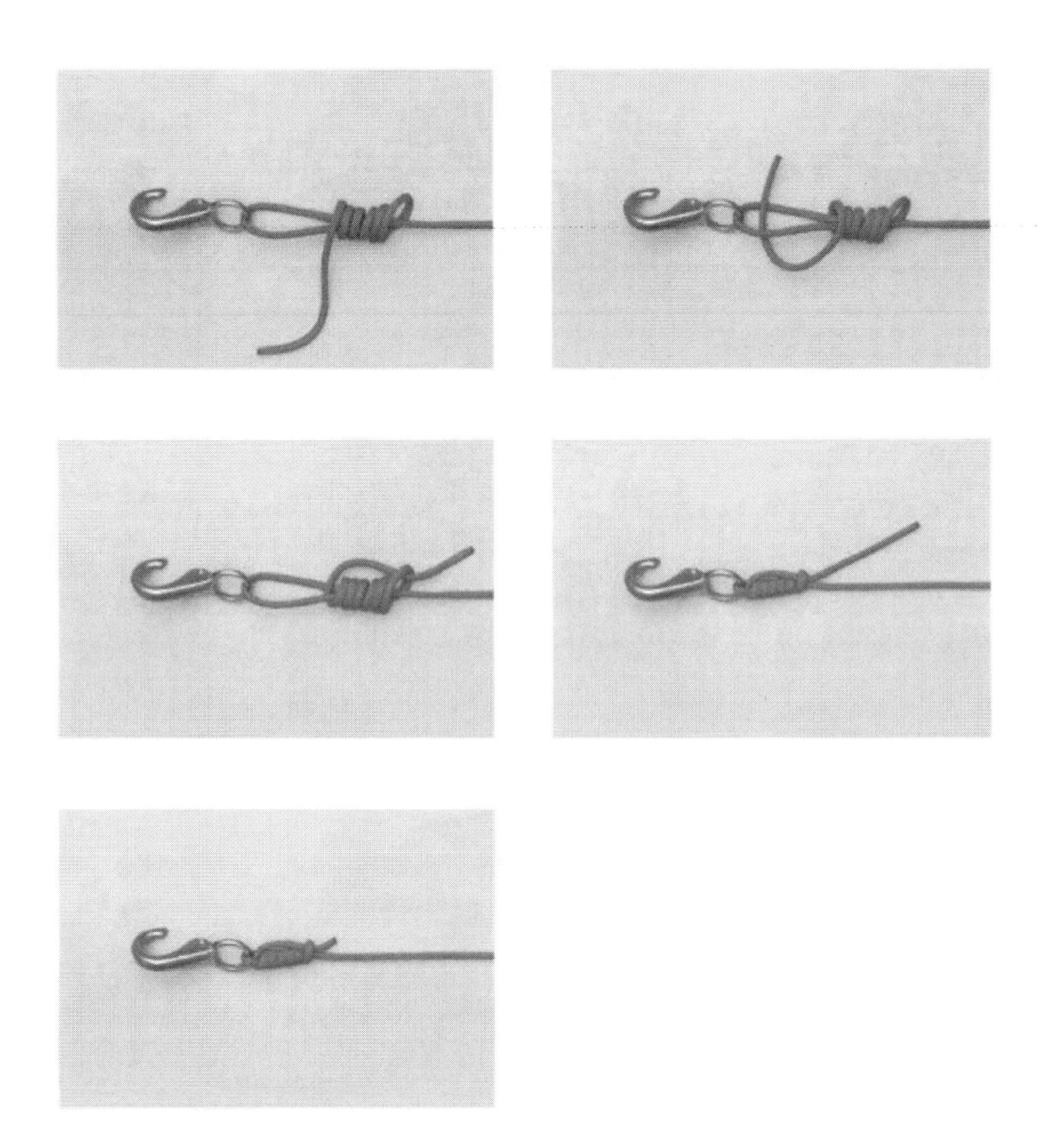

Pass the label end through the eye. Hold the lines to keep a circle and fold the label end over the line and end a few times. Pass the end between the strings close to the eye and back through the circle corresponding to the bar. Grease up, fix cautiously with the goal that the turns don't cover one another, and trim the end.

Uses: The San Diego Jam Knot is otherwise called the Reverse Clinch Knot and the Heiliger Knot. The San Diego Jam Knot was promoted in San Diego, especially with long-range fish anglers. It is sensibly simple to tie adrift and is appropriate for monofilament, plaited, and fluorocarbon fishing lines.

Several turns: The number of turns should be diminished with size, going from around 7 to 8 turns for 10lb line down to 3 turns for 40lb line.

Tying it: When fixing the San Diego Jam Knot, guarantee that the turns structure a perfect winding and don't cover one another.

Strength: Comparison testing proposes that the San Diego Jam Knot likely holds the line's power better than most fishing ties.

Benefits: The San Diego Jam Knot is generally simple to learn and tie, even in antagonistic conditions.

Palomar Knot

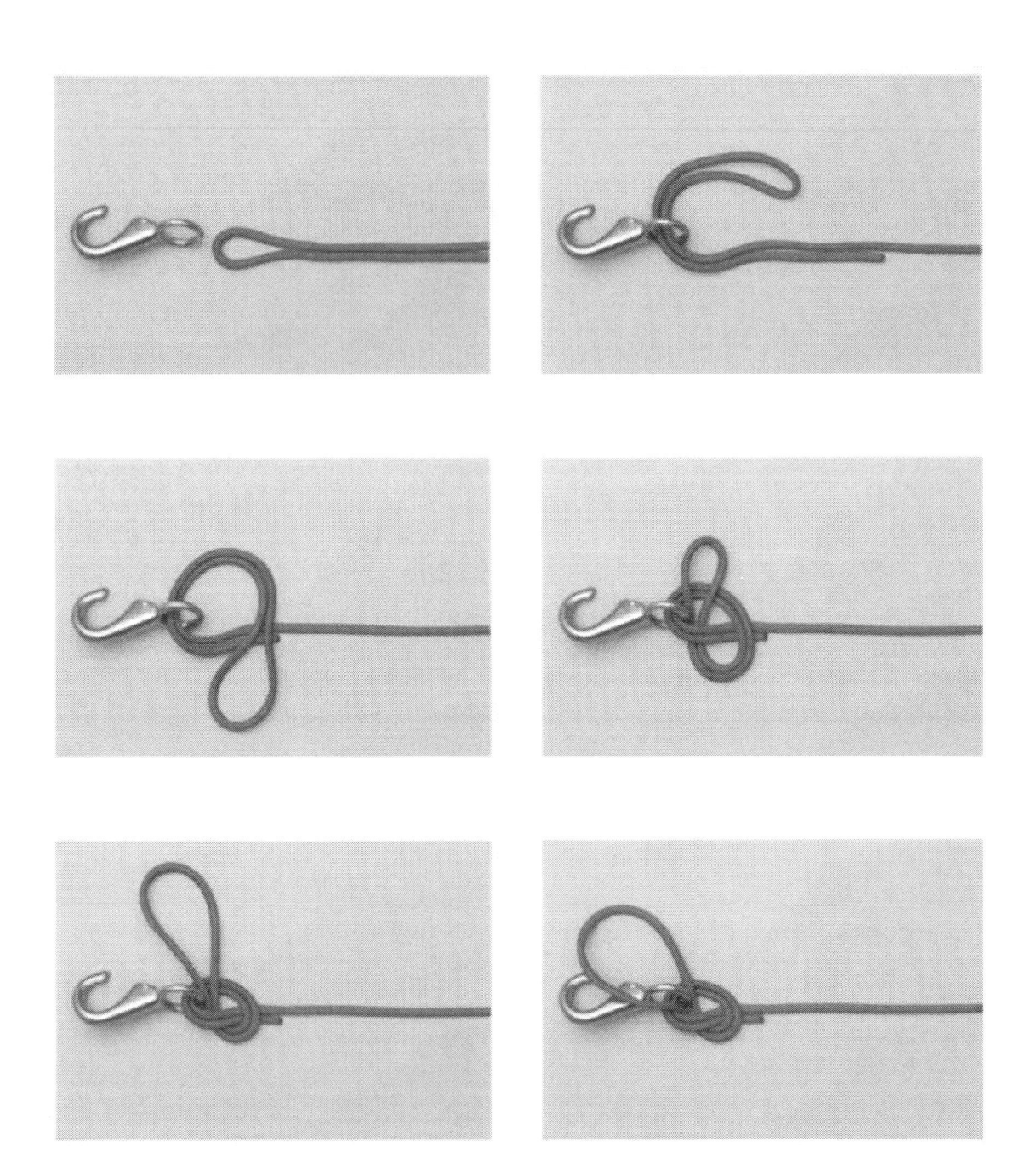

161

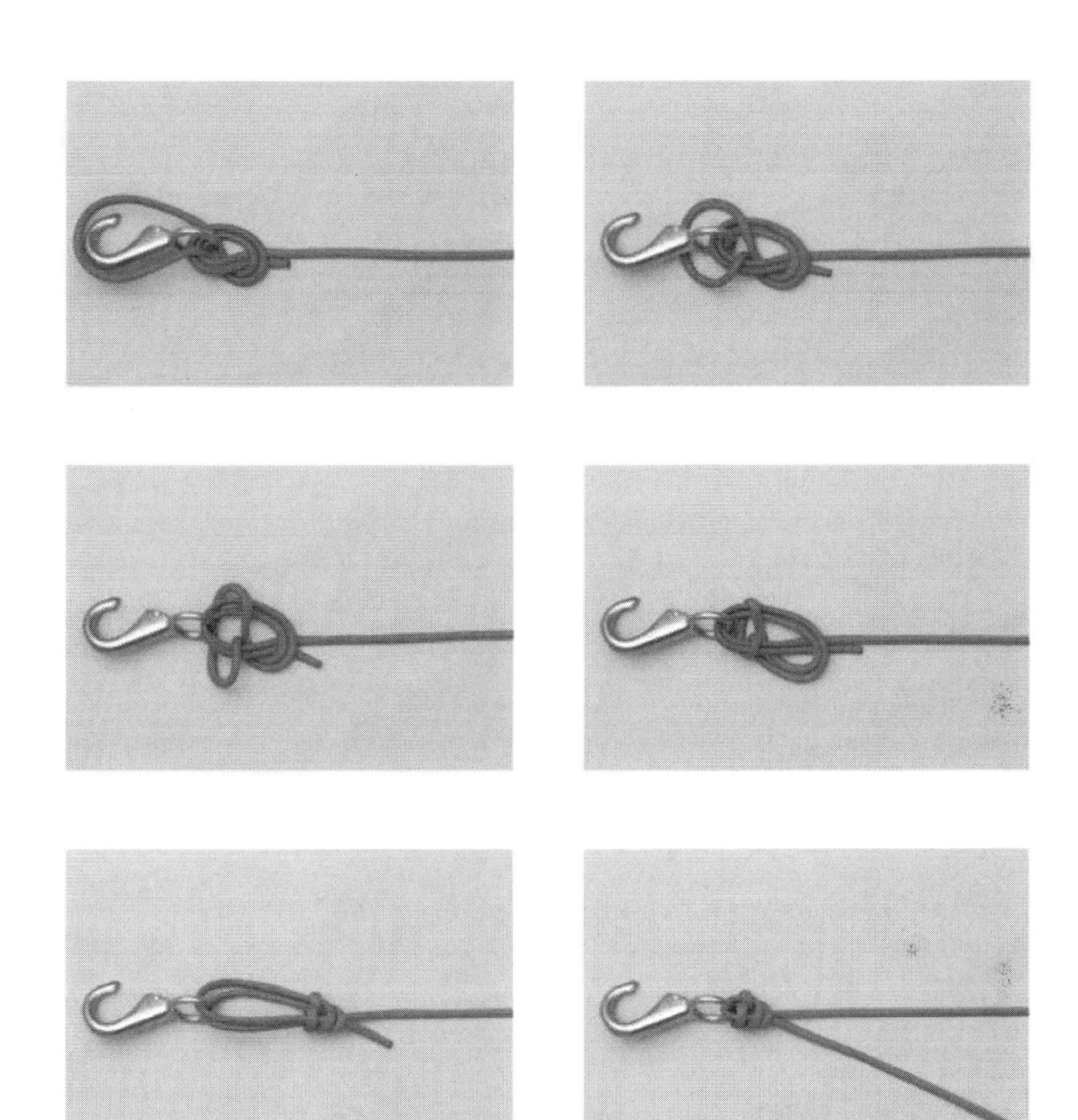

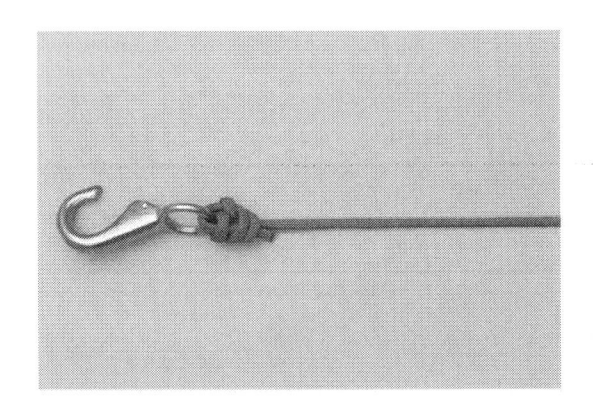

Structure a bight toward as far as it goes. Pass the bight through the eye of the snare. With the bight, tie an overhand bunch. Disregard the bight the loop and down around the bunch. Grease up and pull the standing and label closures to fix the bunch. Trim the label end.

Uses: The Palomar Knot is a straightforward bunch for joining a line to a snare or a fly to a pioneer or scarf, and it is viewed as one of the most grounded and most dependable fishing ties.

Tying it: After the circle is gone through the eye, an overhand bunch is attached to the loop. The process has then ignored the snare and fixed it around the bight underneath the eye. The impact is that this leaves the circle allowed to turn in the bunch.

Alternative: Some depictions of The Palomar Knot show the last circle situated against the shaft of the snare as opposed to being pulled further down around the bight. This restricts the snare's development, and most experienced anglers suggest the procedure showed here.

Benefits: The Palomar Knot is suggested for use with interlaced lines. With a bit of practice, it can tie in a bunch of obscurities.

Burdens: When tying The Palomar Knot, the fly or snare needs to go through the circle, which can be abnormal and requires making the ring sufficiently massive.

Orvis Knot

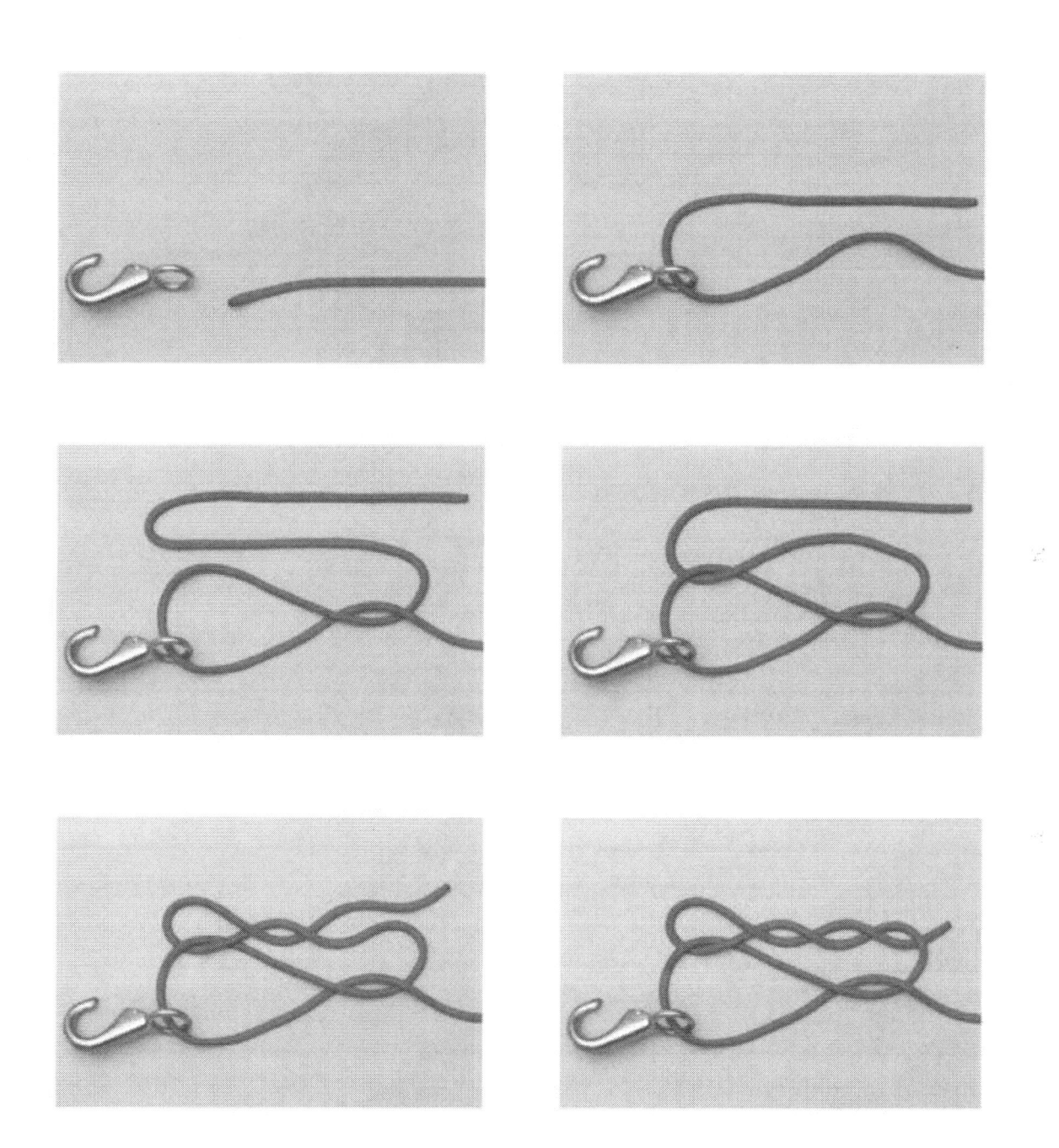

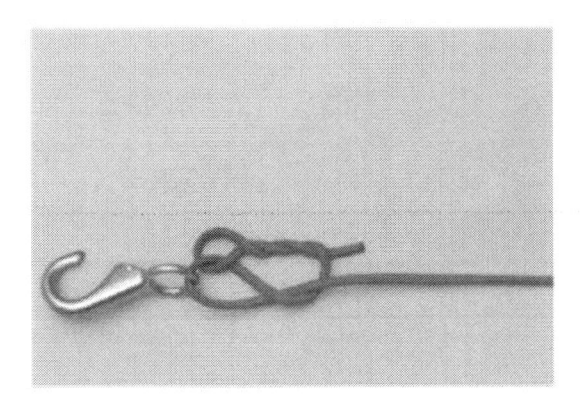

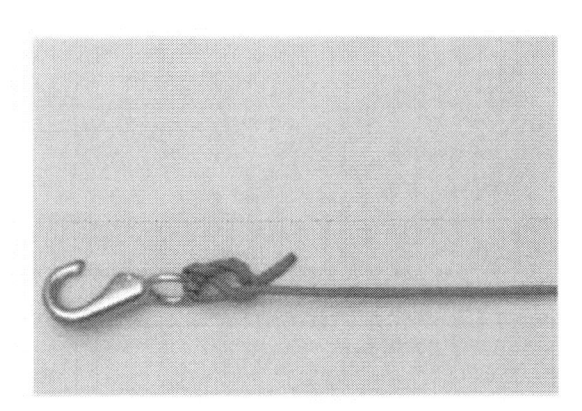

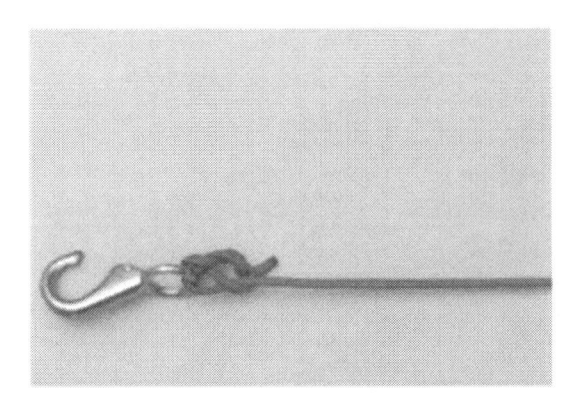

Pass the line through the eye of the hook. Pass the tag end around the line, back through the first loop, and then back through the second loop. Pass the tag end through the second loop again. Lubricate, tighten, and trim the tag end.

Uses: The Orvis Knot was invented by Larry Becker who submitted it in a contest held by the Orvis Company to find the best knot to attach a line to the hook.

Similar Knots: The Orvis Knot performs a similar function as other line-to-hook knots such as the Trilene, Palomar, Uni (Duncan), and Improved Clinch Knots.

Tying it: It is helpful to picture a symmetrical stepladder pattern. Until the final extra twist through the same loop, each step is like the one before.

Advantages: The Orvis Knot is strong, small, light, reliable, and easy to remember and tie. It also works well in light and heavy lines and in any tippet material.

Disadvantages: As it is being tightened, the Orvis knot tends to set up at an angle.

Breaking Strain: The Orvis Knot is claimed to retain much of the line's original breaking strain.

Nail Knot

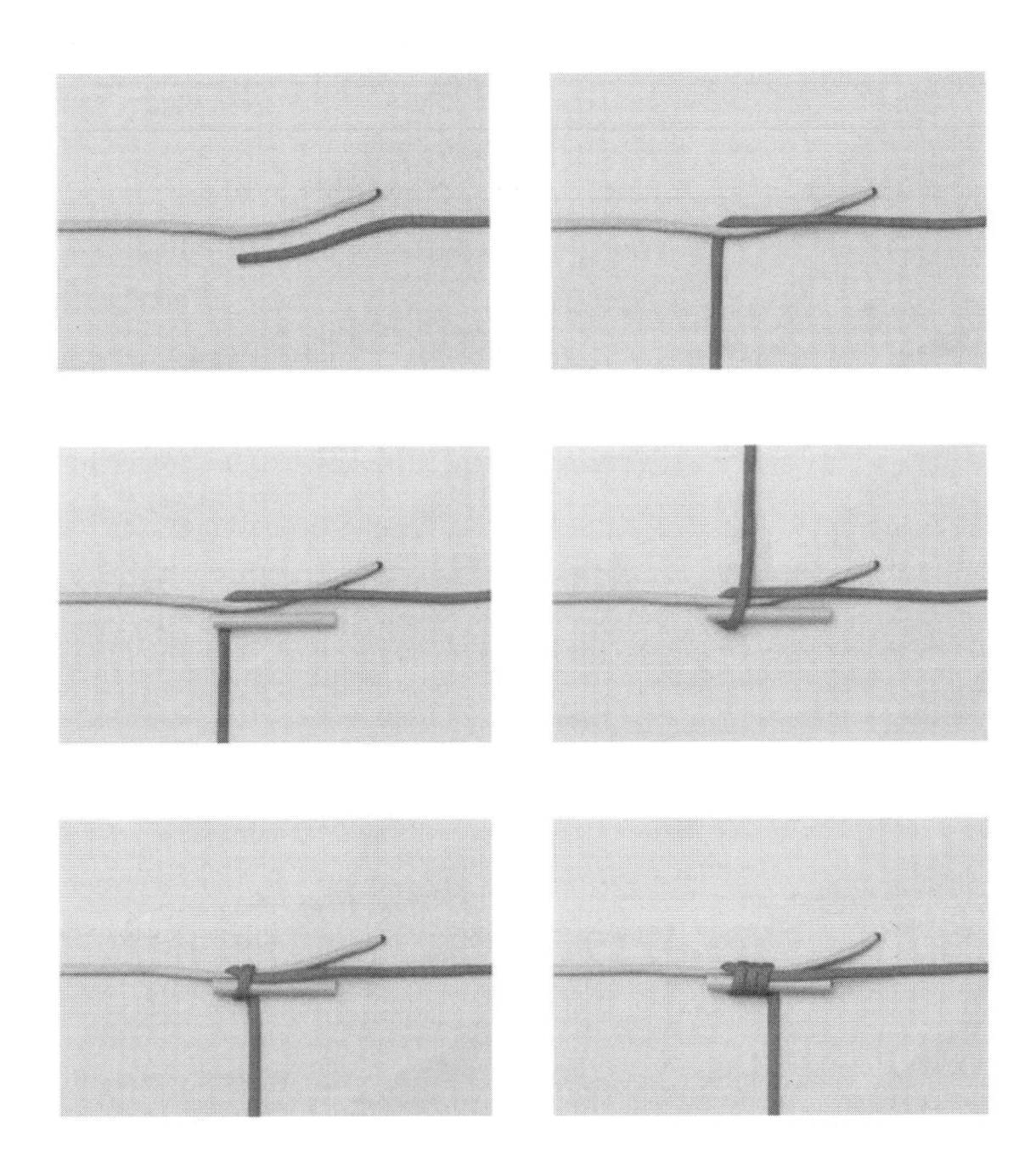

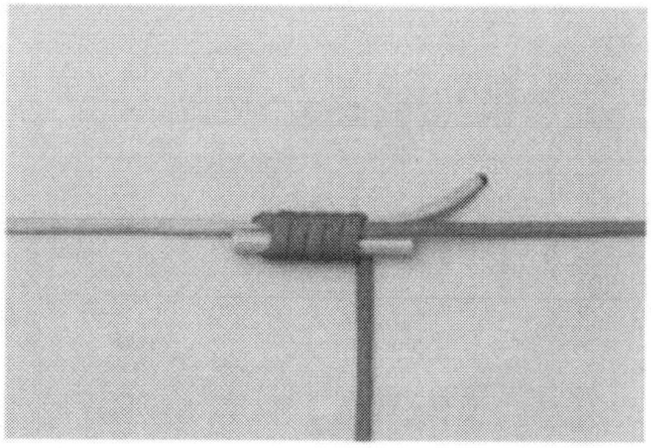

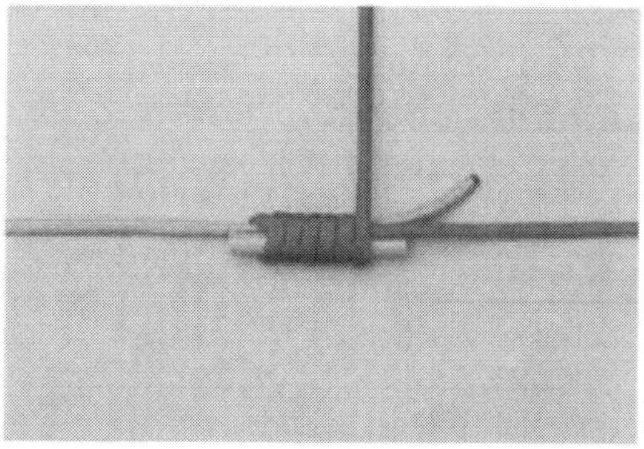

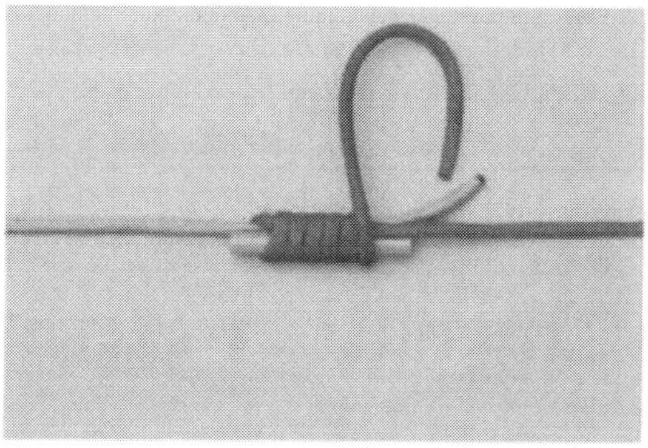

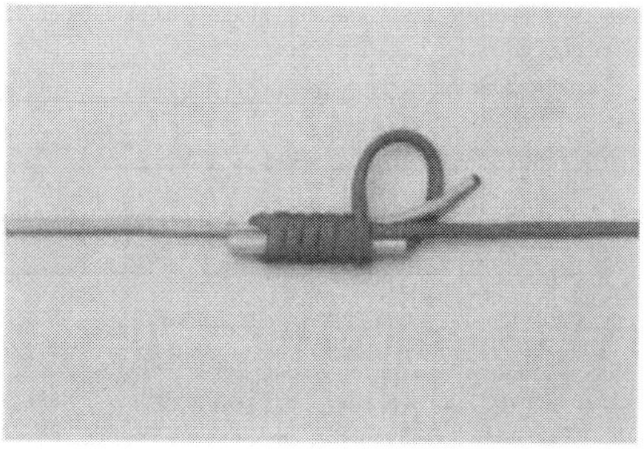

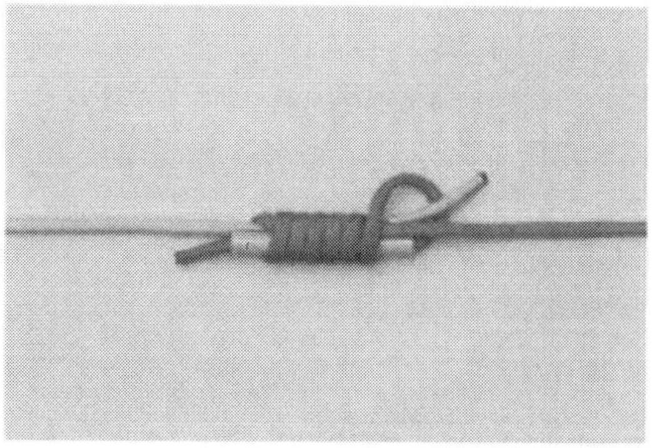

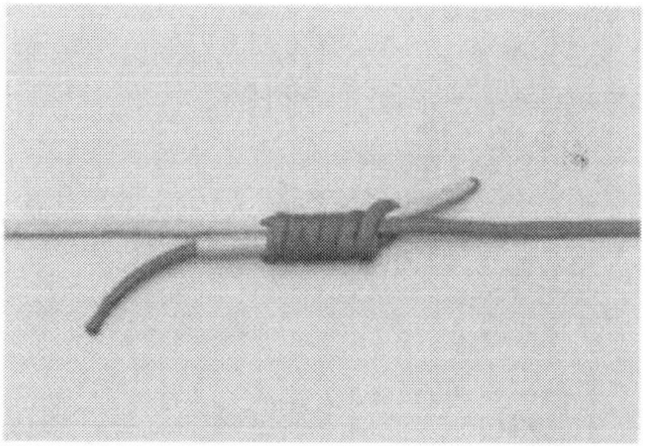

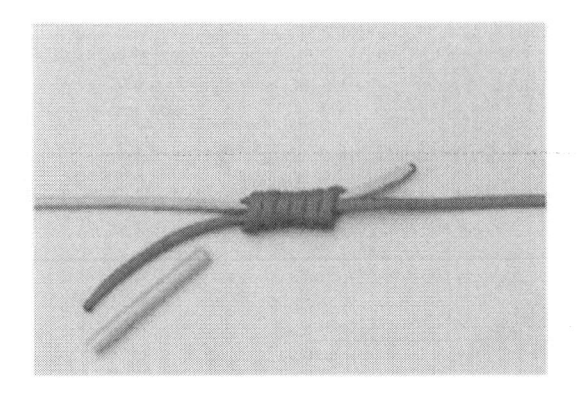

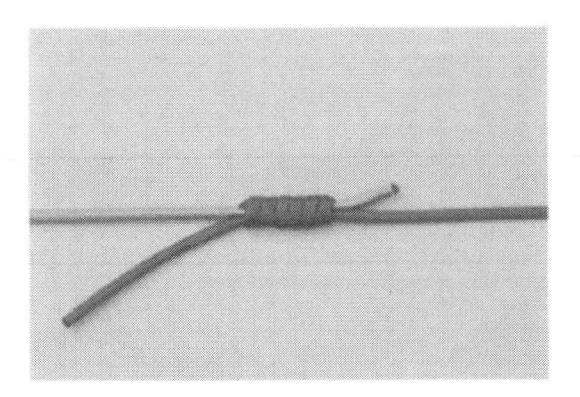

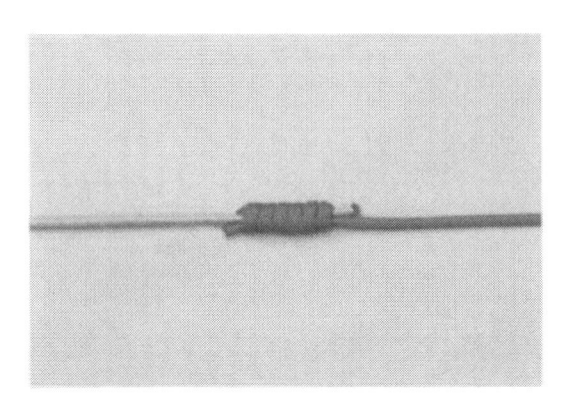

Overlap the two lines. Holding the straw and the lines together, wrap the lighter line around the straw and both lines. Make six complete turns, pass the line through the straw and tighten the knot neatly around the straw. Withdraw the straw. Lubricate, pull the knot tight, and trim the ends.

Description: The Nail Knot is an important fishing knot used to join two lines of different diameters and allows for line diameters to diminish down to the fly, i.e., it is useful for attaching your backing to the fly line, and your fly line to the leader, or tippet.

Name: The Nail Knot was originally named because a nail was inserted as a guide when threading the line. Today, it is easier to use a small straw – if you can find one.

Tying it: There are several ways of tying the Nail Knot. The animation shows the smaller line being threaded through the loops using a straw.

Alternative: Alternatively, the line can be threaded beside a nail (hence its name) or pulled through with a needle.

Advantages: The Nail Knot makes a smooth compact knot that readily goes through the guides.

Improved Clinch Knot

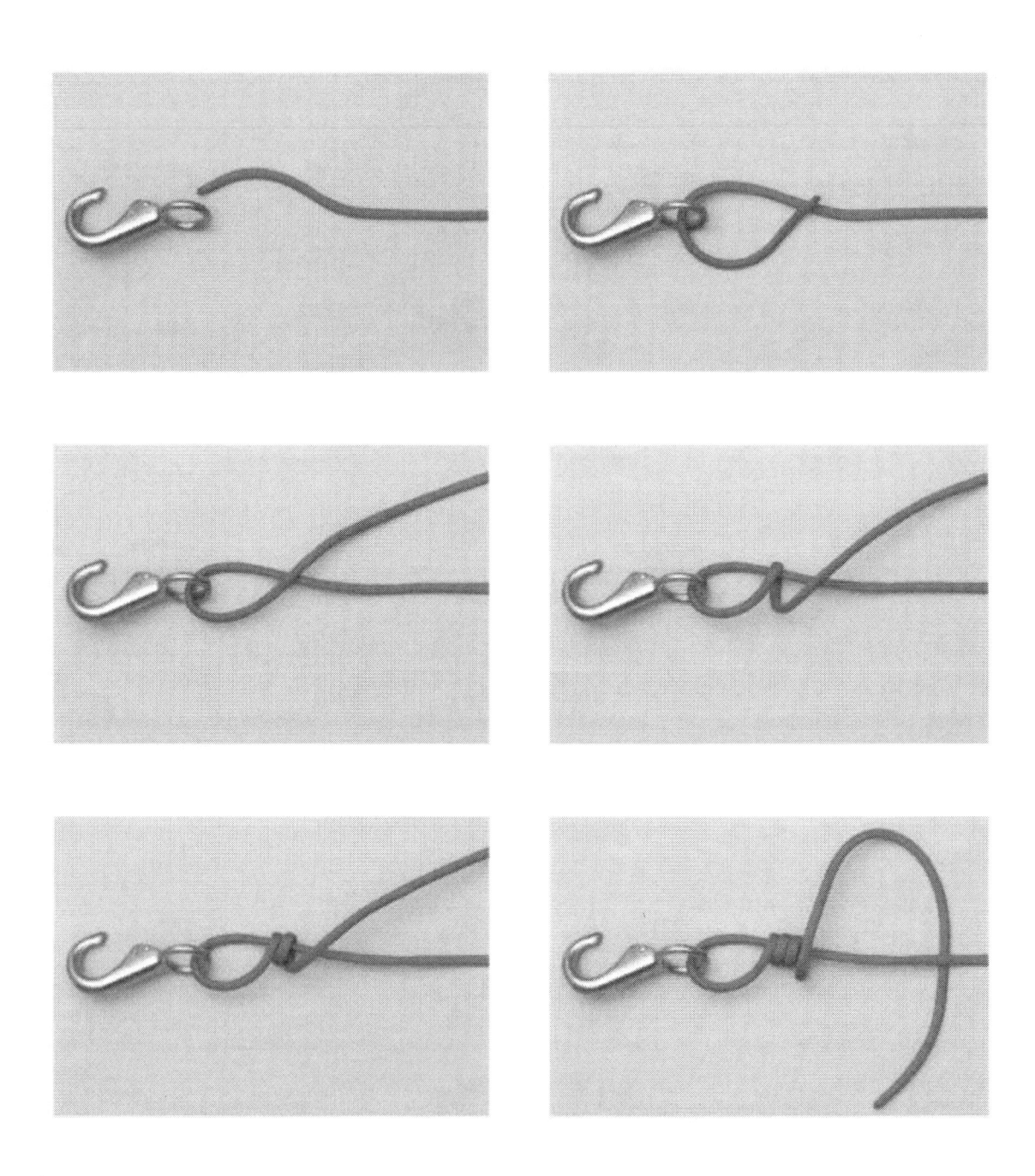

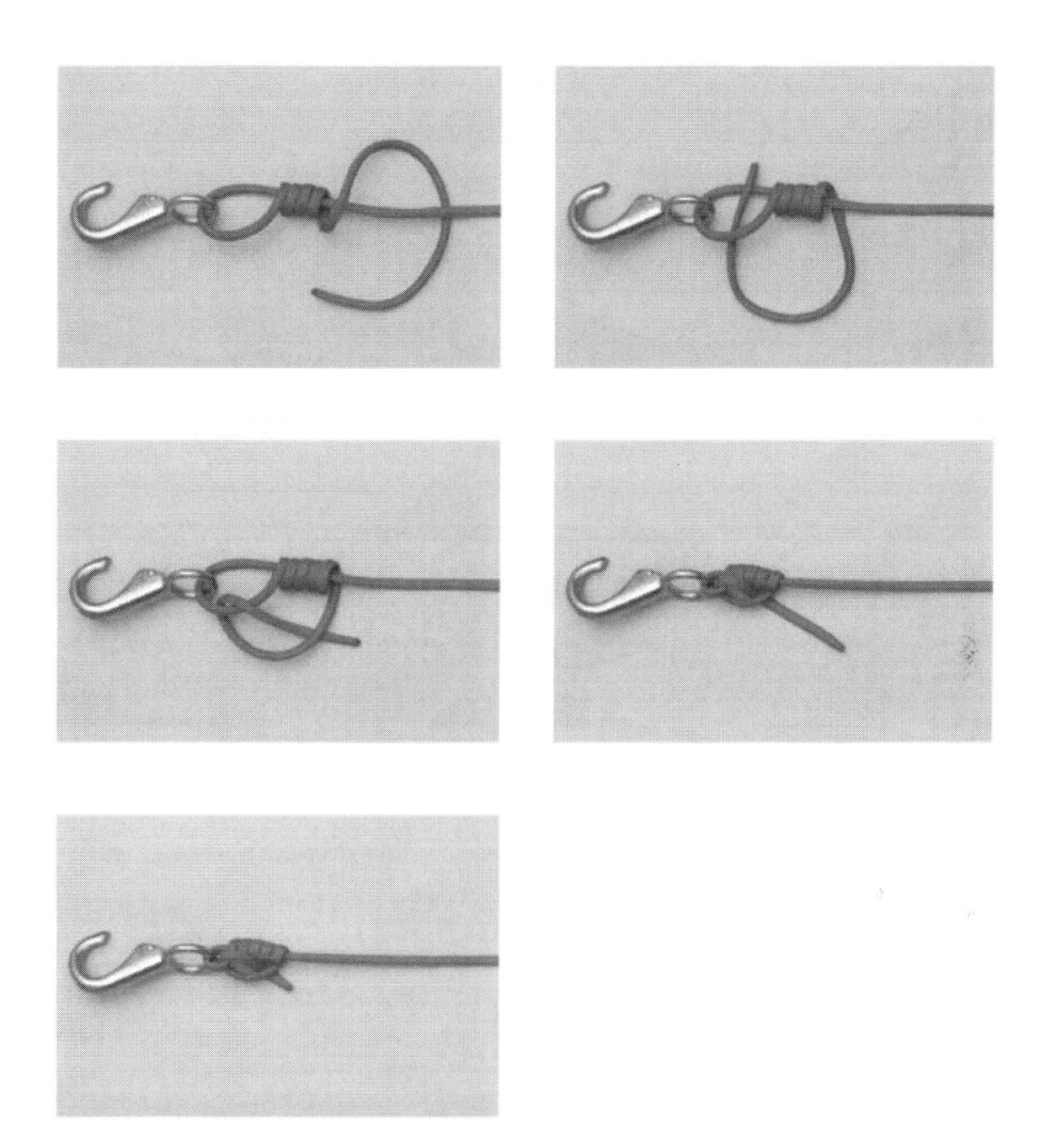

Pass the stopping point through the eye. Fold it over the standing end around five complete turns. Pass the end back through the circle adjacent to the eye. Then, at that point, pass the end under the last turn. Fix the bunch and trim the end.

Uses: The Improved Clinch Knot is one of the most broadly utilized fishing ties. It gives a decent technique for tying down a fishing line to a snare, bait, or turn. The "improved" variant displayed here incorporates a fold under the last turn (stage 9). It is

171

ordinarily used to secure the pioneer to the fly. Since it is more diligently to tie in heavier lines, it isn't suggested if you utilize more than 30 lb test lines.

Tying it: Wind the circles in a slick twisting around the standing line and hold the circles under your fingers as you wind the line on. Albeit at least five turns are suggested, with heavier strings, this might be decreased to four.

Pulling the Improved Clinch Knot Tight: When greased up and pulled tight, the bunch changes its design. Drawing on the line powers, the wrapped rearrange the turns to turn the inner strand into an outer wrap (not delineated in the activity utilizing rope). When fixed, the label end is held intently against the snare.

Elective: Another strategy for tying the Improved Clinch Knot is to hang tight and Tag End in your fingers and, with the other hand, pivot the snare or draw to acquire the ideal number of turns.

Benefits: The Improved Clinch Knot is viewed as an angler's dependable reserve, and it is especially appropriate for appending a little distance across the scarf to a substantial wire snare. The additional last fold works on your odds of holding a solid fish.

FG Knot

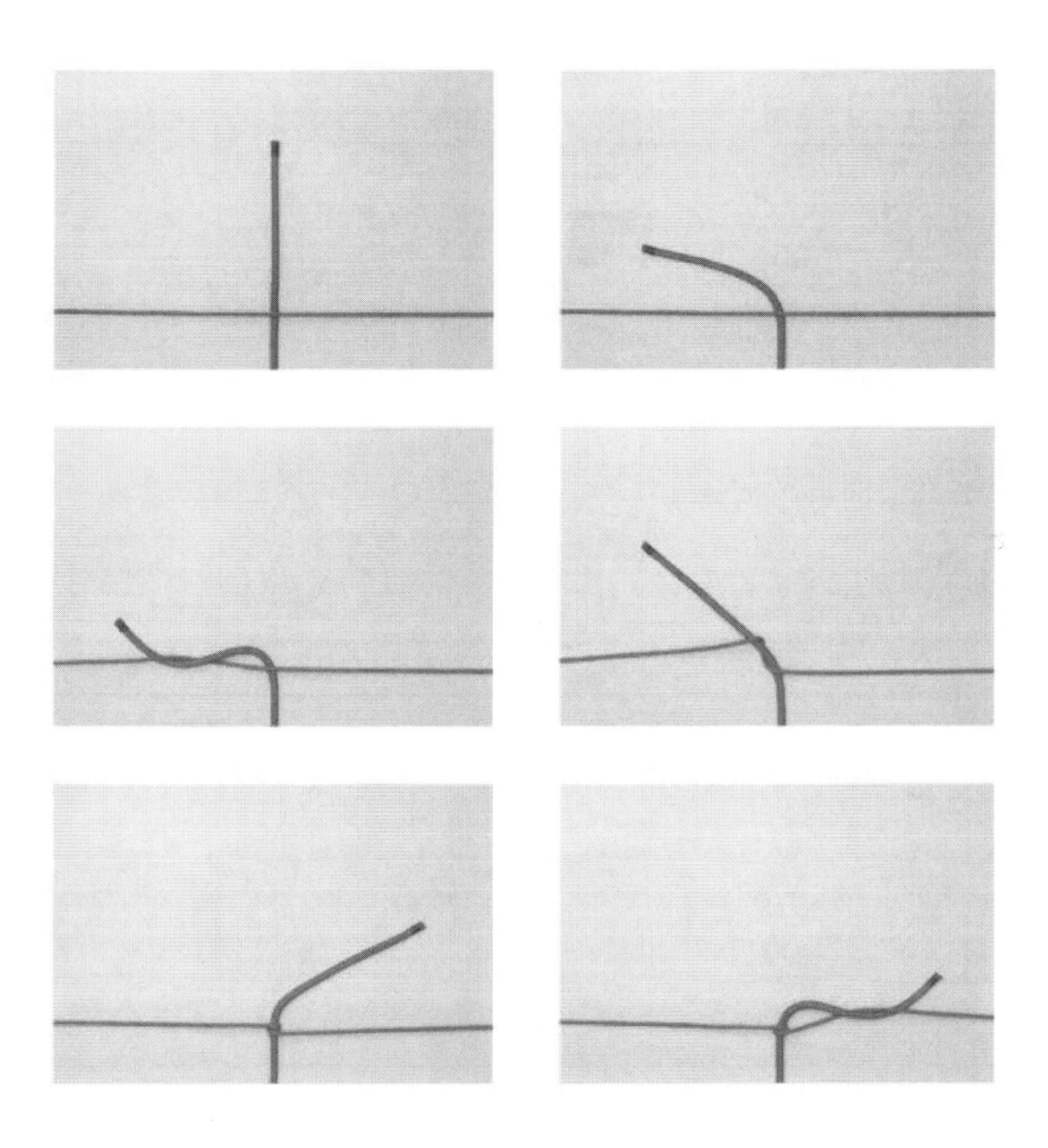

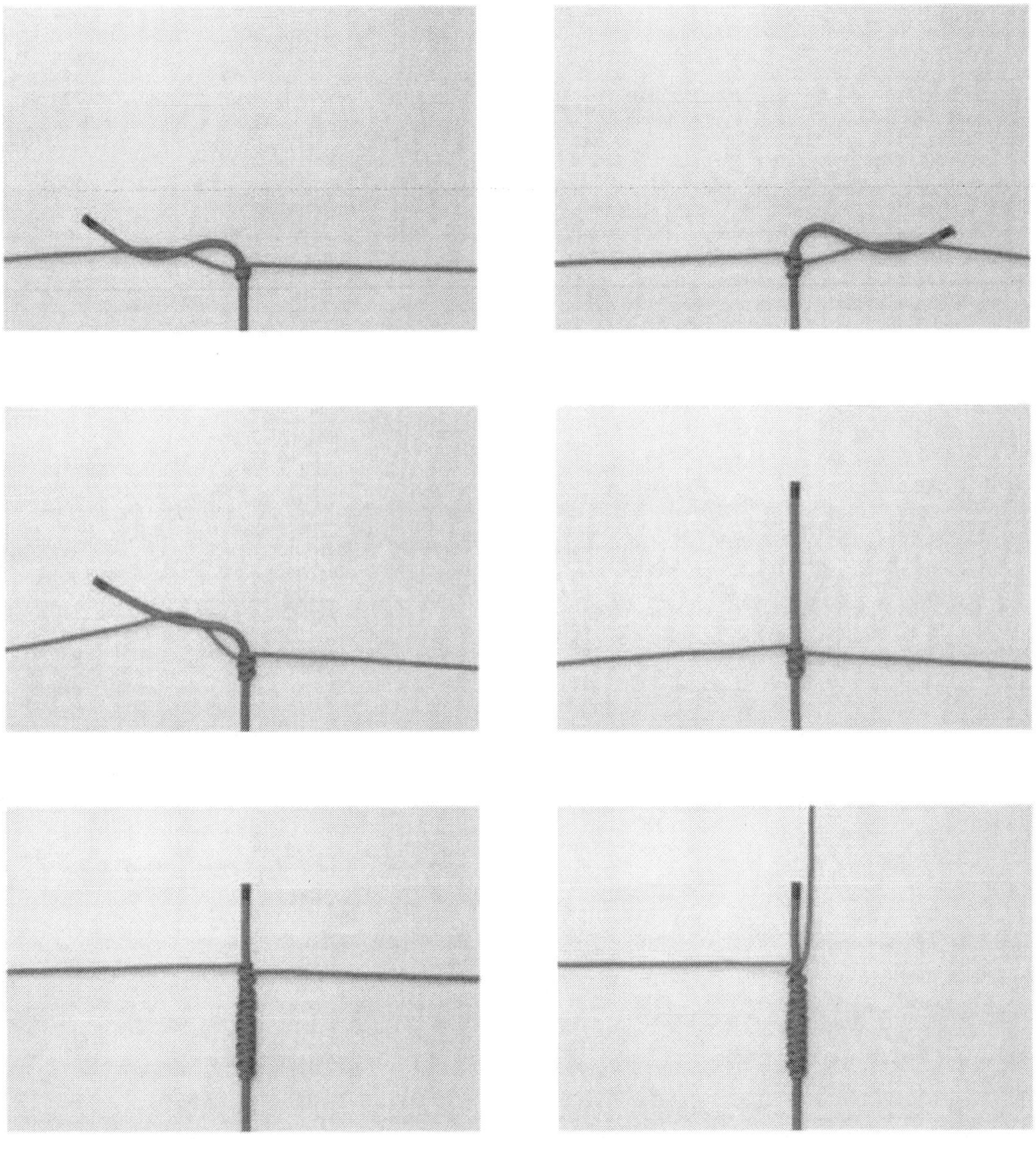

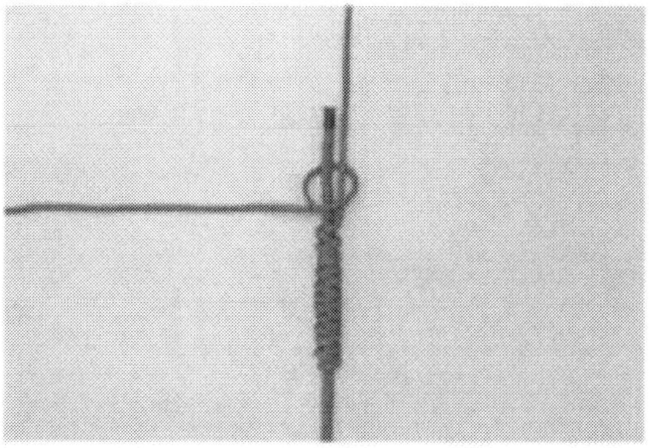
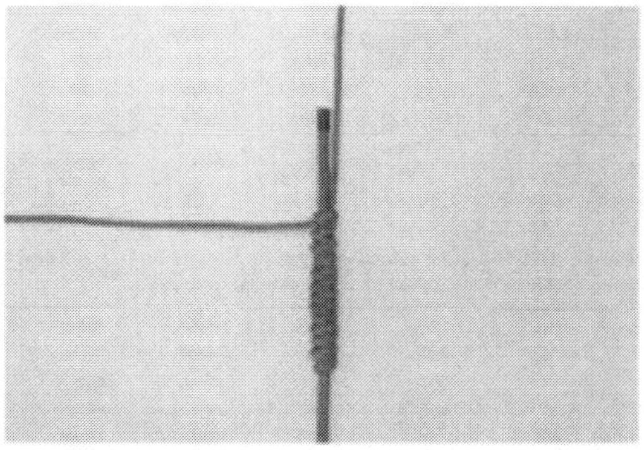
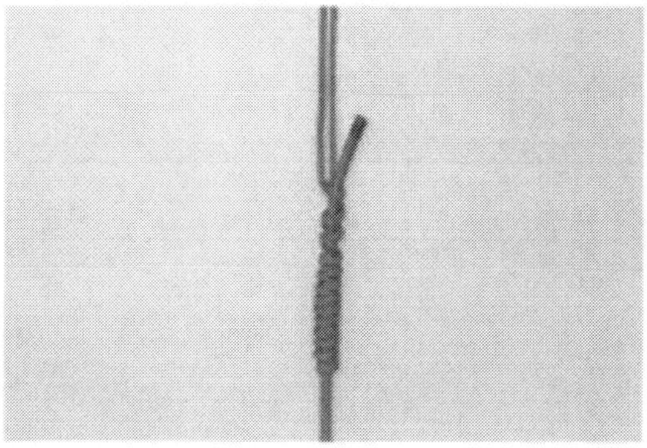
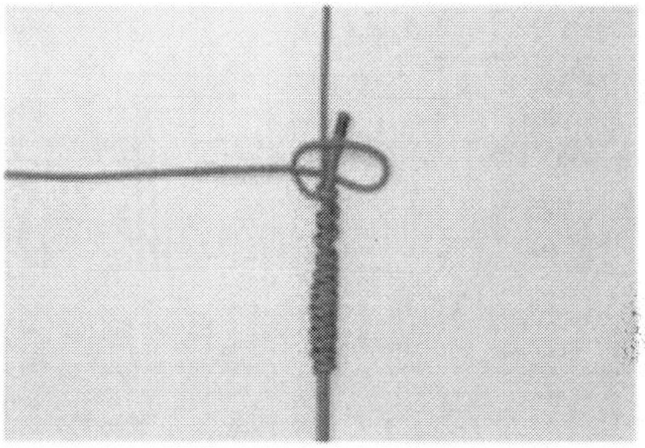
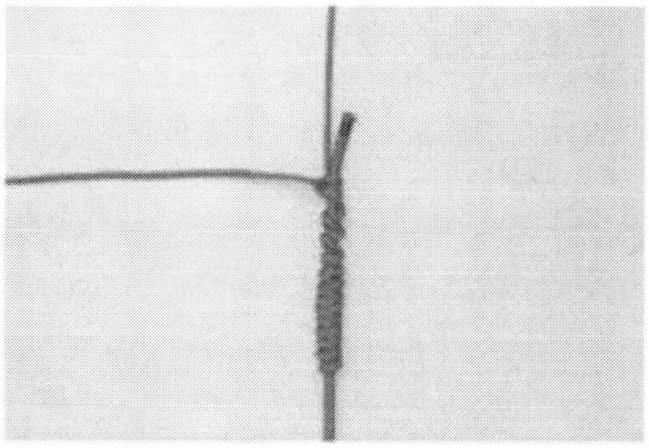
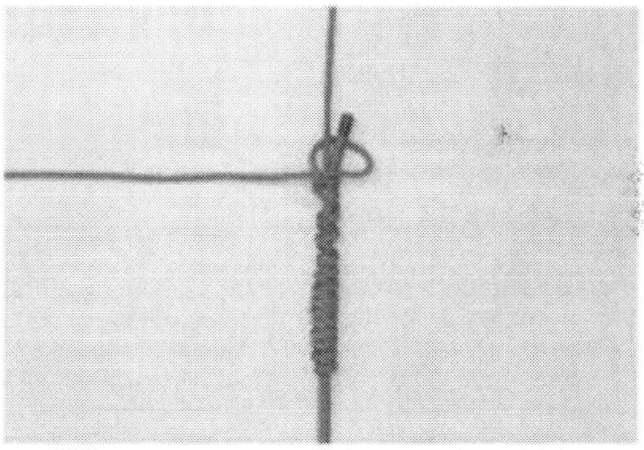

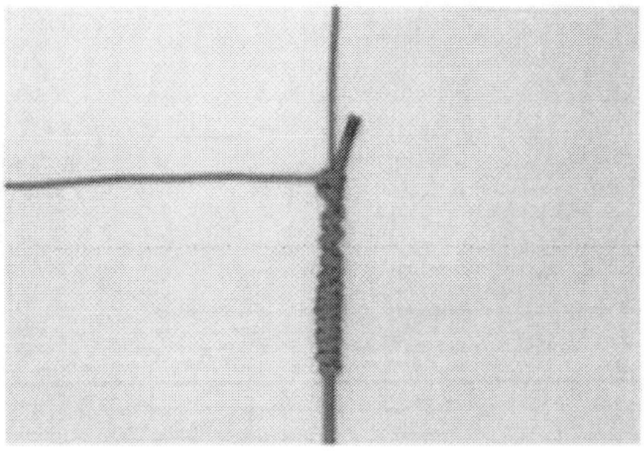

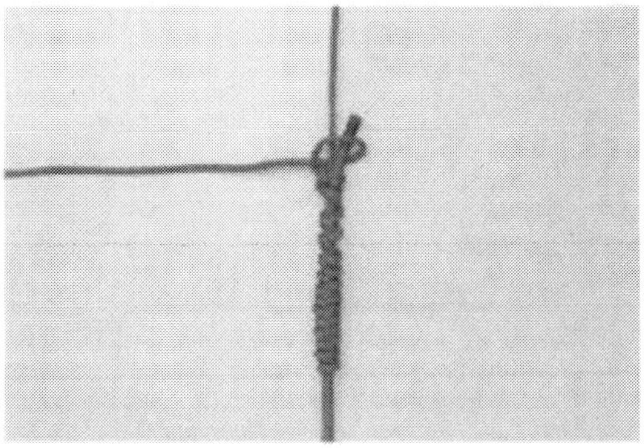

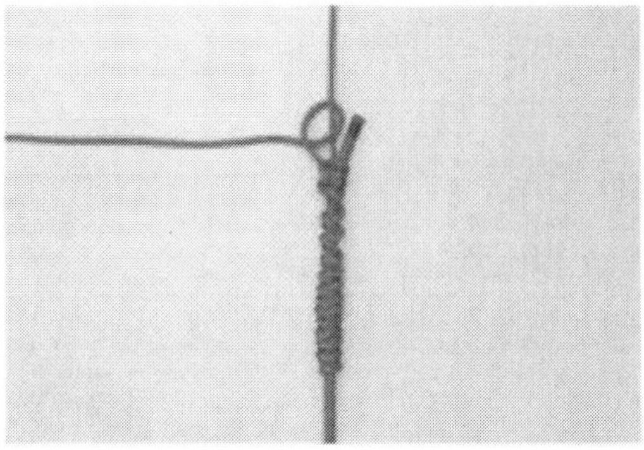

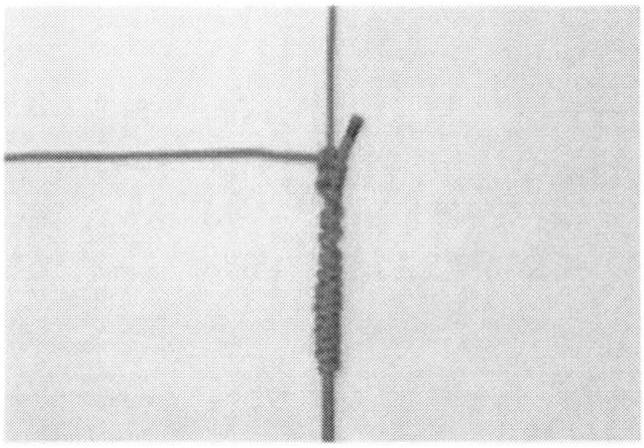

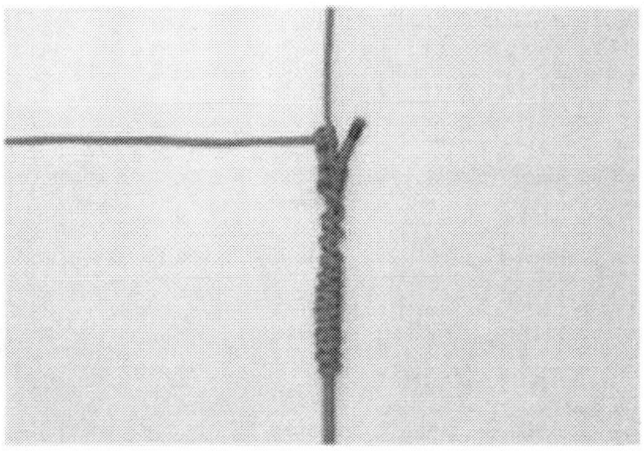

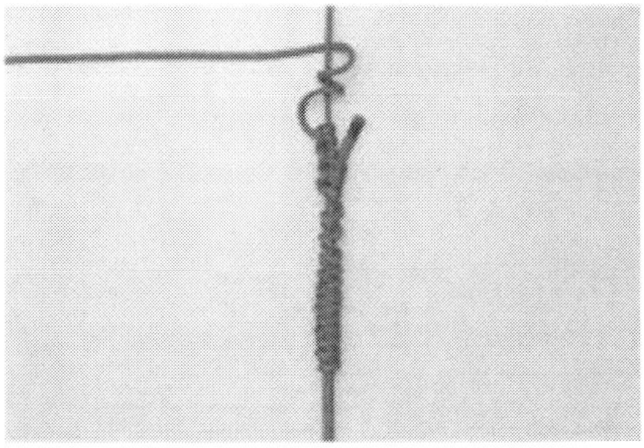

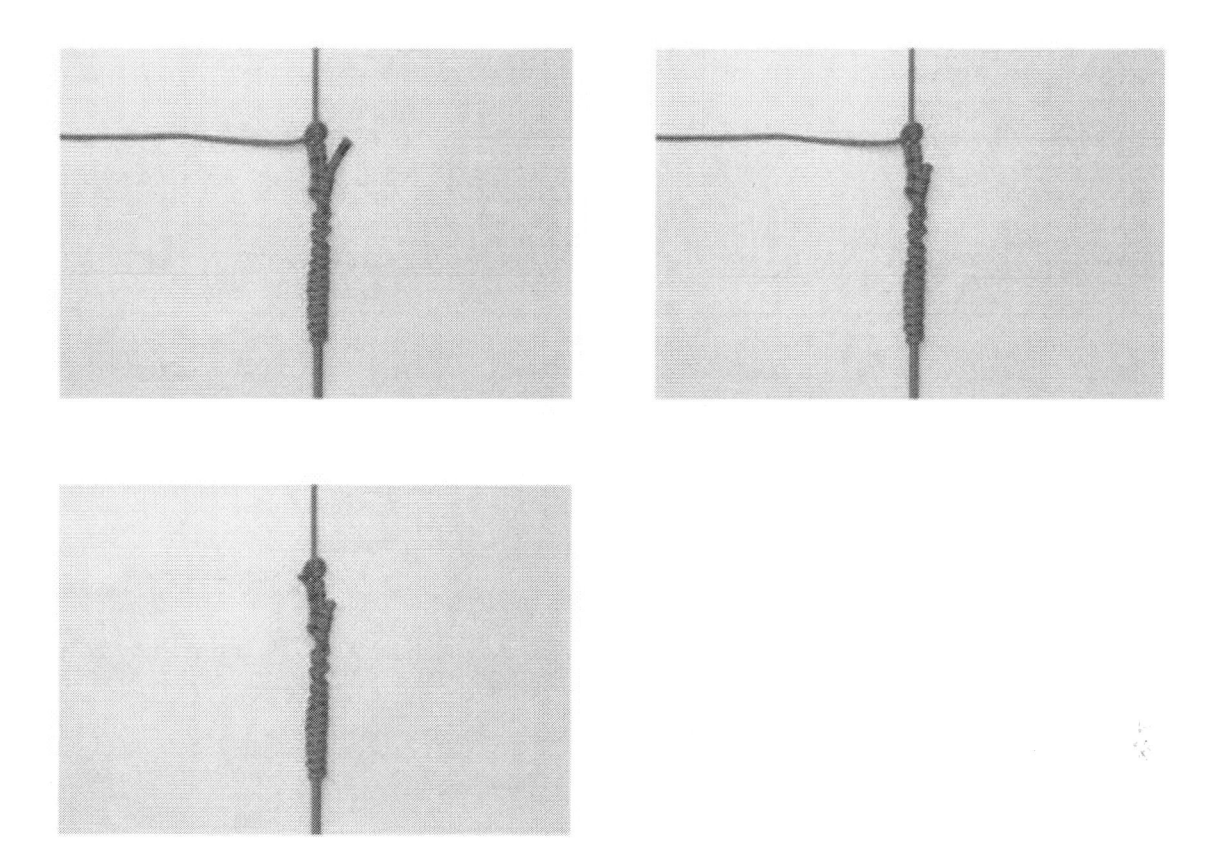

Complete the bunch by tying Half hitches around the two lines and afterward around the Braid. The last locking tie is a three-turn half hitch. Wrap up by cutting the tag-closures of the Leader and Braid.

Use: This bunch is esteemed for its solidarity and its capacity to run uninhibitedly through the aides. Albeit somewhat confounded to learn, it has numerous exciting adherents. We have gotten a more significant number of solicitations for this bunch than some others. With training, it tends to be tied rapidly and dependably.

Tying it: Detail is essential. Pressure on the interlaced line might be applied in different ways – among shaft and foot, finger and thumb, or hand and mouth. Whatever strategy is utilized, the line should be kept tight. As the Head is being wrapped, the turns might fan out. After every five or six sets of wraps, the stack ought to be compacted. The inevitable strength of the FG relies upon the last solid draw toward the end since this stretches the previous six to ten wraps and fixes the Chinese Finger Grip.

Completing Options: Some journalists tie every one of the Half Hitches turning a similar way, and others substitute – as is displayed in the Animation here. Furthermore, there is a wide variety of half hitches tied first around the two lines and afterward around the jagged line. The end can be a Triple Half Hitch or a few Double Half Hitches or a long chain of single Half Hitches.

Egg Loop Knot

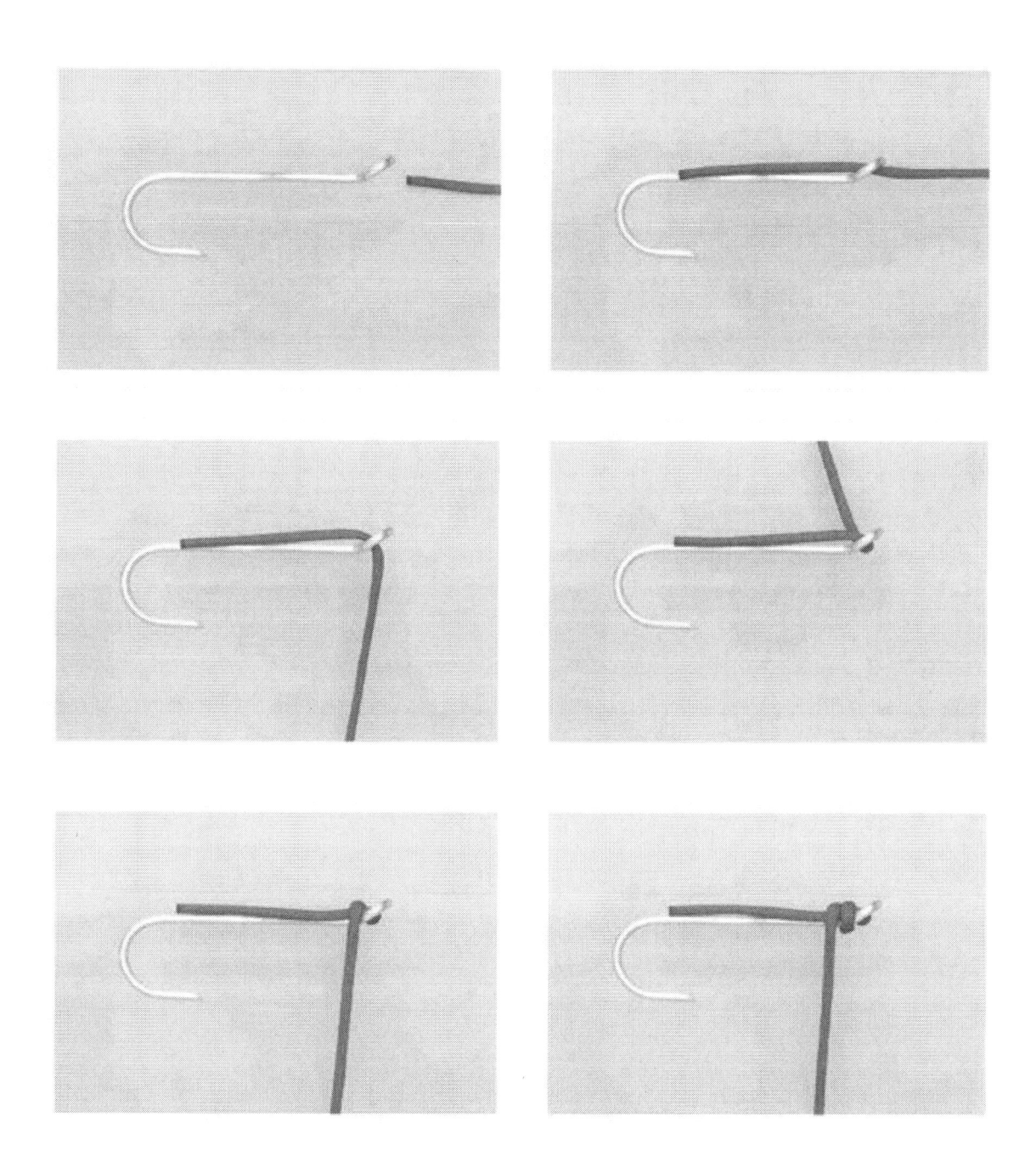

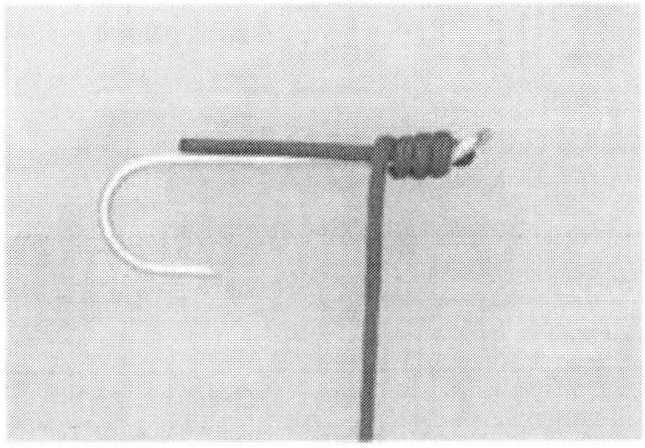

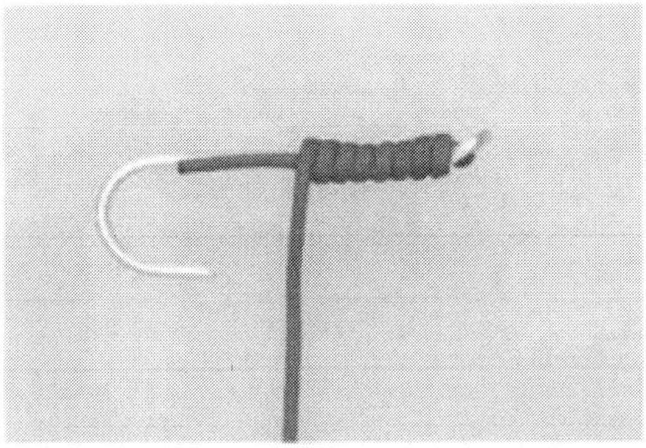

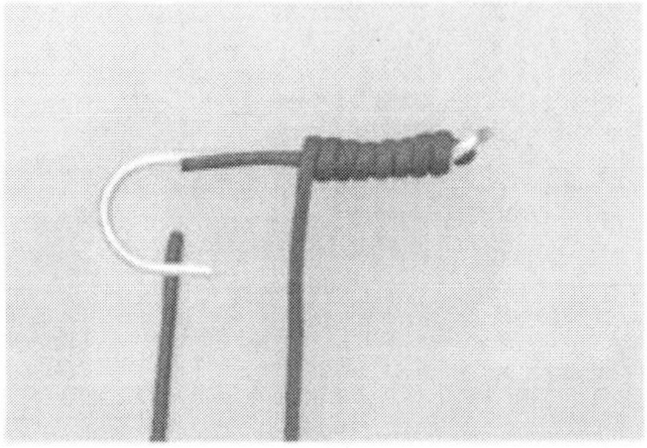

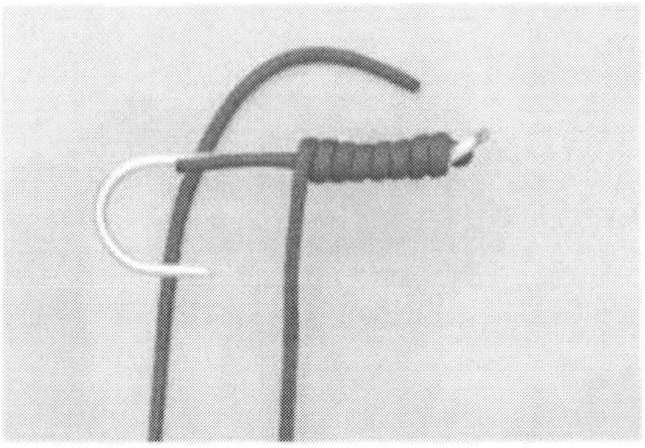

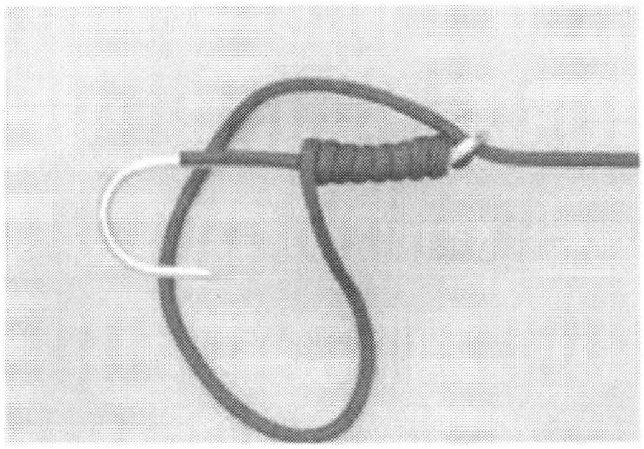

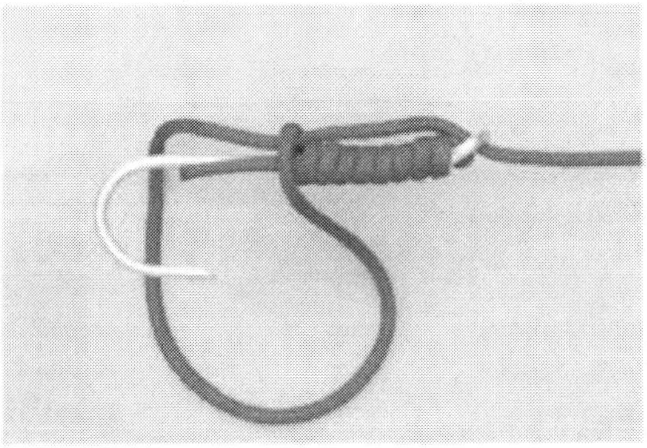

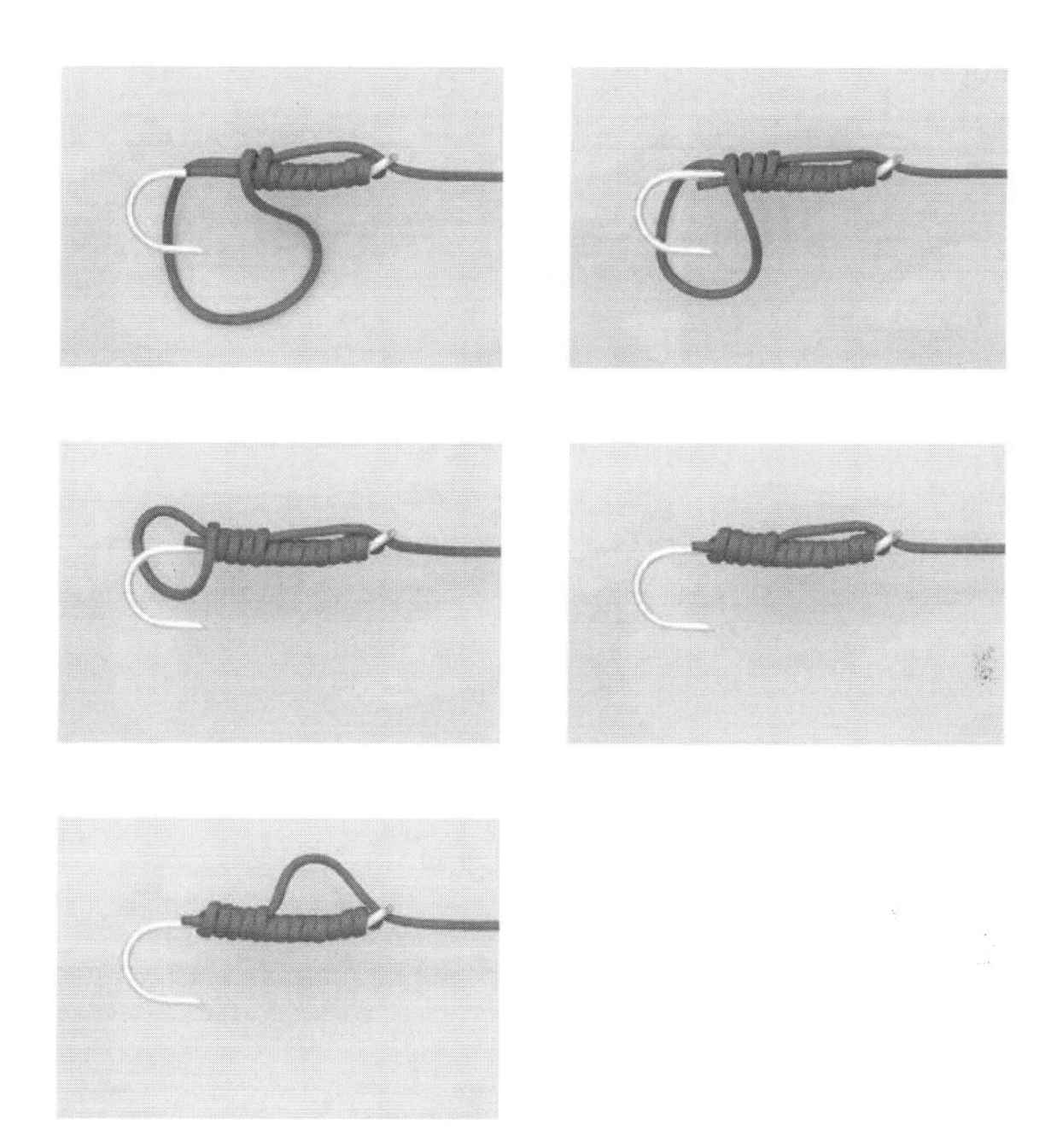

Pass one end of the pioneer through the eye. Fold the long end over the snare and short end multiple times. Pass the long end through the loop to make a circle. Keep wrapping utilizing the circle about another numerous times. Pull the long end to fix the wraps. Open up the egg circle.

Names: The Egg Loop Knot is likewise now and again known as the Bumper Knot. It is an adjustment of the Snell hitch in that turns are wrapped before the end being gone through the eye for the subsequent time.

Uses: The circle in the Egg Loop hitch gives a hold to the lure and is generally utilized when looking for salmon and steelhead trout. Fish eggs, shrimp, and fish roe make a fantastic lure.

Tying the Egg Loop Knot: Keep every one of the turns tight and stay away from covers: foster a hang on the snare and line so you can keep control of the turns. The main turn is usually the most off-kilter. Nonetheless, without a stretch outcome in turns, the circle's wraps can entangle the last draw to finish the Egg Loop Knot (outline 16).

Dropper Loop Knot

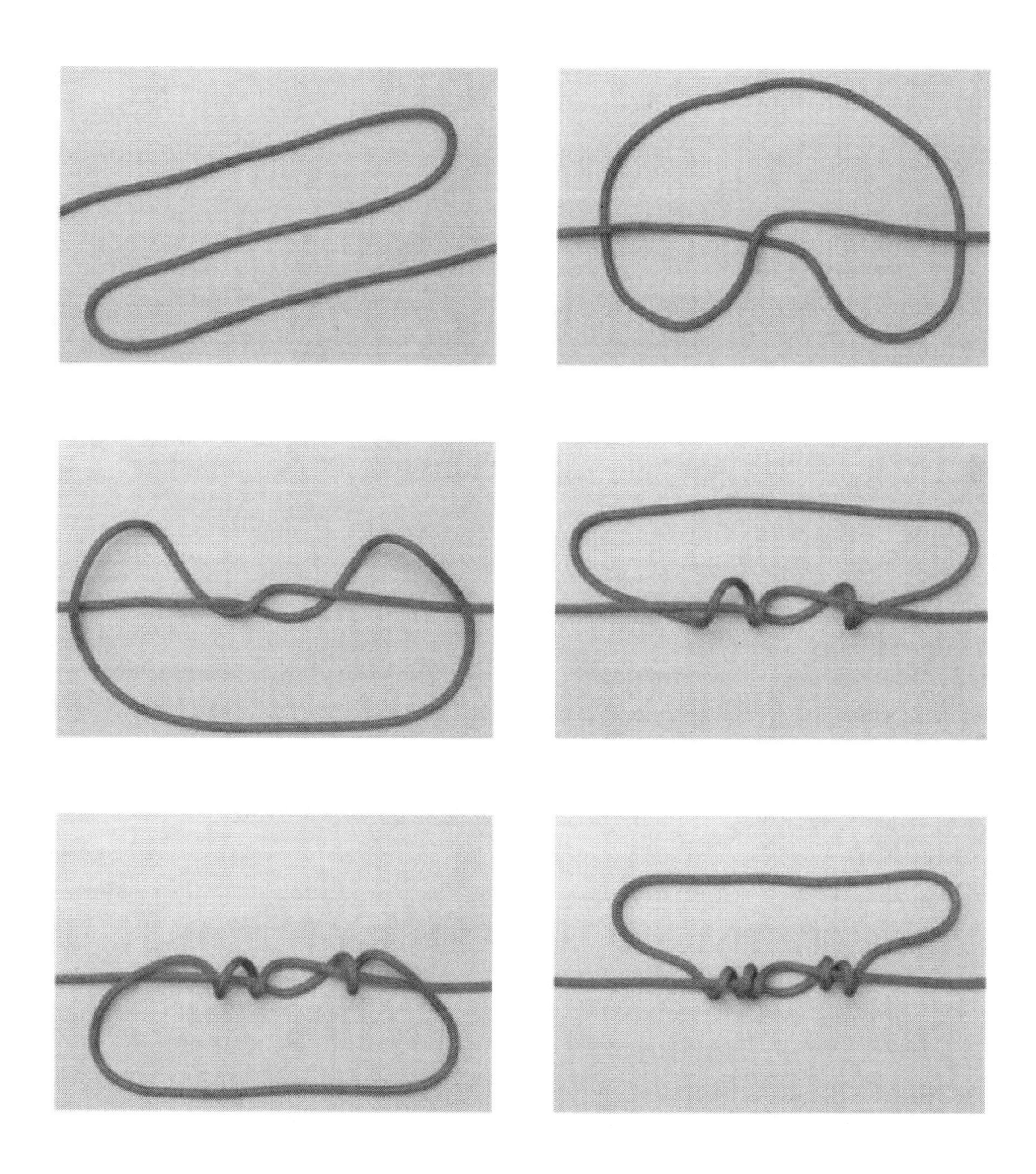

184

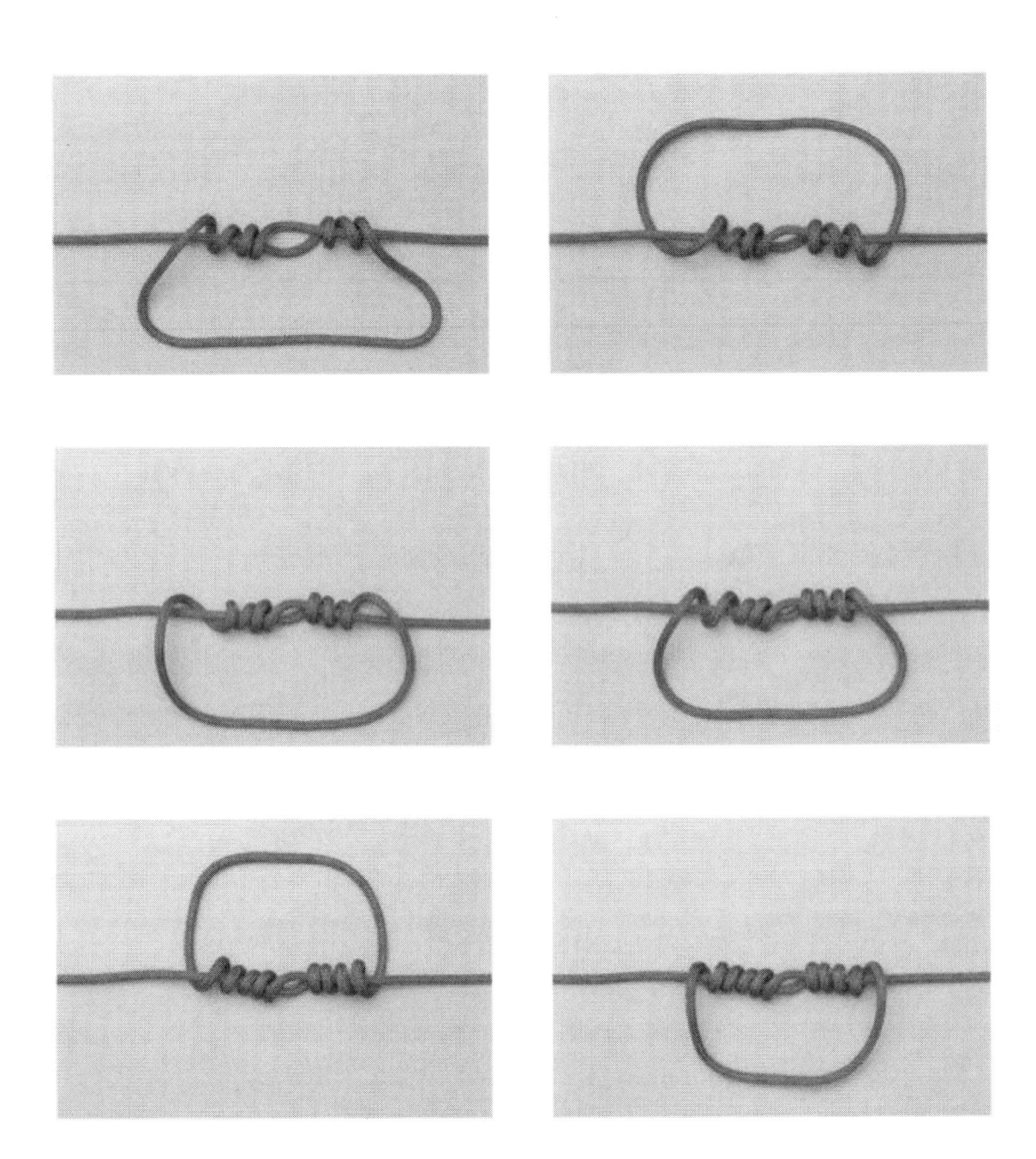

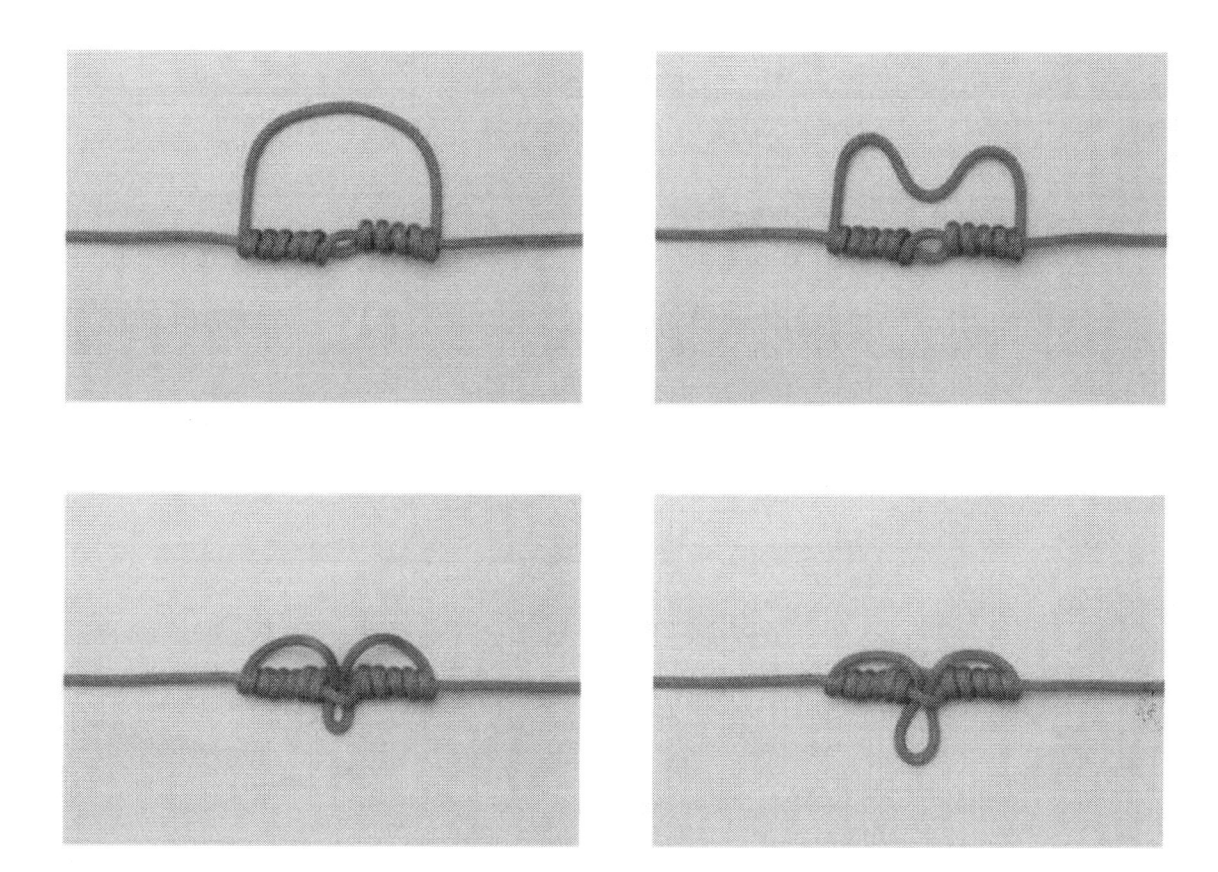

Make a massive circle in a line. Holding the middle, fold the circle over this hybrid point multiple times. Open an opening in the middle and pass the loop through the portal. Grease up, hold the loop with your teeth and pull the bunch tight. Note: in nylon fixing, this bunch adjusts the construction.

Uses: The Dropper Loop Knot makes a circle that stands apart at right points to the center of a line length. It very well may be utilized in your chief or scarf to give an additional connection highlight an extra fly. Whenever wanted, can make the circle long enough to set a snare straightforwardly on it. In any case, to limit the danger of fouling and contorting, this Dropper circle ought not to be excessively long. The Dropper Loop Knot is likewise utilized on multi-snare fishing lines.

Tying it: There are two primary techniques for connecting it. The liveliness shows the circle being wrapped around the cross-over point that is kept still with your fingers.

Pulling the Knot Tight: When greased up and pulled tight, the bunch changes its construction. Drawing on each end powers the wrapped goes to rearrange the turns, so the inner strand turns into an outer wrap (not shown in this liveliness utilizing rope).

Options: a similar outcome can be achieved by keeping the circle still and turning a matchstick in the cross-over to make a twisting. The large circle is then gone through the opening involved by the matchstick. Amos Baehr contributed a thought he found fortunately when he attempted a ballpoint pen rather than a matchstick: Use the clasp in the cap of a ballpoint pen. Clasp it on aside of the circle and turn it as opposed to pivoting a matchstick. The heaviness of the cell is a benefit.

Whichever strategy is utilized, the Dropper Loop Knot should appear practically balanced on either side of the circle.

Benefits: The Dropper Loop points from the line, which assists with staying away from tangles.

Blood Knot

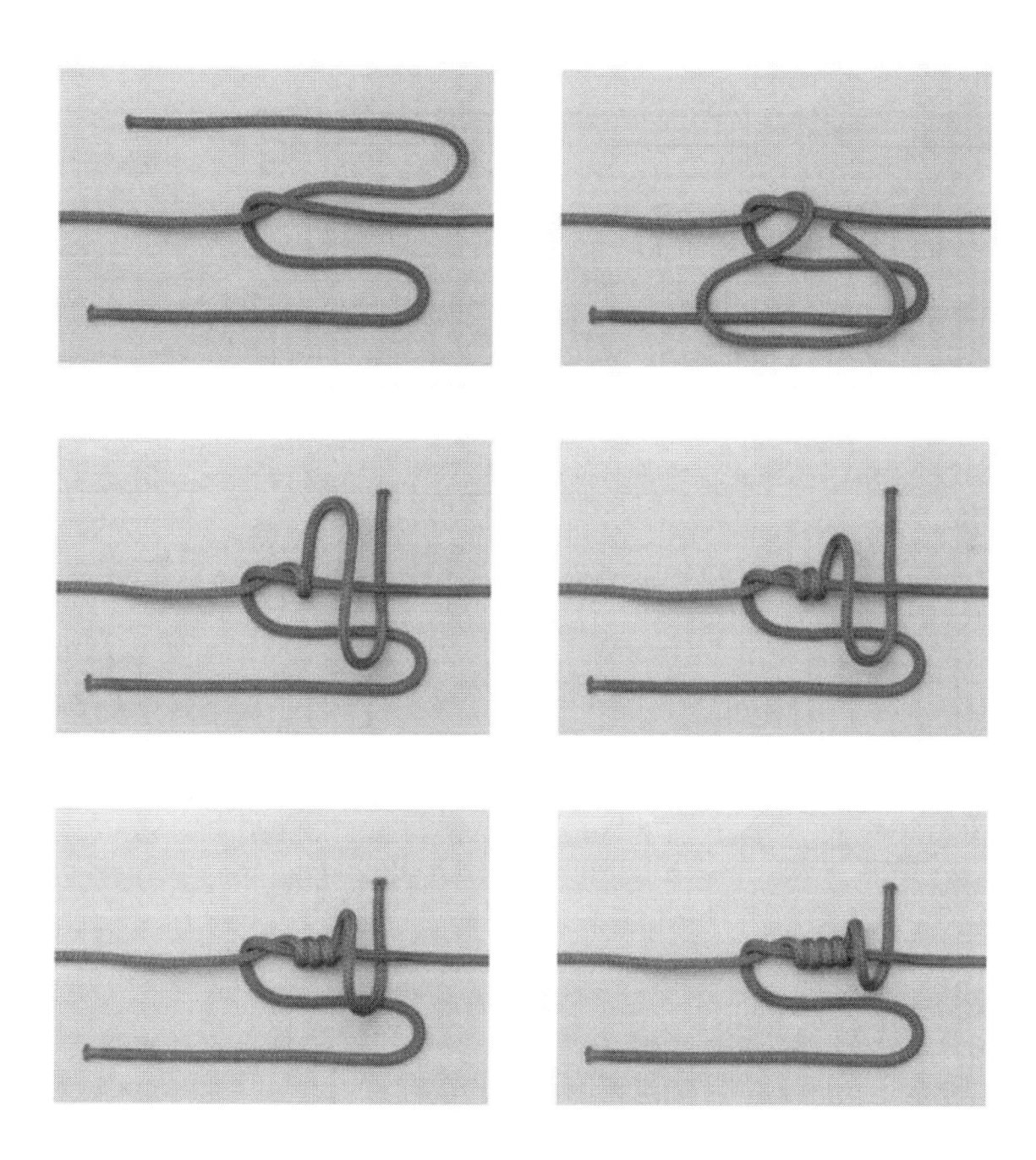

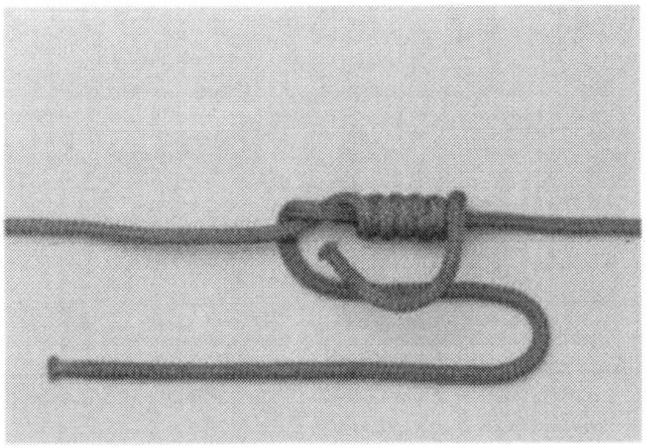
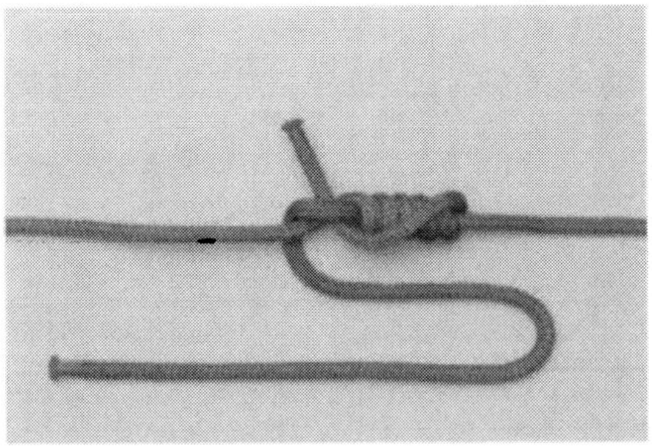
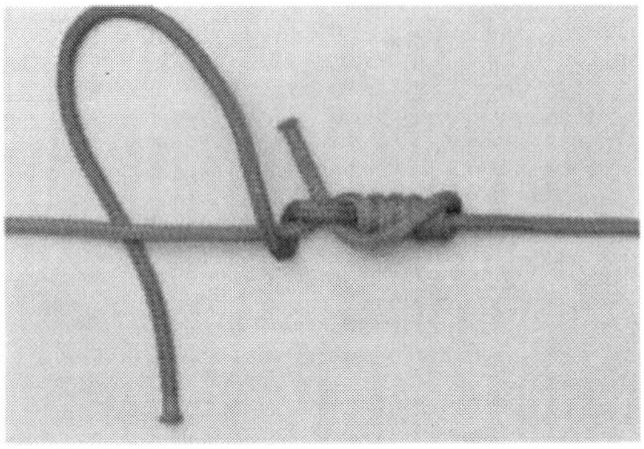
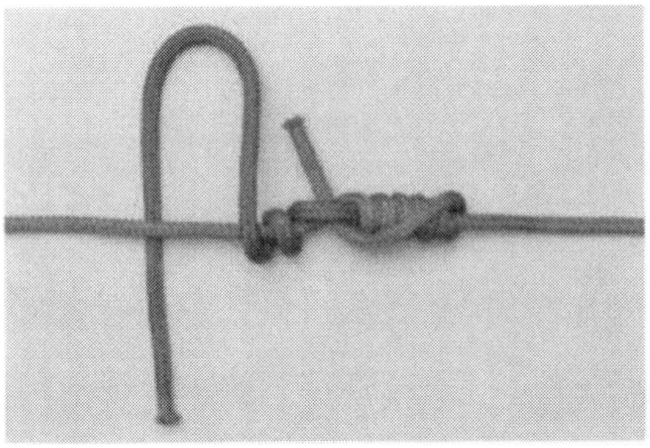
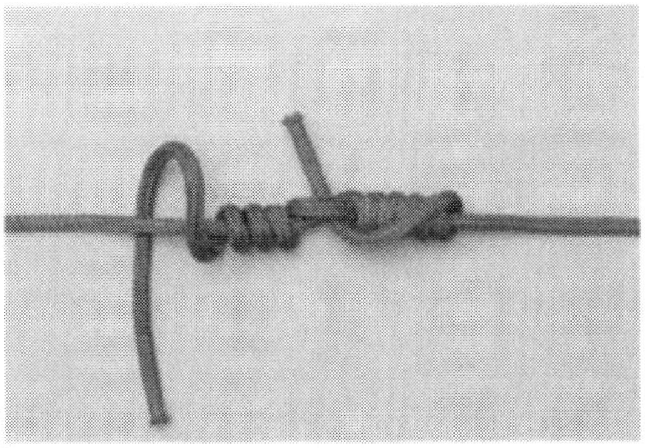
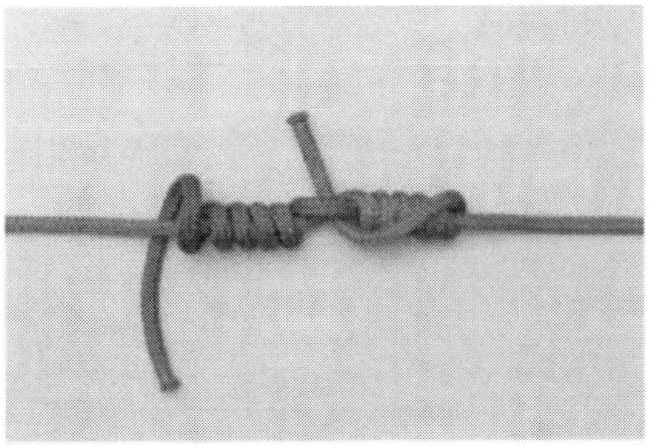

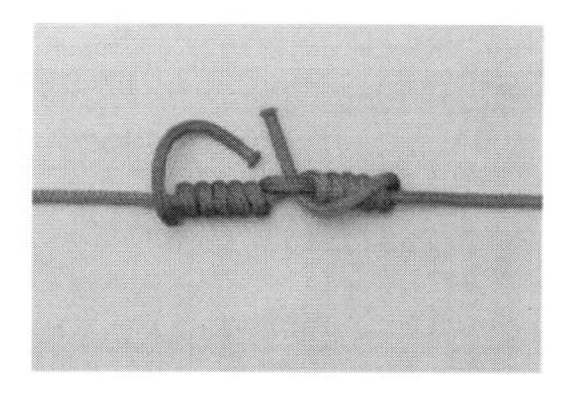

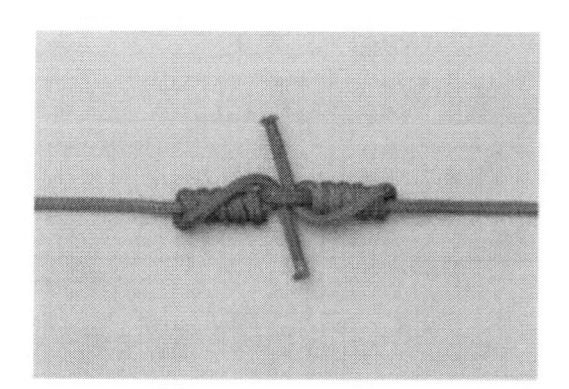

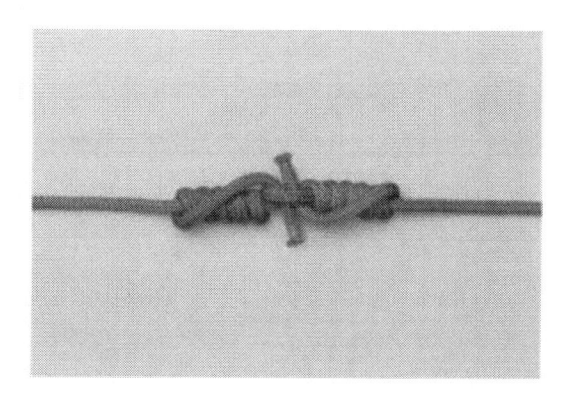

Cross over the two lines to be joined. Fold one end over the other line multiple times. Fold the end back between the lines. Rehash the cycle with the other line, tucking the end back between the pipes the other way. Fix and trim. Note: in nylon, fixing this bunch changes the appearance.

Uses: The Blood Knot is a most loved bunch for the fly angler. It is principally used to join two lines of comparable size, e.g., when joining segments of pioneer or scarf, and is perhaps the best bunch for this reason. The strength of the Blood Knot relies upon making no less than five and up to seven turns on each side of the middle.

Pulling the Knot Tight: When greased up and pulled tight, the Blood Knot changes its construction. Drawing on each line powers the wrapped goes to rearrange the turns so that the inward strand turns into an outer wrap (not represented in the movement utilizing rope).

Tying it: There are a few techniques for tying it. The movement shows every half being made independently, which gives a decent image of the construction of the Blood Knot.

Alternative: An elective technique covers the two closures and bends them together for ten to fourteen turns. Then, at that point, go to the focal point of the turns and make an opening. Pass the two ends a contrary way through the portal.

Whichever strategy is utilized, the Blood Knot is usually balanced with regards to the center. Albeit the turns, for the most part, proceed a similar way on either side of the middle as displayed in the liveliness, it tends to be tied, so the wraps are exact representations of one another.

Benefits: The Blood tie is a primary, effortlessly scholarly, and compelling method of joining two similar estimated lines.

Australian Braid Knot

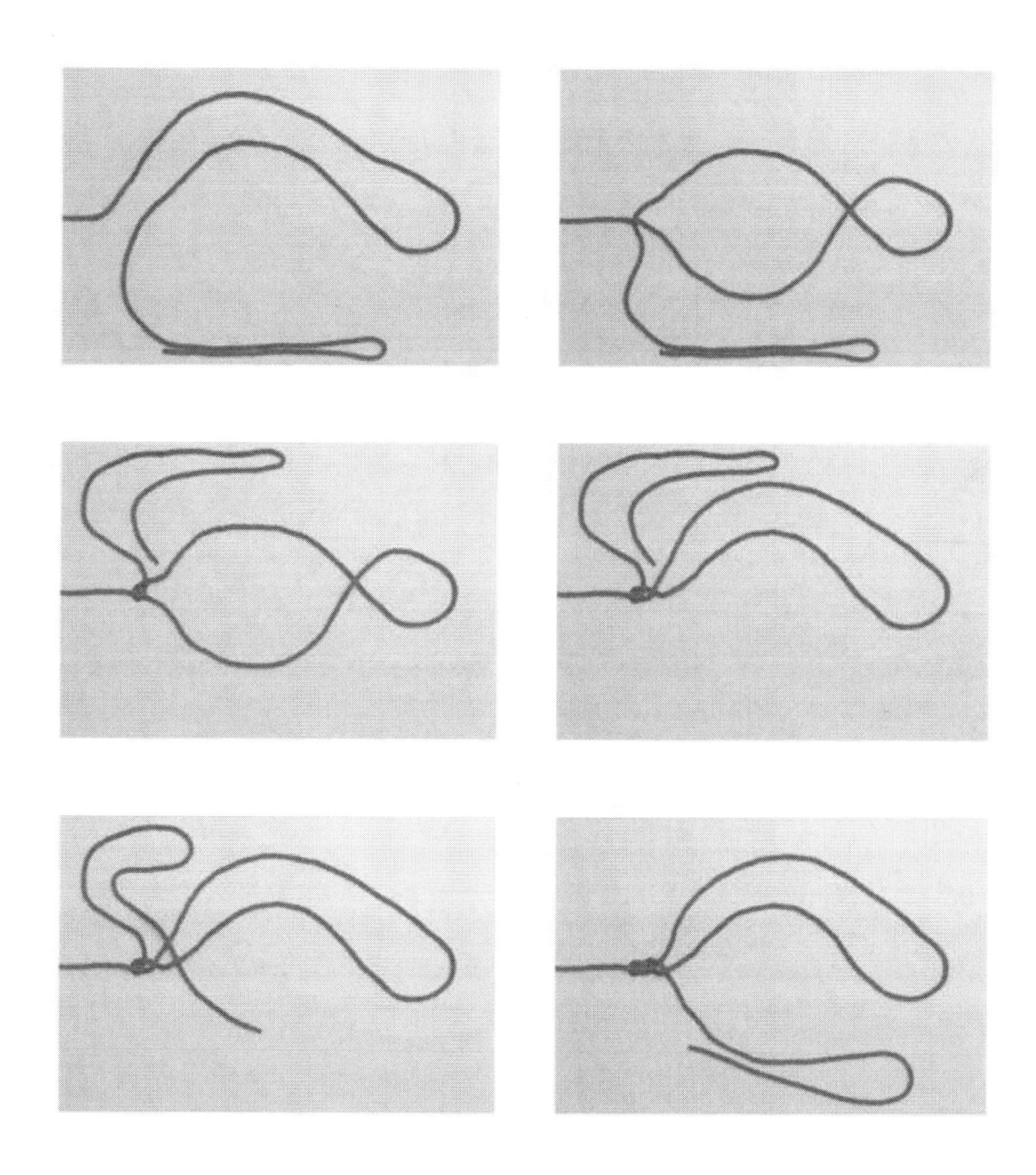

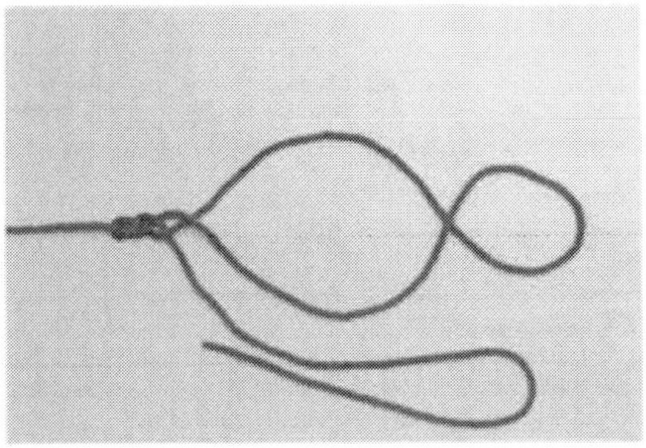
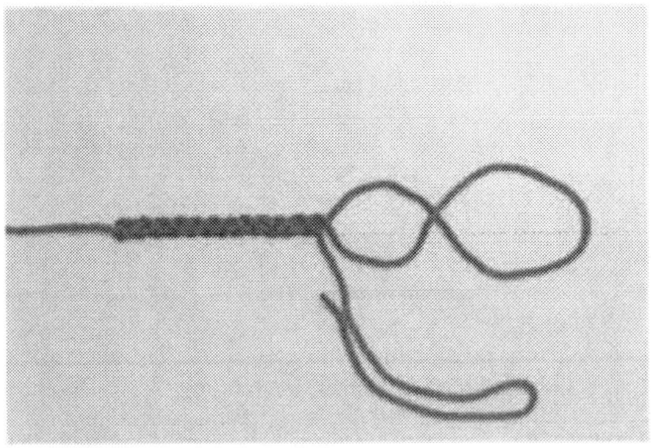
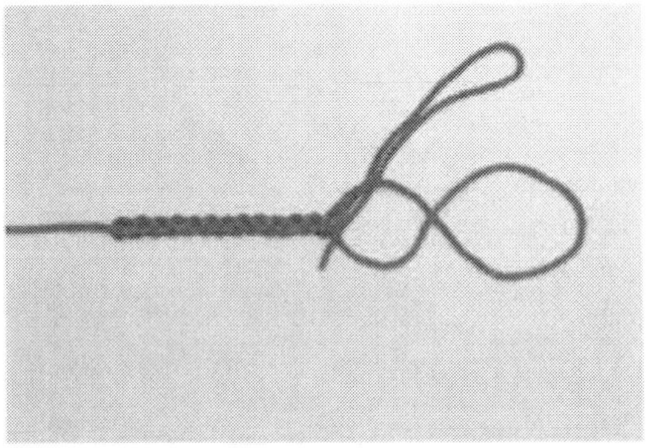
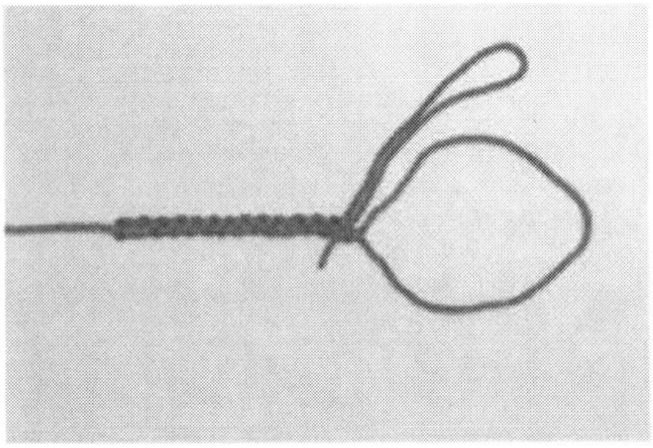
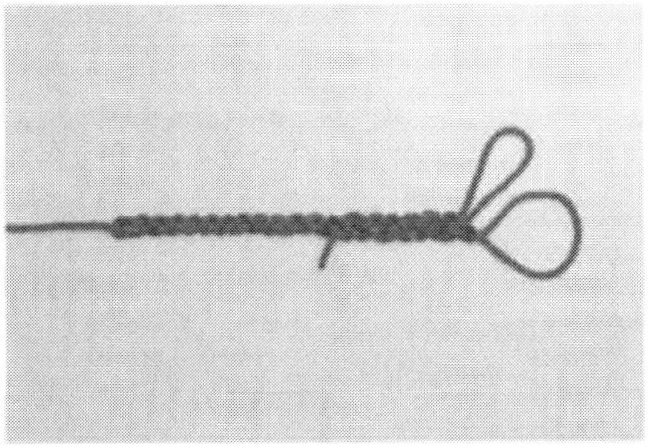
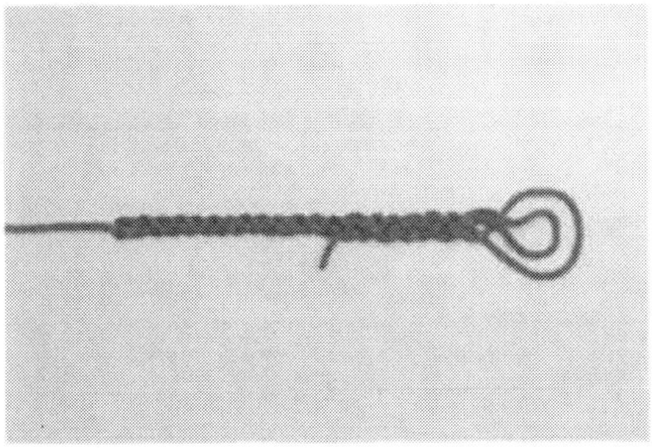

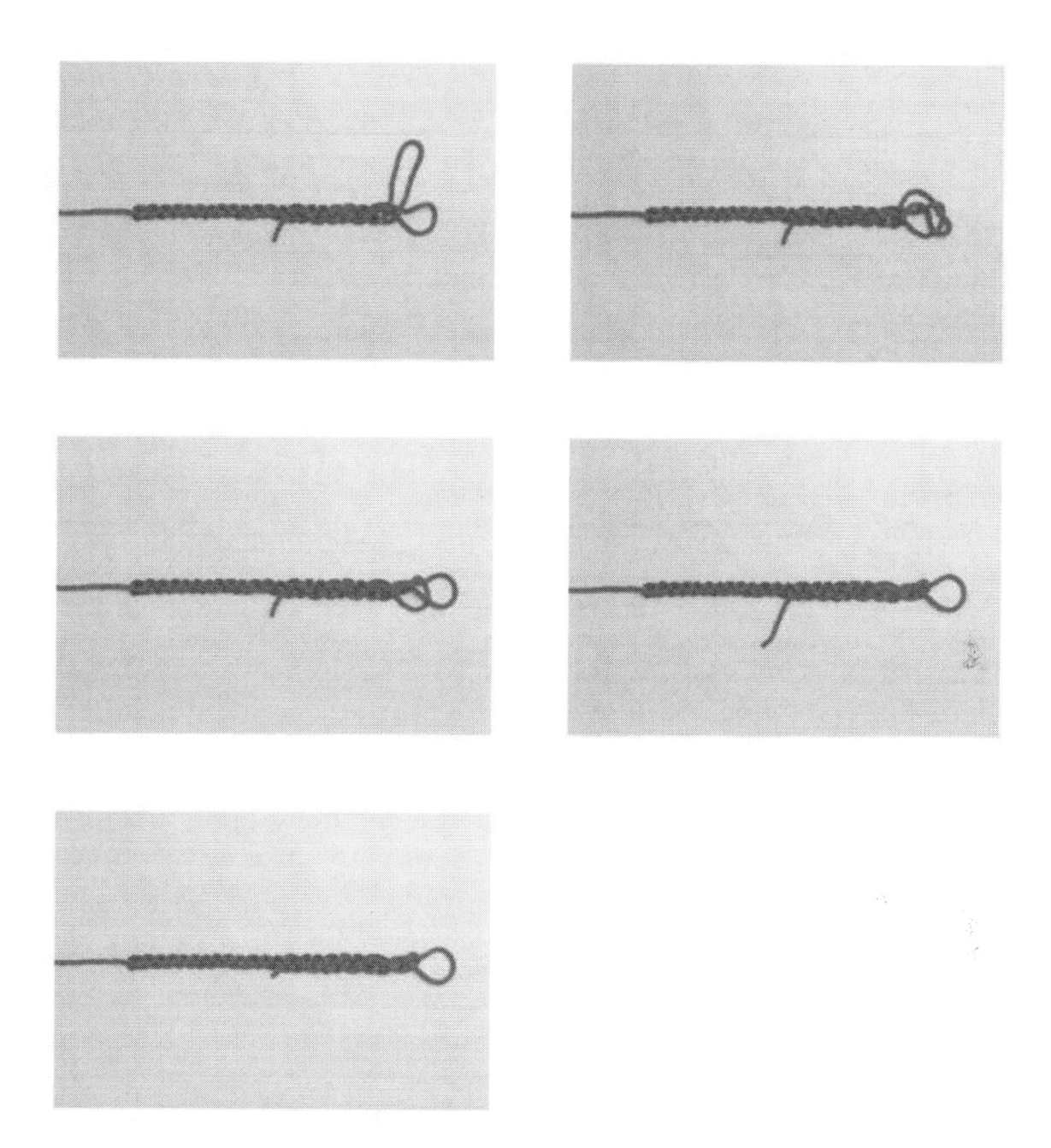

Structure a circle leaving a long label end. Interlace the circle and label end firmly together (the genuine plait length relies upon the line weight). Complete the twist utilizing a bight in the label end. Get the first circle through the bight. Grease up and afterward fix the bight by pulling flawlessly on the label end. Trim the label end.

Uses: The Australian Braid (or Plait) is an option in contrast to the Bimini Twist and makes a solid circle for use as a twofold line pioneer on the end of a fishing line which would then be able to be utilized for a circle to-circle association.

Tying it: The movement exhibits the method as it may, for photography, shows few interlaces. By and by, the Australian Braid requires an extended mesh to function admirably.

Proposals: The qualities in the table depend on suggestions from Leadertec and show the suggested length of plait for various fishing lines.

Methods: An extra defend to forestall unwinding is given by a spot of elastic paste over the managed label end.

Benefits: The Australian Braid moves the strain bit by bit to the bunch over a significant length. Although it isn't as notable as the Bimini Twist, its allies guarantee it is simpler to learn and speedier to tie. It additionally presents the littlest width. If necessary, audit our vivified, bit by bit, instructional exercise for plaits if it's not too much trouble.

Breaking Strain: The Australian Braid (or Plait), like the Bimini Twist, is professed to protect 100% of the line's breaking strain. Notwithstanding, these surprising outcomes are gotten in the lab and may likewise be acquired under ideal conditions – cooled, wet, and without too extraordinary a shock stacking. I have not discovered reports of cautious research center testing for the Australian Braid – and brings about use in all likelihood change. Abrupt jerks produce heat because of contact and are bound to cause disappointment at lower breaking strains.

Arbor Knot

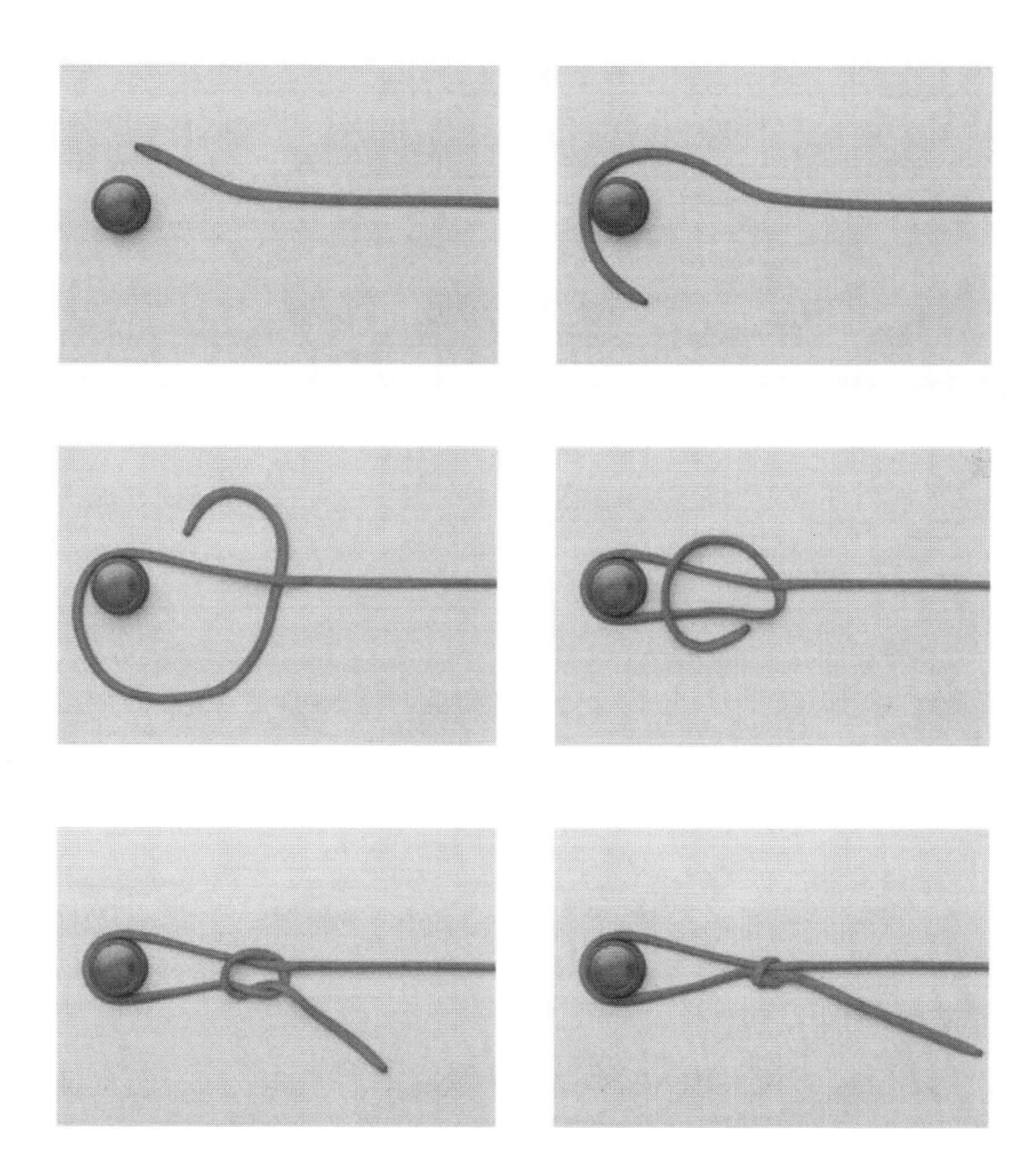

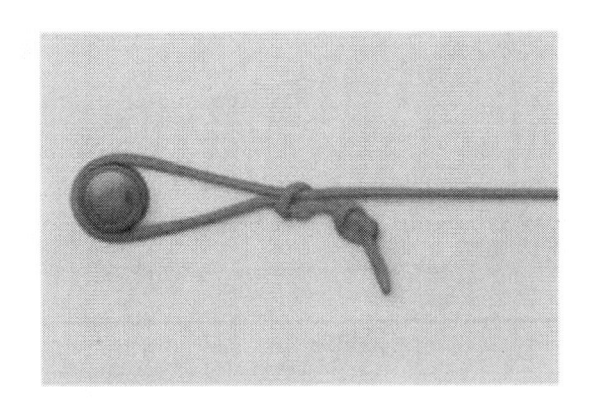

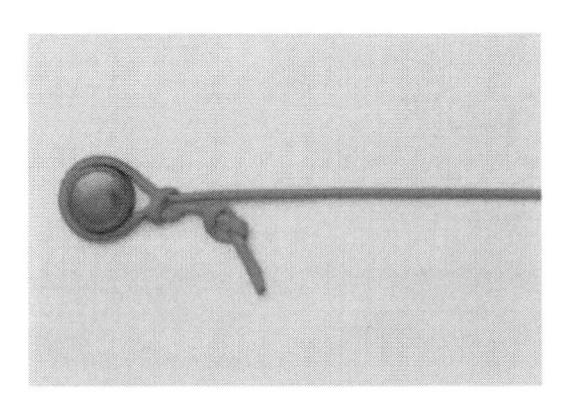

Pass the fishing line around the Arbor. With the free end, tie an overhand bunch around the pipe. Then, at that point, tie a second overhand bunch in the free end to go about as a plug. At last, slide the bunches down close against the Arbor.

Uses: The Arbor Knot is utilized to append the fishing line to the "Arbor" or "Spool Center." Indeed the Arbor Knot is genuinely founded on a noose tie and, accordingly, pulling fixes it. A similar bunch is utilized in Bushcraft under the name Canadian Jam Knot. A light rope, e.g., paracord, is being used to pack a heap like a camping bed or is utilized as the initial phase in making a lashing.

Tying it: When the Arbor is available, the most effortless approach to connect the Arbor tie is to make a Noose, drop it on the Arbor and pull it to fix it. On the off chance that you commit a Slip Knot by error, it will simply remove scattered. On the other hand, as displayed in the movement, first pass the free end around the Arbor or the heap; then, at that point, utilize the free end to tie the primary overhand bunch around the line.

Second Overhand Knot: The extra Overhand Knot in the Tag End is tied closely to the first. It is fundamental: when the Arbor Knot is fixed, the Second Overhand Knot snugs down against the Arbor. Specific individuals prescribe it binds this Overhand Knot first to make it simpler to fold the line over the Arbor.

Further Developed Version: Some anglers wind the circle around the Arbor a few times before making the primary Half Hitch. This builds the grating, which might be valuable on an exceptionally cleaned reel. The course of these turns is introductory. They ought to be wrapped like tying a Tensionless Knot: pivoting the rotation should fix the wraps.

Delivering: Pulling on the free end, the Second Overhand Knot slackens the primary bunch and makes it simple to produce.

Benefits: The Arbor Knot (Canadian Jam Knot) is straightforward, effortlessly scholarly, and successful.

Albright Knot

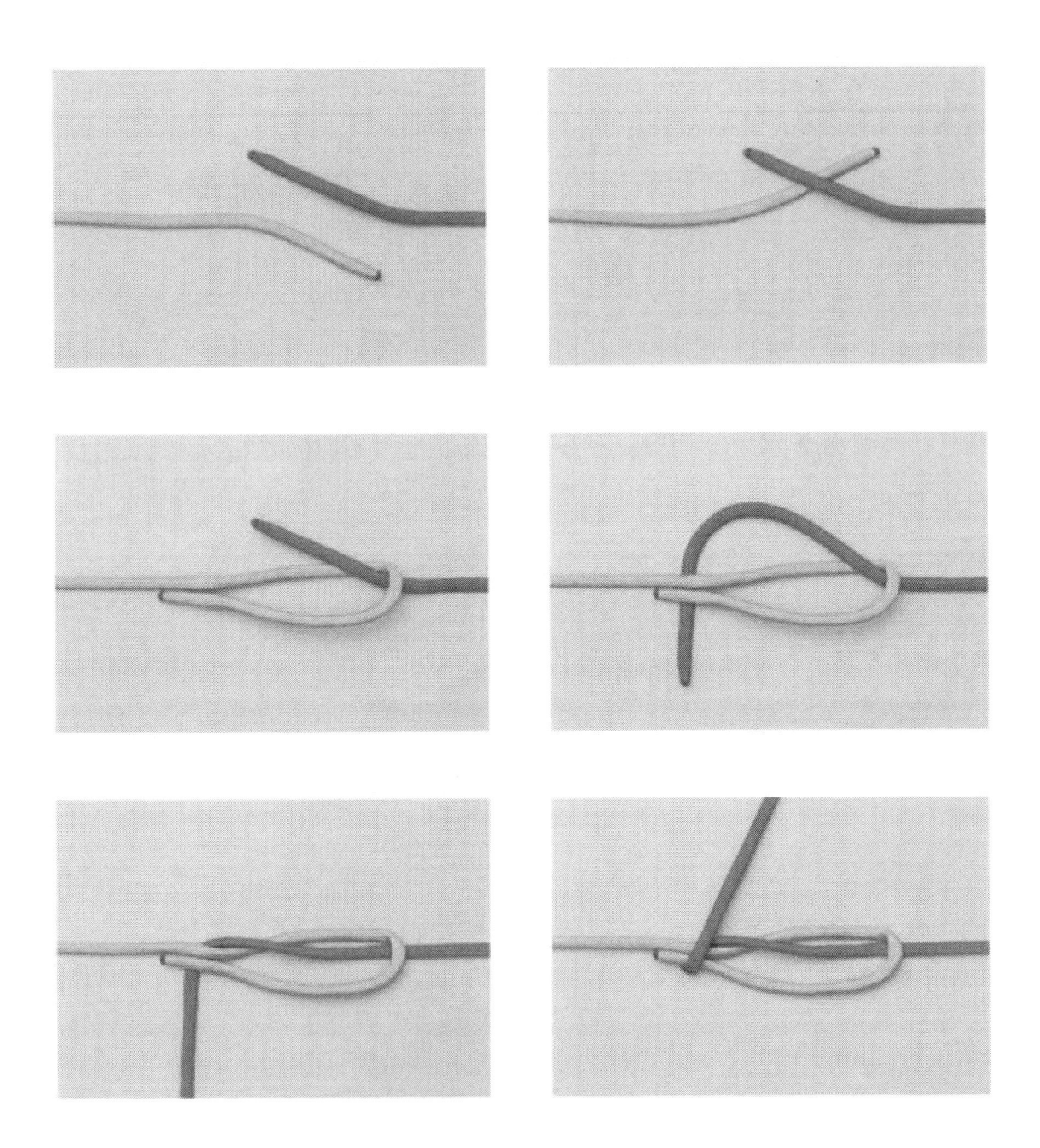

199

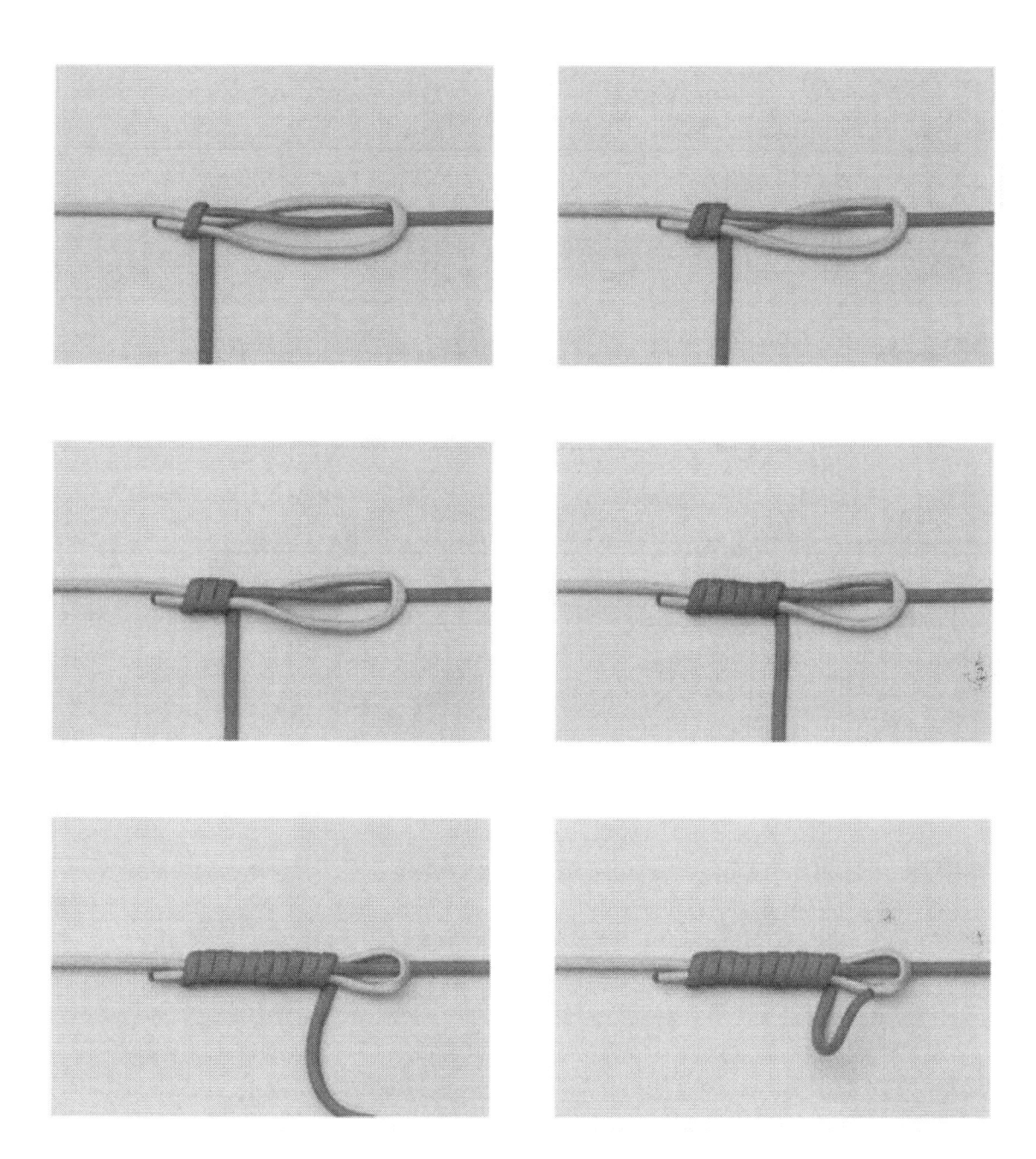

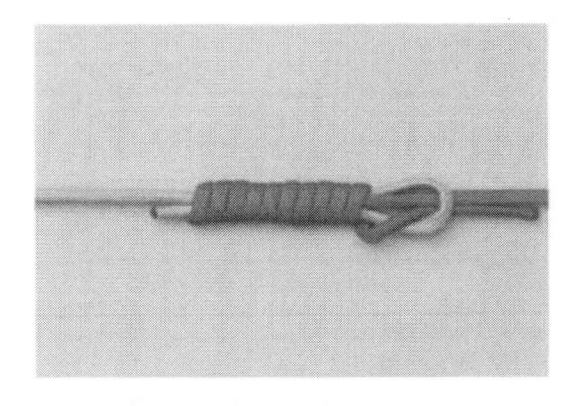

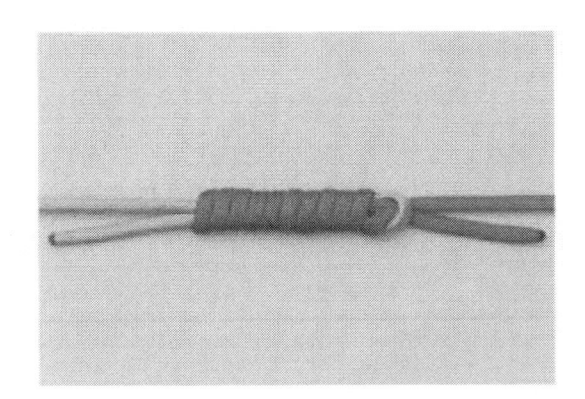

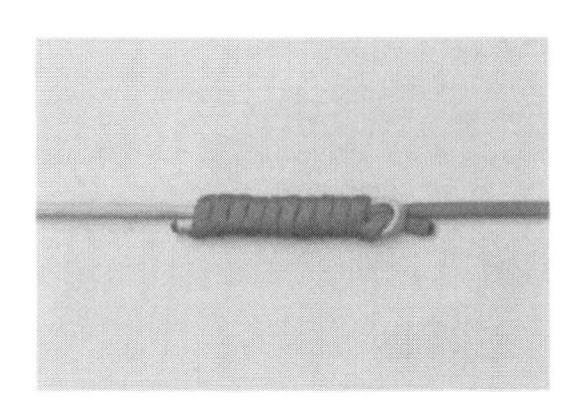

Structure a circle in one line (thicker if inconsistent). Pass the end of the other (slenderer) line through the circle and wrap it perfectly around itself and the loop multiple times. Then, at that point, pass the end back through the loop close to itself. Grease up, pull the bunch tight and trim the ends.

Uses: The Albright Knot is an adaptable bunch that has a broad scope of uses. It is tolerably simple to tie, yet it is appropriate for joining various fishing lines, e.g., Monofilament to Braided or Braided to Wire.

The Albright Knot is additionally helpful when getting monofilaments together with uniquely various measurements. It is usually used to join the fly line to the sponsorship line yet can be utilized when you wish to combine two fishing lines.

Tying it: The underlying circle is made in a more extensive line. Wind the loops flawlessly around this circle. It assists with holding the circles under your fingers as you wind the line on.

Benefits: The Albright Knot is appropriate to slide promptly through the aides when a fish pulls out an excellent line to arrive at your support. A few anglers cover the bunch with elastic-based concrete to make it even smoother and safer.

Stopper Knots

Stopper Loop

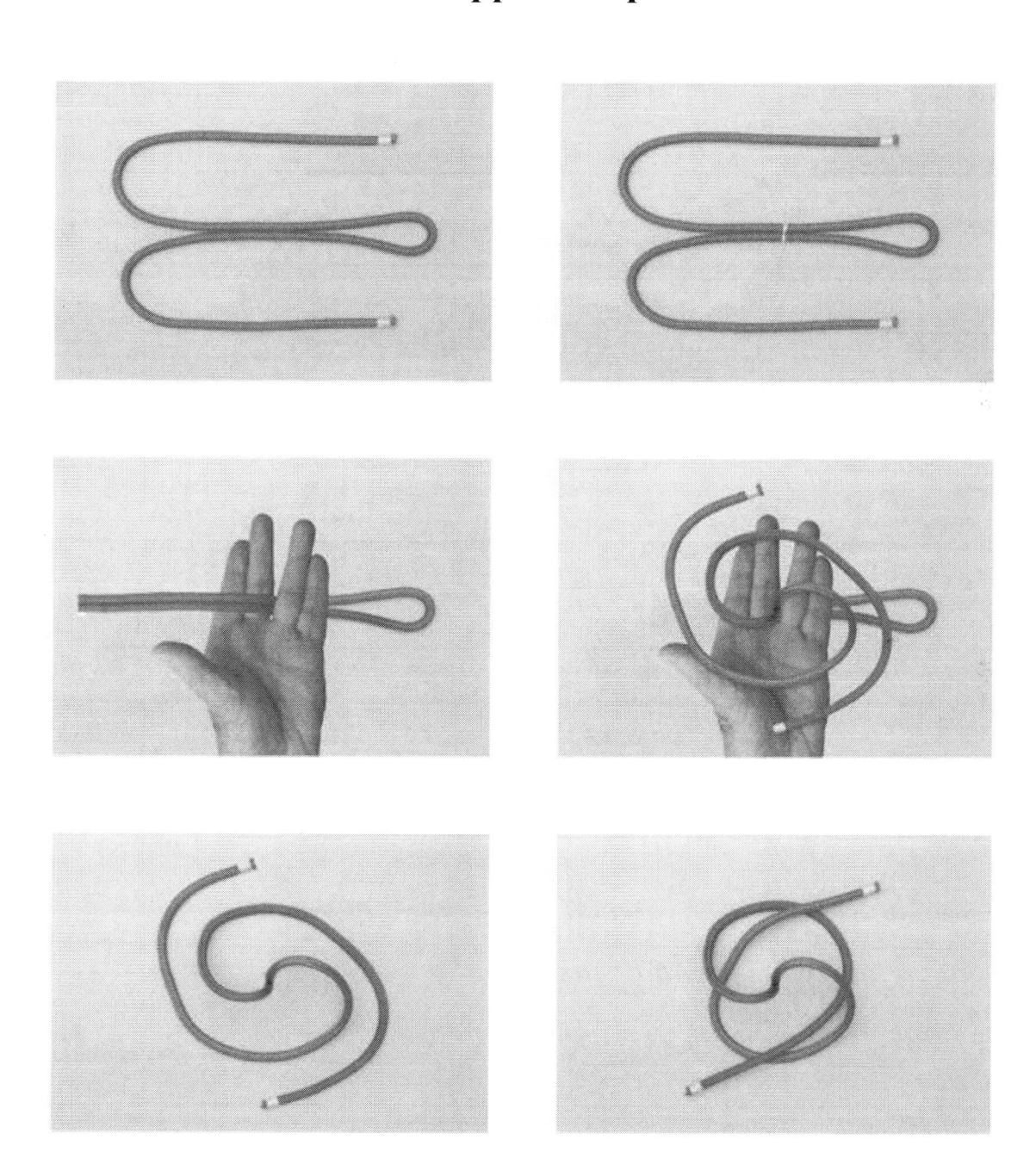

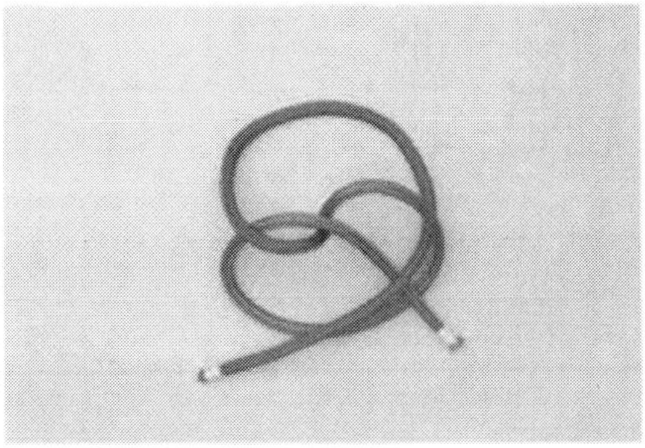
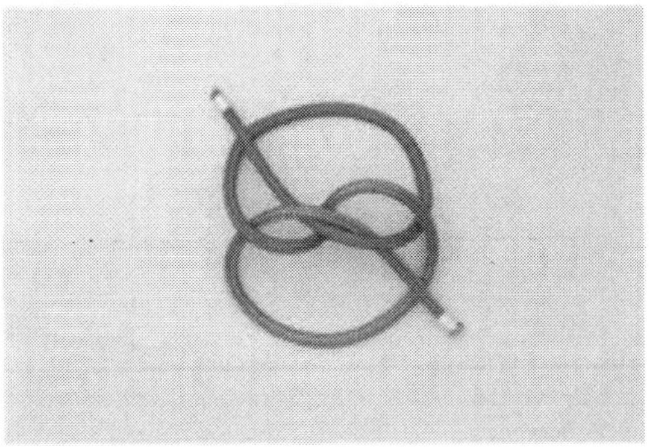
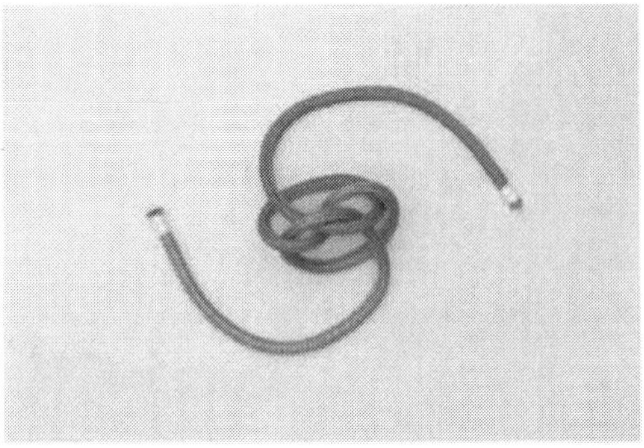
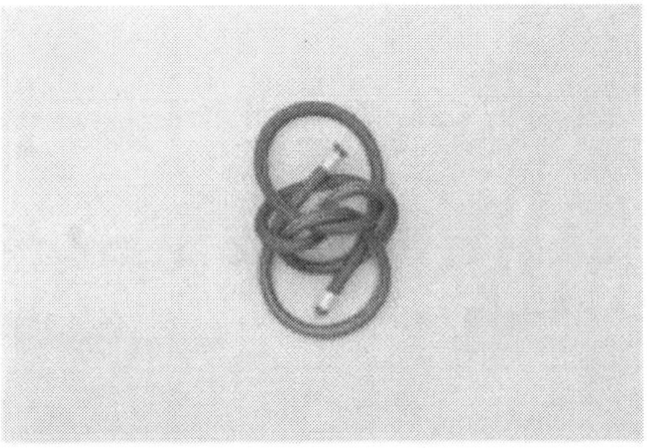
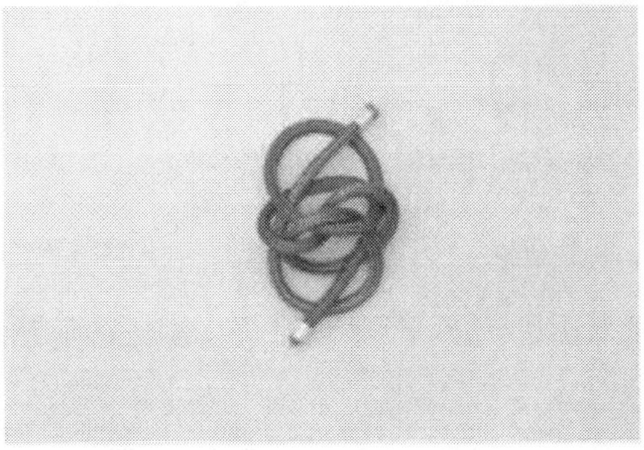
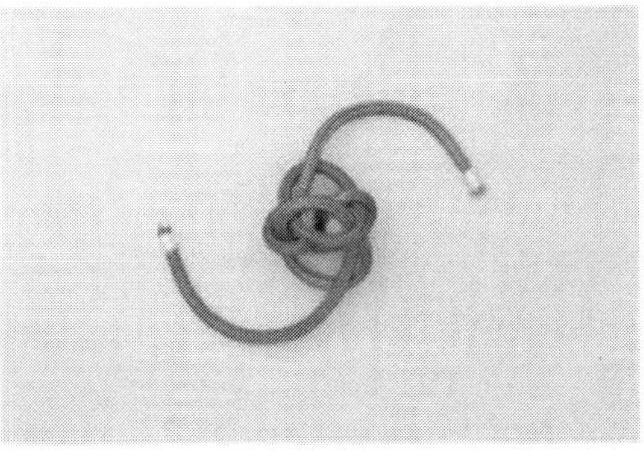

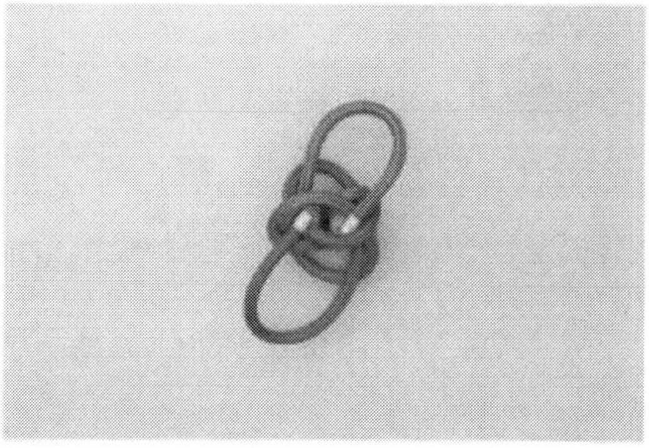
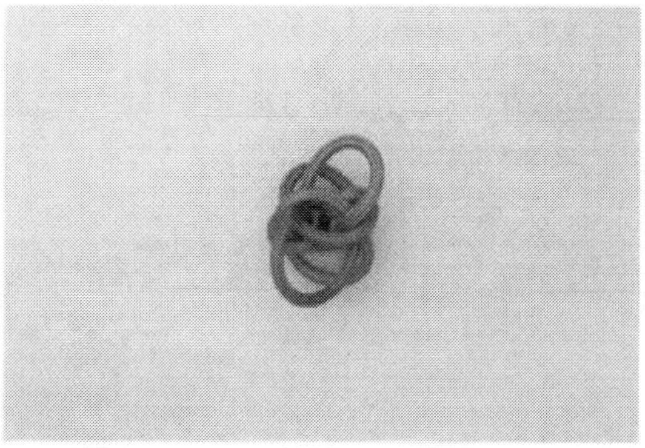
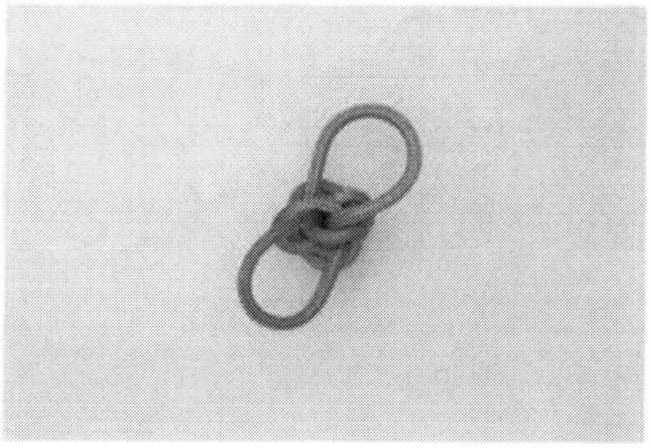
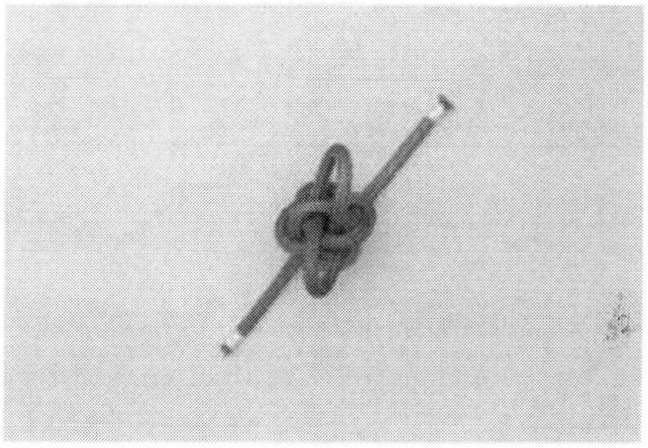
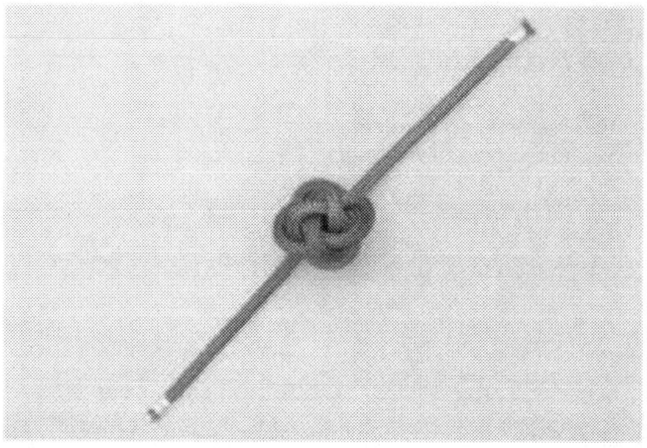
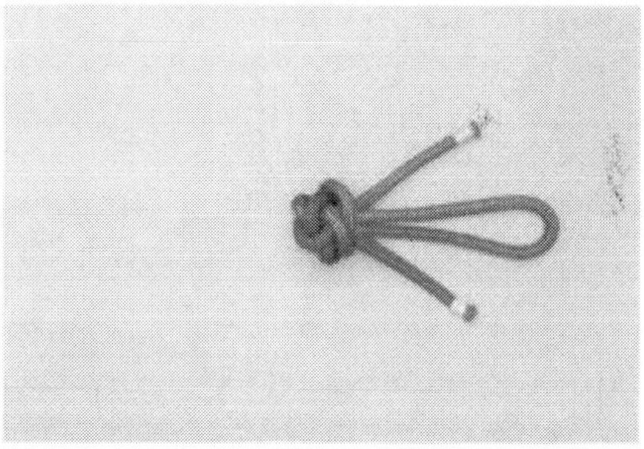

Start by tying a two-strand Wall Knot. Then, at that point, tie a Half Knot (a two abandoned Crown). Pass each end around under the bunch to come up close by its starting point yet inside the other strand. Proceed around and open the Half Knot. String both the closures down through the bunch and out adjacent to the first strands. Trim the closures.

Beginning: The Stopper Loop utilizes a similar Button Knot as the Stronger Rope Shackle and gives its massive expansion in breaking strain. Here the Stopper Loop is made with a circle, and the Button provides an anchor with the highlight a Halyard or Sheets ended utilizing Soft-Shackle processes.

Procedure: Tying this Button Knot appears to welcome slip-ups. The ends are effectively gone through some unacceptable openings. Fix the completed Button Knot cautiously. Each line is fixed from its starting point in the middle and afterward through the bunch to the tails. When selected, each seat is managed.

Double Matthew Walker Knot

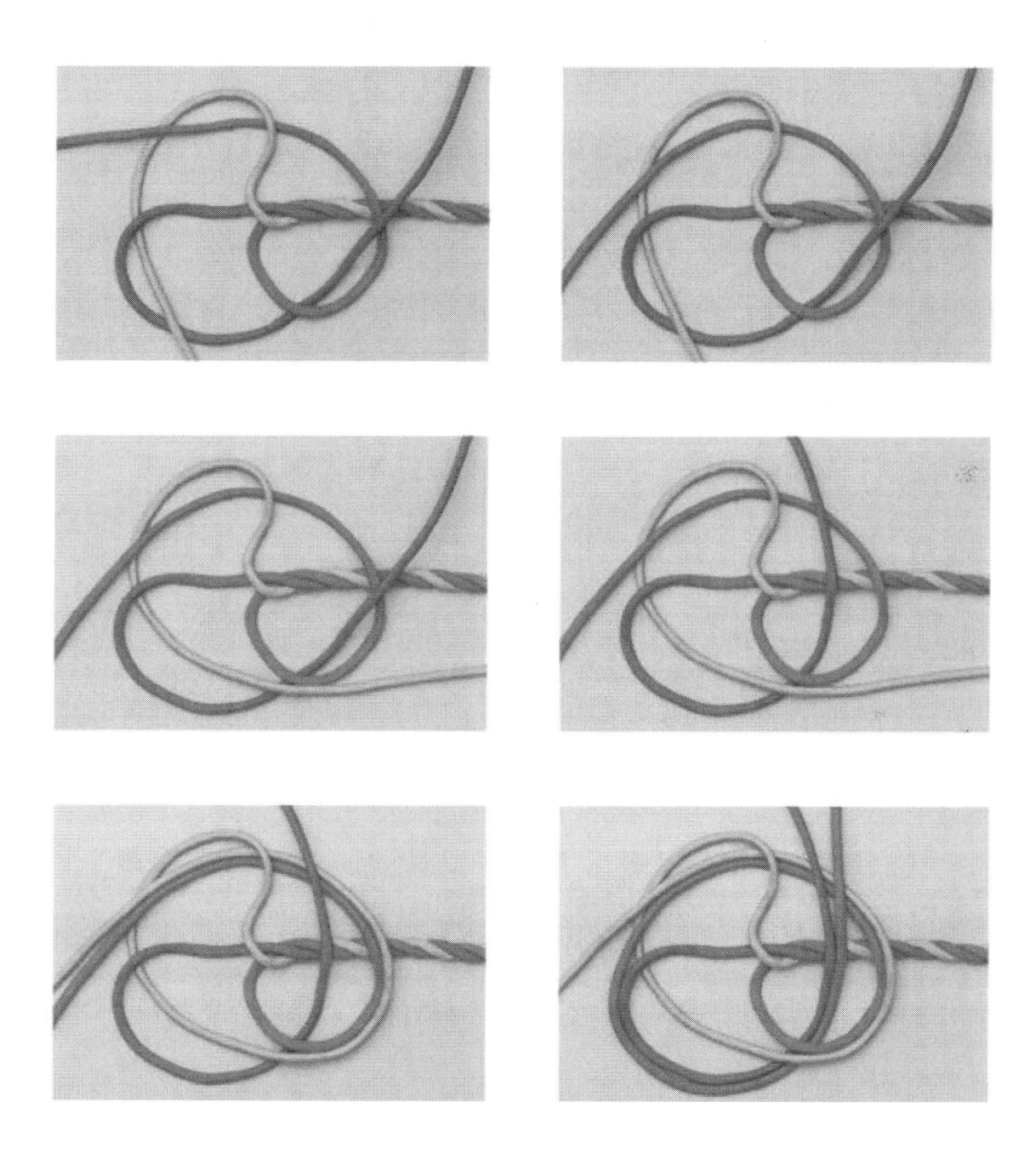

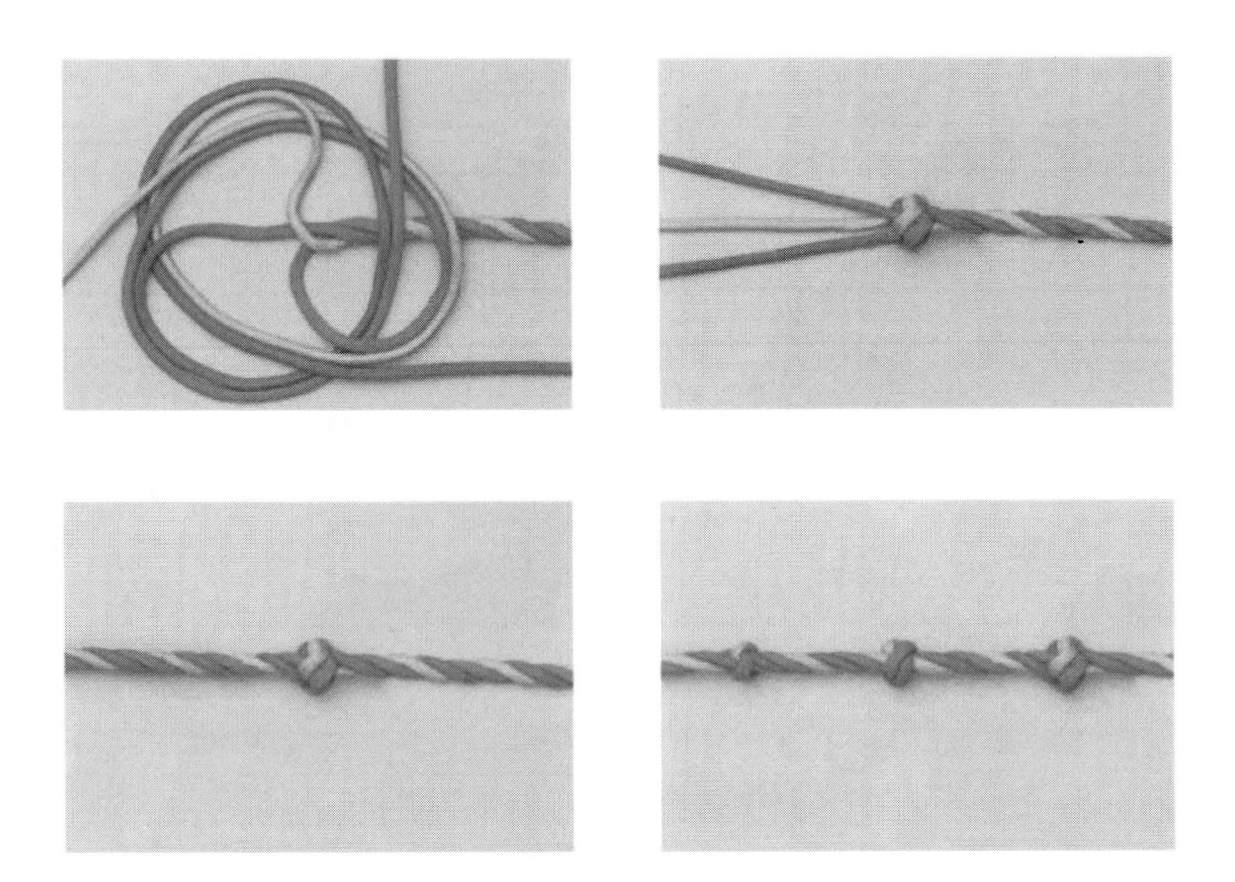

Uses: The Double Matthew Walker Knot gives a safe plug that cannot be unfastened without disentangling the rope.

Applications: Other than enrichment, current yachts do not need a Double Matthew Walker Knot. This is in hitting differently concerning the past when the Double Matthew Walker Knot was broadly utilized.

Drawbacks: The Wall and Matthew Walkers all require the rope to be laid up again and afterward completed, ideally with a rich Sailmaker's Whipping.

Crown Knot

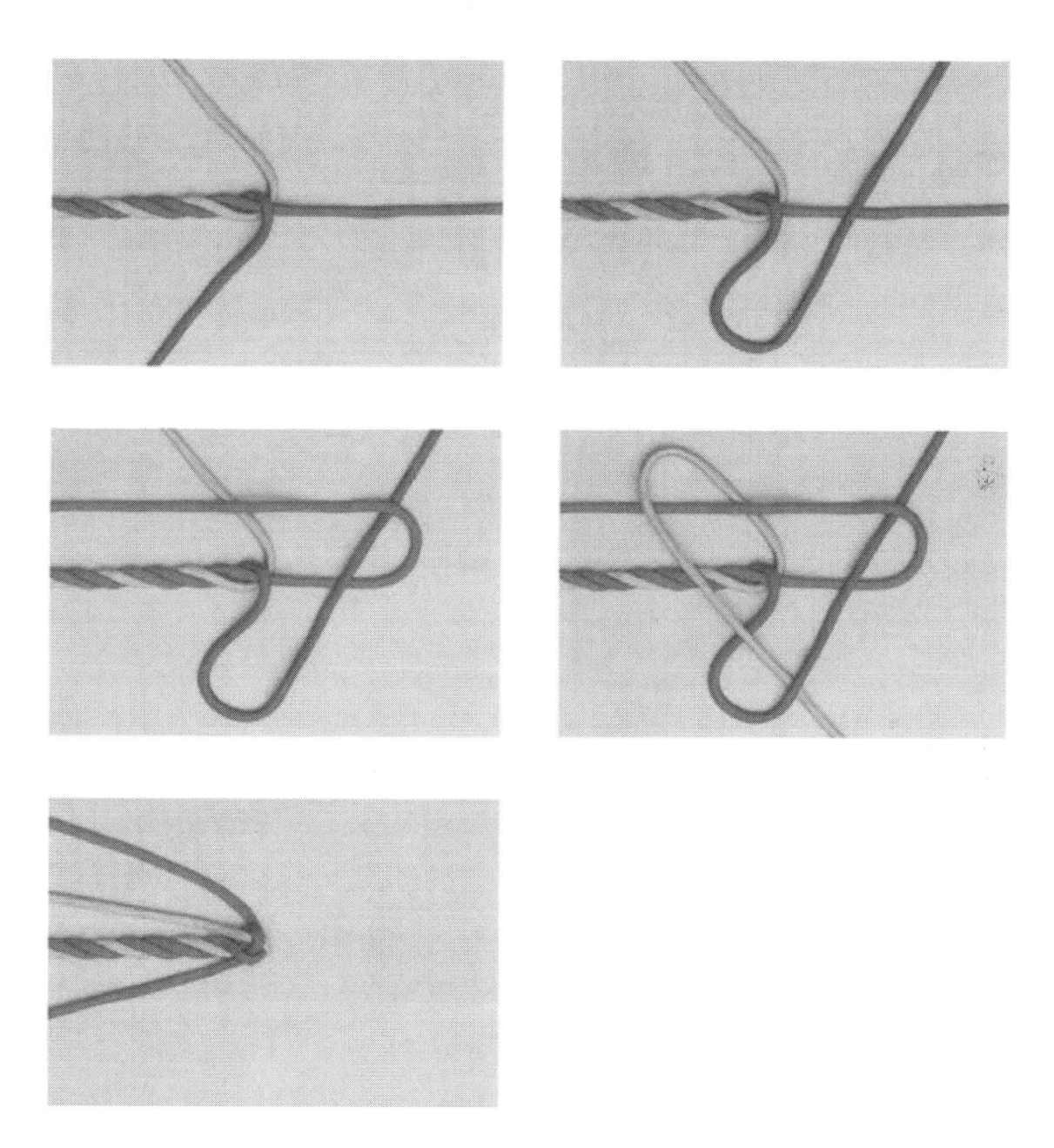

Spread out the strands. Pick one strand and, proceeding around toward the rope's turn, lay it across its neighbor. Rehash with that strand. Rehash with the excess strand tucking it under the first. Fix it to shape the initial segment of a Back Splice.

Uses: The Crown Knot is the primary initial segment of a Back Splice. At the point when the end of a three-abandoned rope begins to shred, a crown ought to be tied promptly with a back graft to follow. This secures the string until the Back Splice can be supplanted with a whipping.

Different uses: The Crown Knot is additionally a fundamental part of a few improving bunches, including the Wall and Crown (Manrope Knot) and the Crown Sinnet.

Relationship to the Wall: The Wall and the Crown are firmly related, and they are simply unique because of how they are attached concerning the rope's end. The crown coordinates the strands down towards the standing back, and the divider blends the strands from the standing end. The two bunches' construction is indistinguishable: if the three strands are relaid to proceed with the rope past the bunch, it is impossible to recognize a Crown Knot from a Wall Knot.

Conclusion

Congratulations on completing Knot Tying for Beginners. I sincerely hope you found all of the knot explanations practical, enjoyable, and worth your time!

I put countless hours into creating this book, and making my readers fulfilled and satisfied is my number one priority!

If you enjoyed this book, please take a few minutes out of your day to leave a review for it on Amazon; it would mean the WORLD to me!

Again, thanks for reading, and I hope to see you in the following guide!

Matthew McCoy

SPECIAL BONUS!

Want these Bonus Books for free?

Get FREE, unlimited access to them and all of my new books by joining the Fan Base

SCAN WITH YOUR CAMERA TO JOIN!

References

Surgeon's Loop Knot | How to tie a Surgeon's Loop Knot ....
https://www.animatedknots.com/surgeons-loop-knot

Rapala Knot | Fishing Knots | Animated Knots by Grog. https://www.animatedknots.com/rapala-knot

Rachmaninoff Hands – Daddy, medium-well..
https://daddymediumwell.wordpress.com/2017/07/10/rachmaninoff-hands/

what is a scaffold knot used for - munituman.gob.pe.
https://www.munituman.gob.pe/o0uqi67o/6195e7-what-is-a-scaffold-knot-used-for

Knots Lesson 3 – Lutheran Pioneers.
https://www.lutheranpioneers.org/courses/climber/lessons/knots-lesson-3/topic/knots-lesson-3/

Perfection loop diagram" Keyword Found Websites Listing ..... https://www.keyword-suggest-tool.com/search/perfection+loop+diagram/

Tips & Tactics: The essential loop knot - Fly Life Magazine. https://flylifemagazine.com/tips-tactics-the-essential-loop-knot/

Double Dragon Loop | How to tie a Double Dragon Loop using ....
https://www.animatedknots.com/double-dragon-loop

Double Davy Knot | How to tie a Double Davy Knot using ....
https://www.animatedknots.com/double-davy-knot

Davy Knot | How to tie a Davy Knot using Step-by-Step ....
https://www.animatedknots.com/davy-knot

Bimini Twist Knot | Fishing Knots | Animated Knots by Grog.
https://www.animatedknots.com/bimini-twist-knot

Figure 8 Knot | How to tie a Figure 8 Knot using Step-by ....
https://www.animatedknots.com/figure-8-knot

Half Hitch Knot | How to tie a Half Hitch Knot using Step ....
https://www.animatedknots.com/half-hitch-knot

Half Knot | How to tie a Half Knot using Step-by-Step .....https://www.animatedknots.com/half-knot

Slip Knot | How to tie a Slip Knot using Step-by-Step .... https://www.animatedknots.com/slip-knot

Noose Knot | How to tie a Noose Knot using Step-by-Step ....

https://www.animatedknots.com/noose-knot

Pioneering Merit Badge - TroopResource.org. http://www.troopresource.org/PPTFiles/Pioneering%20-%20Materials.pdf

Sheet Bend | How to tie a Sheet Bend using Step-by-Step .... https://www.animatedknots.com/sheet-bend-knot

DIY Knot - Useful knots for a day at the beach - D-I-Why Not?. https://vimeo.com/79633542

The 4 Knots You Must Know Before You Go Camping - Leave No https://lnt.org/the-4-knots-you-must-know-before-you-go-camping/

Animated Knots Training - USCG Aux. http://wow.uscgaux.info/content.php?unit=081-07-04&category=knots-know-how

Square Knot | How to tie a Square Knot using Step-by-Step .... https://www.animatedknots.com/square-knot

Alpine Butterfly Bend | How to tie a Alpine Butterfly Bend .... https://www.animatedknots.com/alpine-butterfly-bend-knot

Alpine Butterfly Loop | How to tie a Alpine Butterfly Loop .... https://www.animatedknots.com/alpine-butterfly-loop-knot

Anchor Hitch | How to tie an Anchor Hitch using Step-by .... https://www.animatedknots.com/anchor-hitch-knot

Stevedore Stopper | How to tie a Stevedore Stopper using .... https://www.animatedknots.com/stevedore-stopper-knot

Ashley Stopper Knot | How to tie a Ashley Stopper Knot .... https://www.animatedknots.com/ashley-stopper-knot

Newsletter of Lake Yosemite Sailing Association February 2015. http://www.lakeyosemitesailing.org/uploads/1/1/9/1/11916976/february_2015.pdf

Bowline Knot | How to tie a Bowline Knot using Step-by .... https://www.animatedknots.com/bowline-knot

Types of Knots. https://www.ansaroo.com/types/knots

TS PIONEERING - BSG SCOUT. https://bsgscout.weebly.com/ts-pioneering.html

Buntline Hitch | How to tie a Buntline Hitch using Step-by .... https://www.animatedknots.com/buntline-hitch-knot

Knot tying - SlideShare. https://www.slideshare.net/rolnics/knot-tying

Carrick Bend | How to tie a Carrick Bend using Step-by .... https://www.animatedknots.com/carrick-bend-knot

Chain Splice | How to tie a Chain Splice using Step-by......https://www.animatedknots.com/chain-splice-knot

Cleat Hitch (Dock Line) | How to tie a Cleat Hitch (Dock ....
https://www.animatedknots.com/cleat-hitch-knot-dock-line

Cleat Hitch (Halyard) | How to tie a Cleat Hitch (Halyard ....
https://www.animatedknots.com/cleat-hitch-halyard-knot

Clove Hitch (Rope-End) | How to tie a Clove Hitch (Rope ....
https://www.animatedknots.com/clove-hitch-knot-rope-end

Constrictor Knot (Twisting Method) | How to tie a ....
https://www.animatedknots.com/constrictor-knot-twisting-method

Double Overhand Stopper | How to tie a Double Overhand ....
https://www.animatedknots.com/double-overhand-stopper-knot

EStar Stopper Knot | How to tie a EStar Stopper Knot using ....
https://www.animatedknots.com/estar-stopper-knot

Eye Splice | How to tie a Eye Splice using Step-by-Step ..... https://www.animatedknots.com/eye-splice-knot

Halyard Hitch | How to tie a Halyard Hitch using Step-by ....
https://www.animatedknots.com/halyard-hitch-knot

Heaving Line Knot | How to tie a Heaving Line Knot using ....
https://www.animatedknots.com/heaving-line-knot

Knots Lesson 6 – Lutheran Pioneers.
https://www.lutheranpioneers.org/courses/knots/lessons/knots-lesson-6/topic/knots-lesson-6/

Icicle Hitch (Loop Method) | How to tie a Icicle Hitch .... https://www.animatedknots.com/icicle-hitch-knot-loop-method

Lighterman's Hitch | How to tie a Lighterman's Hitch using ....
https://www.animatedknots.com/lightermans-hitch-knot

Midshipman's Hitch | How to tie a Midshipman's Hitch using ....
https://www.animatedknots.com/midshipmans-hitch-knot

24 End Loops ideas | tie knots, knots, animated knots.
https://www.pinterest.com.au/animatedknots/end-loops/

25 Most Useful Knots – Jackson Raila: Straight To The Point.
https://jacksonraila.wordpress.com/2020/09/03/most-useful-knots/

Rolling Hitch | How to tie a Rolling Hitch using Step-by ....
https://www.animatedknots.com/rolling-hitch-knot

Rolling Hitch and Midshipman's Hitch - 8th Brampton Scouts ....
https://8thbramptonscouts.jimdofree.com/resources/knots/rolling-hitch/

Round Turn & Two Half Hitches | How to tie a Round Turn ....
https://www.animatedknots.com/round-turn-two-half-hitches-knot

Running Bowline | How to tie a Running Bowline using Step ....
https://www.animatedknots.com/running-bowline-knot

Zeppelin Bend | How to tie a Zeppelin Bend using Step-by ....
https://www.animatedknots.com/zeppelin-bend-knot

Netknots :: A forgotten knot - the Zeppelin Bend.
https://www.netknots.com/more/blog/forgotten-knot-zeppelin-bend

Slim Beauty Knot | Fishing Knots | Animated Knots by Grog.
https://www.animatedknots.com/slim-beauty-knot

Knots, Leaders and Tippets - Tackle Tips - Hastings Fly ....
https://www.hastingsflyfishers.org.au/tackle-tips/knots-leaders-tippets/

Uni Knot | How to tie an Uni Knot using Step-by-Step .... https://www.animatedknots.com/uni-knot

Trilene Knot | Fishing Knots | Animated Knots by Grog.
https://www.animatedknots.com/trilene-knot

Surgeon's Join Knot | How to tie a Surgeon's Join Knot ....
https://www.animatedknots.com/surgeons-join-knot

Snell Knot | Fishing Knots | Animated Knots by Grog. https://www.animatedknots.com/snell-knot

San Diego Jam Knot | How to tie a San Diego Jam Knot using ....
https://www.animatedknots.com/san-diego-jam-knot

Palomar Knot | Fishing Knots | Animated Knots by Grog.
https://www.animatedknots.com/palomar-knot

Orvis Knot | Fishing Knots | Animated Knots by Grog. https://www.animatedknots.com/orvis-knot

Nail Knot | Fishing Knots | Animated Knots by Grog. https://www.animatedknots.com/nail-knot

Improved Clinch Knot | Fishing Knots | Animated Knots by Grog.
https://www.animatedknots.com/improved-clinch-knot

FG Knot | How to tie a FG Knot using Step-by-Step .... https://www.animatedknots.com/fg-knot

Egg Loop Knot | Fishing Knots | Animated Knots by Grog.
https://www.animatedknots.com/egg-loop-knot

Dropper Loop Knot | How to tie a Dropper Loop Knot using ....
https://www.animatedknots.com/dropper-loop-knot

Blood Knot | Fishing Knots | Animated Knots by Grog. https://www.animatedknots.com/blood-knot

Australian Braid Knot | Fishing Knots | Animated Knots by Grog.
https://www.animatedknots.com/australian-braid-knot

Arbor Knot | Fishing Knots | Animated Knots by Grog. https://www.animatedknots.com/arbor-knot

Albright Knot | Fishing Knots | Animated Knots by Grog. https://www.animatedknots.com/albright-knot

Stopper Loop | How to tie a Stopper Loop using Step-by .... https://www.animatedknots.com/stopper-loop-knot

Double Matthew Walker Knot | How to tie a Double Matthew .... https://www.animatedknots.com/double-matthew-walker-knot

Crown Knot | How to tie a Crown Knot using Step-by-Step .... https://www.animatedknots.com/crown-knot

Knot Tying for Beginners

An Illustrated Guide
to Tying 65+ Most Useful
Types of Knots

Matthew McCoy

Made in United States
Orlando, FL
22 December 2021